Mastering Geospatial Analysis with Python

Explore GIS processing and learn to work with GeoDjango, CARTOframes and MapboxGL-Jupyter

Paul Crickard
Eric van Rees
Silas Toms

BIRMINGHAM - MUMBAI

Mastering Geospatial Analysis with Python

Commissioning Editor: Merint Mathew
Acquisition Editor: Karan Sadawana
Content Development Editor: Zeeyan Pinheiro
Technical Editor: Gaurav Gala
Copy Editor: Safis Editing
Project Coordinator: Vaidehi Sawant
Proofreader: Safis Editing
Indexer: Aishwarya Gangawane
Graphics: Jason Monteiro
Production Coordinator: Deepika Naik

First published: April 2018

Production reference: 1250418

Published by Packt Publishing Ltd.
Livery Place
35 Livery Street
Birmingham
B3 2PB, UK.

ISBN 978-1-78829-333-4

www.packtpub.com

`mapt.io`

Mapt is an online digital library that gives you full access to over 5,000 books and videos, as well as industry leading tools to help you plan your personal development and advance your career. For more information, please visit our website.

Why subscribe?

- Spend less time learning and more time coding with practical eBooks and Videos from over 4,000 industry professionals

- Improve your learning with Skill Plans built especially for you

- Get a free eBook or video every month

- Mapt is fully searchable

- Copy and paste, print, and bookmark content

PacktPub.com

Did you know that Packt offers eBook versions of every book published, with PDF and ePub files available? You can upgrade to the eBook version at `www.PacktPub.com` and as a print book customer, you are entitled to a discount on the eBook copy. Get in touch with us at `service@packtpub.com` for more details.

At `www.PacktPub.com`, you can also read a collection of free technical articles, sign up for a range of free newsletters, and receive exclusive discounts and offers on Packt books and eBooks.

Contributors

About the authors

Paul Crickard authored a book on the Leaflet JavaScript module. He has been programming for over 15 years and has focused on GIS and geospatial programming for 7 years. He spent 3 years working as a planner at an architecture firm, where he combined GIS with Building Information Modeling (BIM) and CAD. Currently, he is the CIO at the 2nd Judicial District Attorney's Office in New Mexico.

I would like to thank my beautiful wife, Yolanda, for her love and support; my children, Miles and Ivana, for giving up some daddy time; the editors, who have caught all my mistakes and made the book polished; and my coauthors Silas Toms and Eric van Rees. It was a pleasure working with these two great minds. Thank you for inviting me to be a part of this book.

Eric van Rees was first introduced to Geographical Information Systems (GIS) when studying Human Geography in the Netherlands. For 9 years, he was the editor-in-chief of GeoInformatics, an international GIS, surveying, and mapping publication and a contributing editor of *GIS Magazine*. During that tenure, he visited many geospatial user conferences, trade fairs, and industry meetings. He focuses on producing technical content, such as software tutorials, tech blogs, and innovative new use cases in the mapping industry.

I would like to thank my wife, Regina, for her support. I'd like to thank my coauthors, Paul Crickard and Silas Toms, for their assistance during the writing of this book. I would like to thank Eric Pimpler for giving me the opportunity to write technical content on his website and for inspiring me to contribute to this book.

Silas Toms is a geographer and geospatial developer from California. Over the last decade, Silas has become an expert in the use of Python programming for geospatial analysis, publishing two books on the use of ArcPy. Now, as a President of Loki Intelligent Corporation, Silas develops ETL automation tools, interactive web maps, enterprise GIS, and location data for businesses and governments. Silas teaches classes on programming for GIS with BayGeo, and co-hosts *The Mappyist Hour* podcast.

I would like to thank Maureen Stewart for her love and support. I want to thank my good friends Rowena Harris, Sacha Selim, Dara O'Beirne, Sam Oakley, Karla King, Todd Barr, and Michelle Toennies. Thanks also to BayGeo, HSU & SFSU Geography Depts., and all of my students. A big thanks to Paul and Eric. Good luck to Devon and Zsa Zsa!

About the reviewer

Karla King is a Solutions Engineer at a satellite imagery and machine learning start-up. Before joining Descartes Labs, she worked at a handful of geospatial companies in the Bay Area, developing software to create maps for autonomous vehicles and writing technical documentation for Google Earth Engine. Karla got her start in remote sensing monitoring the health of cloud forests in Honduras.

Packt is searching for authors like you

If you're interested in becoming an author for Packt, please visit `authors.packtpub.com` and apply today. We have worked with thousands of developers and tech professionals, just like you, to help them share their insight with the global tech community. You can make a general application, apply for a specific hot topic that we are recruiting an author for, or submit your own idea.

Table of Contents

Preface

Over time, Python has become the programming language of choice for spatial analysis, resulting in many packages that read, convert, analyze, and visualize spatial data. With so many packages available, it made sense to create a reference book for students and experienced professionals containing essential geospatial Python libraries for Python 3.

This book also comes at an exciting moment: new technology is transforming how people work with geospatial data – IoT, machine learning, and data science are areas where geospatial data is used constantly. This explains the inclusion of new Python libraries, such as CARTOframes and MapboxGL, and Jupyter is included as well, to explore these new trends. At the same time, web and cloud-based GIS is increasingly becoming the new standard. This is reflected in the chapters of the second part of this book, where interactive geospatial web maps and REST APIs are introduced.

These newer libraries are combined with a number of older ones that have become essential over the years, and are still very popular to this day, such as Shapely, Rasterio, and GeoPandas. Readers who are new to this field will be given a proper introduction to popular libraries, putting them into perspective and comparing their syntax through code examples using real-world data.

Finally, this books marks the transition from Python 2 to 3.x. All of the libraries covered in this book were written in Python 3.x so that the readers can access all of them using Jupyter Notebook, which is also the recommended Python coding environment for this book.

Who this book is for

This book is for anyone who works with location information and Python. Students, developers, and geospatial professionals can all use this reference book, as it covers GIS data management, analysis techniques, and code libraries built with Python 3.

What this book covers

Chapter 1, *Package Installation and Management*, explains how to install and manage the code libraries used in the book.

Chapter 2, *Introduction to Geospatial Code Libraries*, covers the major code libraries used to process and analyze geospatial data.

Chapter 3, *Introduction to Geospatial Databases*, introduces the geospatial databases used for data storage and analysis.

Chapter 4, *Data Types, Storage, and Conversion*, focuses on the many different data types (both vector and raster) that exist within GIS.

Chapter 5, *Vector Data Analysis*, covers Python libraries such as Shapely, OGR, and GeoPandas. which are used for analyzing and processing vector data.

Chapter 6, *Raster Data Processing*, explores using GDAL and Rasterio to process raster datasets in order to perform geospatial analysis.

Chapter 7, *Geoprocessing with Geodatabases*, shows the readers how to use Spatial SQL to perform geoprocessing with database tables containing a spatial column.

Chapter 8, *Automating QGIS Analysis*, teaches the readers how to use PyQGIS to automate analysis within the QGIS mapping suite.

Chapter 9, *ArcGIS API for Python and ArcGIS Online*, introduces the ArcGIS API for Python, which enables users to interact with Esri's cloud platform, ArcGIS Online, using Python 3.

Chapter 10, *Geoprocessing with a GPU Database*, covers using Python tools to interact with cloud-based data to search and process data.

Chapter 11, *Flask and GeoAlchemy2*, describes how to use the Flask Python web framework and the GeoAlchemy ORM to perform spatial data queries.

Chapter 12, *GeoDjango*, covers using the Django Python web framework and the GeoDjango ORM to perform spatial data queries.

Chapter 13, *Geospatial REST API*, teaches the readers how to create a REST API for geospatial data.

Chapter 14, *Cloud Geodatabase Analysis and Visualization*, introduces the readers to the CARTOframes Python package, enabling the integration of Carto maps, analysis, and data services into data science workflows.

Chapter 15, *Automating Cloud Cartography*, covers a new location data visualization library for Jupyter Notebooks.

Chapter 16, *Python Geoprocessing with Hadoop*, explains how to perform geospatial analysis using distributed servers.

To get the most out of this book

As this book covers Python, it is assumed that the reader has a basic understanding of the Python language, can install Python libraries, and knows how to write and run Python scripts. As for additional knowledge, the first six chapters can easily be understood without any previous knowledge of geospatial data analysis. However, later chapters assume some knowledge of spatial databases, big data platforms, data science, web APIs, and Python web frameworks.

Download the example code files

You can download the example code files for this book from your account at `www.packtpub.com`. If you purchased this book elsewhere, you can visit `www.packtpub.com/support` and register to have the files emailed directly to you.

You can download the code files by following these steps:

1. Log in or register at `www.packtpub.com`.
2. Select the **SUPPORT** tab.
3. Click on **Code Downloads & Errata**.
4. Enter the name of the book in the **Search** box and follow the onscreen instructions.

Once the file is downloaded, please make sure that you unzip or extract the folder using the latest version of:

- WinRAR/7-Zip for Windows
- Zipeg/iZip/UnRarX for Mac
- 7-Zip/PeaZip for Linux

The code bundle for the book is also hosted on GitHub at `https://github.com/PacktPublishing/Mastering-Geospatial-Analysis-with-Python`. In case there's an update to the code, it will be updated on the existing GitHub repository.

We also have other code bundles from our rich catalog of books and videos available at `https://github.com/PacktPublishing/`. Check them out!

Download the color images

We also provide a PDF file that has color images of the screenshots/diagrams used in this book. You can download it here: https://www.packtpub.com/sites/default/files/downloads/MasteringGeospatialAnalysiswithPython_ColorImages.pdf.

Conventions used

There are a number of text conventions used throughout this book.

CodeInText: Indicates code words in text, database table names, folder names, filenames, file extensions, pathnames, dummy URLs, user input, and Twitter handles. Here is an example: "Select a folder and save the key, which will now have a .ppk file extension."

A block of code is set as follows:

```
cursor.execute("SELECT * from art_pieces")
data=cursor.fetchall()
data
```

When we wish to draw your attention to a particular part of a code block, the relevant lines or items are set in bold:

```
from pymapd import connect
connection = connect(user="mapd", password= "{password}",
    host="{my.host.com}", dbname="mapd")
cursor = connection.cursor()
sql_statement = """SELECT name FROM county;"""
cursor.execute(sql_statement)
```

Any command-line input or output is written as follows:

```
conda install -c conda-forge geos
```

Bold: Indicates a new term, an important word, or words that you see onscreen. For example, words in menus or dialog boxes appear in the text like this. Here is an example: "To generate the pair from the **EC2 Dashboard**, select **Key Pairs** from the **NETWORK & SECURITY** group in the left panel after scrolling down."

 Warnings or important notes appear like this.

Tips and tricks appear like this.

Get in touch

Feedback from our readers is always welcome.

General feedback: Email `feedback@packtpub.com` and mention the book title in the subject of your message. If you have questions about any aspect of this book, please email us at `questions@packtpub.com`.

Errata: Although we have taken every care to ensure the accuracy of our content, mistakes do happen. If you have found a mistake in this book, we would be grateful if you would report this to us. Please visit `www.packtpub.com/submit-errata`, selecting your book, clicking on the Errata Submission Form link, and entering the details.

Piracy: If you come across any illegal copies of our works in any form on the Internet, we would be grateful if you would provide us with the location address or website name. Please contact us at `copyright@packtpub.com` with a link to the material.

If you are interested in becoming an author: If there is a topic that you have expertise in and you are interested in either writing or contributing to a book, please visit `authors.packtpub.com`.

Reviews

Please leave a review. Once you have read and used this book, why not leave a review on the site that you purchased it from? Potential readers can then see and use your unbiased opinion to make purchase decisions, we at Packt can understand what you think about our products, and our authors can see your feedback on their book. Thank you!

For more information about Packt, please visit `packtpub.com`.

1
Package Installation and Management

This book focuses on important code libraries for geospatial data management and analysis for Python 3. The reason for this is simple—as Python 2 is near the end of its life cycle, it is quickly being replaced by Python 3. This new Python version comes with key differences in organization and syntax, meaning that developers need to adjust their legacy code and apply new syntax in their code. Fields such as machine learning, data science, and big data have changed the way geospatial data is managed, analyzed, and presented today. In all these areas, Python 3 has quickly become the new standard, which is another reason for the geospatial community to start using Python 3.

The geospatial community has been relying on Python 2 for a long time, as many dependencies weren't available for Python 3 or not working correctly. But now that Python 3 is mature and stable, the geospatial community has taken advantage of its capabilities, resulting in many new libraries and tools. This book aims to help developers understand open source and commercial modules for geospatial programs written in Python 3, offering a selection of major geospatial libraries and tools for doing geospatial data management and data analysis.

This chapter will explain how to install and manage the code libraries that will be used in this book. It will cover the following topics:

- Installing Anaconda
- Managing Python packages using Anaconda Navigator, Anaconda Cloud, `conda`, and `pip`
- Managing virtual environments using Anaconda, `conda`, and `virtualenv`
- Running a Jupyter Notebook

Introducing Anaconda

Anaconda is a freemium open source distribution of the Python programming language for large-scale data processing, predictive analytics, and scientific computing, that aims to simplify package management and deployment. It is also the world's most popular Python data science platform, with over 4.5 million users and 1,000 data science packages. It is not to be confused with `conda`, a package manager that is installed with Anaconda.

For this book, we recommend installing and using Anaconda as it provides you everything you need—Python itself, Python libraries, the tools to manage these libraries, a Python environment manager, and the Jupyter Notebook application to write, edit, and run your code. You can also choose to use an alternative to Anaconda or install Python through `www.python.org/downloads` and use any IDE of your choice combined with a package manager such as `pip` (covered as we proceed further). We recommend using Python version 3.6.

Installing Python using Anaconda

A free download of the latest version of Anaconda, available for Windows, macOS, and Linux is available at the homepage of Continuum Analytics. At the time of writing, the latest version is Anaconda 5.0.1, released in October 2017 and available in 32 and 64-bit versions from `https://www.continuum.io/downloads`. This page also offers extensive download instructions for each operating system, a 30-minute tutorial that explains how to use Anaconda, a cheat sheet on how to get started, and an FAQ section. There's also a slimmed-down version of Anaconda called Miniconda that only installs Python and the `conda` package manager, leaving out the 1000+ software packages that come with the standard installation of Anaconda: `https://conda.io/miniconda.html`. If you decide to use this, make sure you download the Python 3.6 version.

Anaconda will install Python 3.6.2 as the default Python version on your machine. The Python version that is used in all chapters of this book is Python 3.6, so you're good with any version that starts with 3.6 or higher. With Anaconda, you get more than 1,000 Python packages, as well as a number of applications, such as Jupyter Notebook, and a variety of Python consoles and IDEs.

Please note that you are not forced to always use Python version 3.6 after installing it—using Anaconda Navigator (a GUI for managing local environments and installing packages), you can also choose to use Python 3.5 or 2.7 in a virtual environment. This gives you more flexibility in switching between different Python versions for various projects.

To begin the installation, download the 32-or 64-bit Anaconda installer, depending on your system capabilities. Open the installation and follow the setup guide to install Anaconda on your local system.

Running a Jupyter Notebook

Jupyter Notebooks are a novel idea, which has been adopted by many companies (including Esri and the new ArcGIS API for Python). Managed by Project Jupyter, the open source project (which is based on IPython, an earlier interactive code environment), is a fantastic tool for both learning and production environments. While the code can also be run as a script, as seen in other chapters, using the Jupyter Notebooks will make coding even more fun.

The idea of the code Notebooks is to make coding interactive. By combining a Python terminal with direct output that results from the code being run, the Notebooks (which are saveable) become a tool for sharing and comparing code. Each section can be edited later or can be saved as a separate component for demonstration purposes.

 Check out the documentation for Jupyter Notebooks here: http://jupyter.org/documentation.

Running a Notebook

To start the local server that powers the Notebooks, activate the virtual environment and pass the `jupyter notebook` command:

```
C:\PythonGeospatial3>cartoenv\Scripts\activate
(cartoenv) C:\PythonGeospatial3>jupyter notebook
[I 17:30:46.338 NotebookApp] Serving notebooks from local directory:
C:\PythonGeospatial3
[I 17:30:46.338 NotebookApp] 0 active kernels
[I 17:30:46.339 NotebookApp] The Jupyter Notebook is running at:
[I 17:30:46.339 NotebookApp]
http://localhost:8888/?token=5376ed8c704d0ead295a3c0464e52664e367094a9e74f7
0e
[I 17:30:46.339 NotebookApp] Use Control-C to stop this server and shut
down all kernels (twice to skip confirmation).
[C 17:30:46.344 NotebookApp]
```

```
    Copy/paste this URL into your browser when you connect for the first
time,
    to login with a token:
http://localhost:8888/?token=5376ed8c704d0ead295a3c0464e52664e367094a9e74f7
0e
[I 17:30:46.450 NotebookApp] Accepting one-time-token-authenticated
connection from ::1
[I 17:30:49.490 NotebookApp] Kernel started: 802159ef-3215-4b23-
b77f-4715e574f09b
[I 17:30:50.532 NotebookApp] Adapting to protocol v5.1 for kernel
802159ef-3215-4b23-b77f-4715e574f09b
```

This will start running the server that will power the Notebooks. This local server can be accessed on port 8888, using a browser, by navigating to: http://localhost:8888. It should automatically open a tab like this one when started:

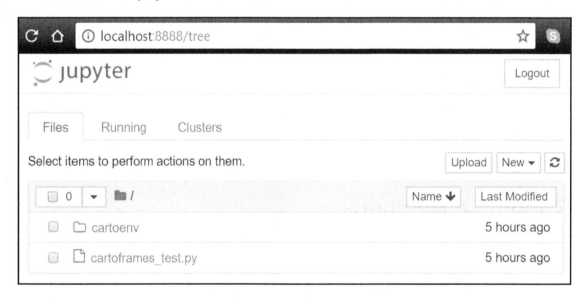

If you log out, use the token provided in the text generated when the jupyter notebook command is passed to log back in, as in this example:

```
http://localhost:8888/?token=5376ed8c704d0ead295a3c0464e52664e367094a9e74f7
0e
```

Creating a new Notebook

To create a new Notebook, click on the **New** button in the upper-right, and select **Python 3** from the Notebook section. It will open the Notebook in a new tab:

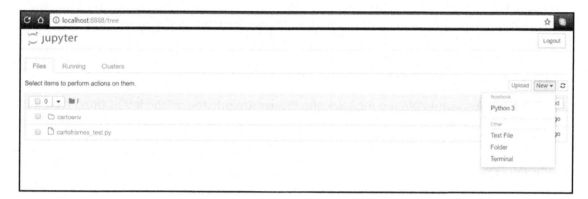

Adding code

In Jupyter Notebooks, code is added in the **In** sections. The code can be added line by line, as the code variables and imported modules will be saved in memory, or it can be added in blocks/multiple lines, like a script. The **In** sections can be edited and run over and over, or they can be left alone, and a new section can be started. This creates a record of the scripting efforts, along with the interactive output.

 Here is a GIST explaining lots of useful keyboard shortcuts for Jupyter Notebooks:
https://gist.github.com/kidpixo/f4318f8c8143adee5b40

Managing Python packages

After installing Anaconda, it's time to discuss how to manage different Python packages. Anaconda offers several options to do this—Anaconda Navigator, Anaconda Cloud, and the conda package manager.

Managing packages with Anaconda Navigator

After installing Anaconda, you will notice a working folder with various applications inside of it. One of these is Anaconda Navigator, which provides a **Graphical User Interface (GUI)**. You can compare it to Windows File Explorer, that is, an environment to manage projects, packages, and environments. The term *environment* refers to a collection of packages and a Python install. Notice that this is similar to how you would use `virtualenv`, but this time using a GUI instead of a command prompt to create one (`virtualenv` is covered in more detail later in this chapter).

After opening Anaconda Navigator, click the **Environments** tab on the left of the screen and Anaconda Navigator will provide an overview of existing environments and the packages it contains. There's one pre-defined environment available, a so-called **root** environment that provides you with 150+ pre-installed Python packages. New environments can be made by clicking the **Create** button on the bottom of the screen. This will automatically install five default Python packages, including `pip`, which means you're free to use that too for package management. What's interesting about Anaconda Navigator is that, with every new environment, you can choose a preferred Python version and install from a list of 1000+ packages that are available locally if you installed the default Anaconda version and not Miniconda. This list is available by selecting the option **Not Installed** from the drop-down menu next to the **Channels** button. You can easily search and select the packages of your choice by using the **Search Packages** field and hitting *Enter*. Mark the packages and install them for the environment of your choice. After installation, the package will be listed by name in the environment. If you click the green box with a checkmark next to the package name, you can choose to mark a package for an upgrade, removal, or specific version installation.

After installing the packages, you can start working with an environment by opening up a terminal, Jupyter Notebook, or another Anaconda application with one mouse click on the arrow button inside of the environment of your choice. If you wish to use an IDE instead of one of the options that Anaconda Navigator offers you, be sure to redirect your IDE to the right `python.exe` file that is used by Anaconda. This file can usually be found at the following path, which is the default installation path of Anaconda:

```
C:\Users\<UserName>\Anaconda3\python.exe.
```

Online searching for packages using Anaconda Cloud

If you are searching for a Python package that is not found in the local list of available Python packages, you can use Anaconda Cloud. This application is also part of Anaconda3 and you can use the Anaconda Cloud application for sharing packages, Notebooks, and environments with others. After clicking on the Anaconda Cloud desktop icon, an internet page will open where you can sign up to become a registered user. Anaconda Cloud is similar to GitHub, as it lets you create a private online repository for your own work. These repositories are called **channels**.

If you create a user account, you can use Anaconda Cloud from inside Anaconda Navigator. After creating a user account for Anaconda Cloud, open Anaconda Navigator and use your login details to sign into Anaconda Cloud in the upper-right corner of the screen where it says **Sign in to Anaconda Cloud**. Now, you can upload your own packages and files to a private package repository and search for existing files or packages.

Managing Python packages with conda

Apart from using Anaconda Navigator and Cloud for package management, you can use conda, a binary package manager, as a command-line tool to manage your package installations. conda quickly installs, runs, and updates packages and their dependencies. conda easily creates, saves, loads, and switches between environments on your local computer. The best ways to install conda are through installing either Anaconda or Miniconda. A third option is a separate installation through **Python Package Index (PyPI)**, but may not be up-to-date so this option is not recommended.

Installing packages with conda is straightforward, as it resembles the syntax of pip. However, it is good to know that conda cannot install packages directly from a Git server. This means that the latest version of many packages under development cannot be downloaded with conda. Also, conda doesn't cover all the packages available on PyPI as pip does itself, which is why you always have access to pip when creating a new environment with Anaconda Navigator (more on pip as we proceed further).

You can verify if conda is installed by typing the following command in a terminal:

```
>> conda -version
```

If installed, conda will display the number of the version that you have installed. Installing the package of your choice can be done with the following command in a terminal:

```
>> conda install <package-name>
```

Updating an already installed package to its latest available version can be done as follows:

```
>> conda update <package-name>
```

You can also install a particular version of a package by pointing out the version number:

```
>> conda install <package-name>=1.2.0
```

You can update all the available packages simply by using the --all argument:

```
>> conda update --all
```

You can uninstall packages too:

```
>> conda remove <package-name>
```

Extensive conda documentation is available at: https://conda.io/docs/index.html.

Managing Python packages using pip

As stated earlier, Anaconda users always have pip available in every new environment, as well as the root folder—it comes pre-installed with every version of Anaconda, including Miniconda. As pip is a Python package manager used to install and manage software packages written in Python, it runs in the command line, as opposed to Anaconda Navigator and Cloud. If you decide not to use Anaconda or anything similar to it, and use a default Python installation from python.org, you can either use easy_install or pip as a package manager. As pip is seen as an improvement over easy_install and the preferred Python package manager for Python 3, we will only discuss pip here. It is recommended to use either pip, conda, Anaconda Navigator, or Cloud for Python package management in the upcoming chapters.

Optionally, as you install Anaconda, three environment variables will be added to your list of user variables. This enables you to access commands such as pip from any system location if you open a terminal. To check if pip is installed on your system, open a terminal and enter:

```
>> pip
```

If you don't receive any error message, it means `pip` is installed correctly and you can use `pip` to install any package of your choice from the PyPI by using:

```
>> pip install <package-name>
```

For Anaconda users, the `pip` command file should be stored at the following path:

`C:\Users\<User Name>\Anaconda3\Scripts\pip.exe.`

If `pip` is not available on your system, you can install `pip` by following the instructions given at: `https://pip.pypa.io/en/latest/installing`.

Upgrading and uninstalling the package with pip

Whereas Anaconda Cloud automatically displays a version number of a certain installed package, users choosing to use a default Python installation can use `pip` to display it through the following command:

```
>> import pandas
>> pandas.__version__ # output will be a version number, for example:
u'0.18.1'
```

Upgrading a package, for example when there's a new version you'd like to use, can be done as follows:

```
>> pip install -U pandas==0.21.0
```

Upgrading it to the latest available version can be done as follows:

```
>> pip install -U pandas
```

Uninstalling a package can be done with the following command:

```
>> pip uninstall <package name>
```

Python virtual environments

The recommended approach to using Python, in general, is a project-based one. This means that each project uses a separate Python version, along with the packages required and their mutual dependencies. This approach gives you the flexibility to switch between different Python versions and installed package versions. Not following this approach would mean that, every time you update a package or install a new one, its dependencies will be updated too, resulting in a different setup. This may cause problems, for example, code that won't run correctly because of changes under the hood, or packages that do not communicate correctly with each other. While this book focuses on Python 3, there won't be any need to switch to a different Python version, but maybe you can imagine using different versions of the same packages for different projects.

Before Anaconda, this project-based approach would require using `virtualenv`, a tool for creating isolated Python environments. This approach has gotten a lot easier with Anaconda, which offers the same approach but in a more simplified way. Both options are covered in detail as we proceed further.

Virtual environments using Anaconda

As stated before, Anaconda Navigator has a tab called **Environments**, that when clicked will display an overview of all local environments created by the user on a local file system. You can easily create, import, clone, or remove environments, specify the preferred Python version, and install packages by version number inside such an environment. Any new environment will automatically install a number of Python packages, such as `pip`. From there, you are free to install more packages. These environments are the exact same virtual environments that you would create by using the `virtualenv` tool. You can start working with them by opening a terminal or by running Python, which opens a terminal and runs `python.exe`.

Anaconda stores all environments in a separate `root` folder, keeping all your virtual environments in one place. Note that each environment in Anaconda Navigator is treated as a virtual environment, even the root environment.

Managing environments with conda

Both Anaconda and Miniconda offer the `conda` package manager, which can also be used to manage virtual environments. Open a terminal and use the following command to list all available environments on your system:

```
>> conda info -e
```

Use the following command for creating a virtual environment based on Python version 2.7:

```
>> conda create -n python3packt python=2.7
```

Activate the environment next as follows:

```
>> activate python3packt
```

Multiple additional packages can now be installed with a single command:

```
>> conda install -n python3packt <package-name1> <package-name2>
```

This command calls conda directly.

Deactivate the environment you've been working in as follows:

```
>> deactivate
```

More on managing environments with conda can be found at: https://conda.io/docs/user-guide/tasks/manage-environments.html

Virtual environments using virtualenv

If you don't want to use Anaconda, virtualenv needs to be installed first. Use the following command to install it locally:

```
>> pip install virtualenv
```

Next, a virtual environment can be created by assigning with the virtualenv command followed by the name of the new environment, for example:

```
>> virtualenv python3packt
```

Navigate to the directory with the same name:

```
>> cd python3packt
```

Next, activate the virtual environment with the activate command:

```
>> activate
```

Your virtual environment is now ready for use. Use `pip install` to install packages exclusively to this environment and use them in your code. Use the `deactivate` command to stop the virtual environment from working:

```
>> deactivate
```

If you have multiple Python versions installed, use the argument `-p` together with the desired Python version or path to the `python.exe` file of your choice, for example:

```
>> -p python2.7
```

You can also do it as follows:

```
>> -p c:\python34\python.exe
```

This step follows creation of the virtual environment and precedes installation of the required packages. For more information on `virtualenv`, see: `http://virtualenv.readthedocs.io/en/stable`

Summary

This introductory chapter discussed how to install and manage the code libraries that will be used in this book. We'll be working mainly with Anaconda, a freemium open source distribution of the Python programming language that aims to simplify package management and deployment. We discussed how to install Anaconda, and the options for Python package management using Anaconda Navigator, Anaconda Cloud, `conda`, and `pip`. Finally, we discussed virtual environments and how to manage these using Anaconda, `conda`, and `virtualenv`.

The recommended installation for this book is the Anaconda3 version, that will install not only a working Python environment, but also a large repository of local Python packages, the Jupyter Notebook application, as well as the `conda` package manager, Anaconda Navigator, and Cloud. In the next chapter, we will introduce the major code libraries used to process and analyze geospatial data.

Introduction to Geospatial Code Libraries

2

This chapter will introduce the major code libraries used to process and analyze geospatial data. You will learn the characteristics of each library, how they are related to each other, how to install them, where to find additional documentation, and typical use cases. These instructions assume that the user has a recent (2.7 or later) version of Python on their machine, and do not cover installing Python. Next, we'll discuss how all of these packages fit together and how they are covered in the rest of this book.

The following libraries will be covered in this chapter:

- GDAL/OGR
- GEOS
- Shapely
- Fiona
- Python Shapefile Library (`pyshp`)
- `pyproj`
- Rasterio
- GeoPandas

Geospatial Data Abstraction Library (GDAL) and the OGR Simple Features Library

The **Geospatial Data Abstraction Library (GDAL)/OGR Simple Features Library** combines two separate libraries that are generally downloaded together as a GDAL. This means that installing the GDAL package also gives access to OGR functionality, which is why they're covered together here. The reason GDAL is covered first is that other packages were written after GDAL, so chronologically, it comes first. As you will notice, some of the packages covered in this chapter extend GDAL's functionality or use it under the hood.

GDAL was created in the 1990s by Frank Warmerdam and saw its first release in June 2000. Later, the development of GDAL was transferred to the **Open Source Geospatial Foundation (OSGeo)**. Technically, GDAL is a little different than your average Python package as the GDAL package itself was written in C and C++, meaning that in order to be able to use it in Python, you need to compile GDAL and its associated Python bindings. However, using `conda` and Anaconda makes it relatively easy to get started quickly. Because it was written in C and C++, the online GDAL documentation is written in the C++ version of the libraries. For Python developers, this can be challenging, but many functions are documented and can be consulted with the built-in `pydoc` utility, or by using the `help` function within Python.

Because of its history, working with GDAL in Python also feels a lot like working in C++ rather than pure Python. For example, a naming convention in OGR is different than Python's since you use uppercase for functions instead of lowercase. These differences explain the choice for some of the other Python libraries such as Rasterio and Shapely, which are also covered in this chapter, that has been written from a Python developer's perspective but offer the same GDAL functionality.

GDAL is a massive and widely used data library for raster data. It supports the reading and writing of many raster file formats, with the latest version counting up to 200 different file formats that are supported. Because of this, it is indispensable for geospatial data management and analysis. Used together with other Python libraries, GDAL enables some powerful remote sensing functionalities. It's also an industry standard and is present in commercial and open source GIS software.

The OGR library is used to read and write vector-format geospatial data, supporting reading and writing data in many different formats. OGR uses a consistent model to be able to manage many different vector data formats. We'll discuss this model when working with vector data in `Chapter 5`, *Vector Data Analysis*. You can use OGR to do vector reprojection, vector data format conversion, vector attribute data filtering, and more.

GDAL/OGR libraries are not only useful for Python programmers but are also used by many GIS vendors and open source projects. The latest GDAL version at the time of writing is 2.2.4, which was released in March 2018.

Installing GDAL

The installation of GDAL for Python used to be quite complicated, requiring you to fiddle with system settings and path variables. It is still possible to install GDAL in various ways, however, we recommend that you use either Anaconda3 or `conda`, as this is the quickest and easiest way to get started. Other options are using `pip` install, or using an online repository such as `http://gdal.org` or Tamas Szekeres Windows binaries (`http://www.gisinternals.com/release.php`).

However, this might be a little more involved than the options described here. The catch with installing GDAL is that a particular version of the library (that comes in the C language and is installed in a separate system directory from your local Python files) has an accompanying Python version, and needs to be compiled in order for you to use it in Python. In addition, GDAL for Python is dependent on some extra Python libraries that come with an installation. While it is possible to use multiple versions of GDAL on the same machine, the recommended approach here is to install it in a virtual environment, using Anaconda3, `conda`, or `pip` installations. This will keep your system settings clean of additional path variables or stop things from working.

Installing GDAL using Anaconda3

If you're using Anaconda3, the easiest way to install GDAL is to create a virtual environment through Anaconda Navigator, choosing Python 3.6 as the preferred version. Then, choose `gdal` from the list of uninstalled Python packages. This will install `gdal` version 2.1.0.

After installation, you can check if everything works OK by entering a Python shell and typing:

```
>> import gdal
>> import ogr
```

You can check GDAL's version number as follows:

```
>> gdal.VersionInfo() # returns '2010300'
```

This means you're running GDAL version 2.1.3.

Installing GDAL using conda

Using `conda` to install GDAL gives you more flexibility in choosing a preferred Python version than Anaconda3. If you open up a terminal, you can use the `conda search gdal` command to print a list of available `gdal` versions and the corresponding Python version. If you want to know the dependencies for each package, type `conda info gdal`. Particular versions of GDAL depend on a specific package version, which can be a problem if you have these already installed, for example, NumPy. Then, you can create a virtual environment to install and run GDAL and their dependencies with the accompanying Python version, for example:

```
(C:\Users\<UserName> conda create -n myenv python=3.4
(C:\Users\<UserName> activate myenv # for Windows only. macOS and Linux
users type "source activate myenv"
(C:\Users\<UserName> conda install gdal=2.1.0
```

You will be asked to proceed or not. If you confirm with y and hit *Enter*, a set of additional packages will be installed. These are called **dependencies**, which are packages that GDAL requires in order to function.

As you can see, `conda` does not list the latest GDAL version, 2.2.2, when you type in `conda search gdal`. Remember that in Chapter 1, *Package Installation and Management*, we stated that `conda` does not always have the latest test versions of packages available for installation that are available in other ways. This is one such case.

Installing GDAL using pip

The **Python Package Index** (PyPI) also offers GDAL, meaning you can use `pip` to install it on your machine. The installation is similar to the `conda` installation procedure described earlier, but this time using the `pip install` command. Again, it is recommended to use a virtual environment when installing GDAL instead of a root installation that requires you to create path variables in your system environment setting if you're using Windows.

Installing a second GDAL version using pip

If you have a Windows machine and already have a working version of GDAL on your machine, but would like to install an extra one using `pip`, you can use the following link to install the GDAL version of your choice and then run the following command from your activated virtual environment to install it correctly:

GDAL download repository: `https://www.lfd.uci.edu/~gohlke/pythonlibs/#gdal`

```
>> pip install path\to\GDAL-2.1.3-cp27-cp27m-win32.whl
```

`GDAL-2.1.3-cp27m-win32.whl` is the name of the downloaded GDAL repository.

Other recommended GDAL resources

The full documentation of the GDAL/OGR Python API is available at: `http://gdal.org/python/`.

The homepage, `http://gdal.org`, also offers download links to GDAL as well as extensive documentation for developers and users.

GEOS

The **Geometry Engine Open Source (GEOS)** is the C/C++ port of a subset of the **Java Topology Suite (JTS)** and selected functions. GEOS aims to contain the complete functionality of JTS in C++. It can be compiled on many platforms, including Python. As you will see later on, the Shapely library uses functions from the GEOS library. In fact, there are many applications using GEOS, including PostGIS and QGIS. GeoDjango, covered in `Chapter 12`, *GeoDjango*, also uses GEOS, as well as GDAL, among other geospatial libraries. GEOS can also be compiled with GDAL, giving OGR all of its capabilities.

The JTS is an open source geospatial computational geometry library written in Java. It provides various functionalities, including a geometry model, geometric functions, spatial structures and algorithms, and i/o capabilities. Using GEOS, you have access to the following capabilities—geospatial functions (such as `within` and `contains`), geospatial operations (union, intersection, and many more), spatial indexing, **Open Geospatial Consortium (OGC) well-known text (WKT)** and **well-known binary (WKB)** input/output, the C and C++ APIs, and thread safety.

Installing GEOS

GEOS can be installed using `pip` install, `conda`, and Anaconda3:

```
>> conda install -c conda-forge geos
>> pip install geos
```

Detailed installation info about GEOS and other documentation is available here: `https://trac.osgeo.org/geos/`

Shapely

Shapely is a Python package for manipulation and analysis of planar features, using functions from the GEOS library (the engine of PostGIS) and a port of the JTS. Shapely is not concerned with data formats or coordinate systems but can be readily integrated with packages that are. Shapely only deals with analyzing geometries and offers no capabilities for reading and writing geospatial files. It was developed by Sean Gillies, who was also the person behind Fiona and Rasterio.

Shapely supports eight fundamental geometry types that are implemented as a class in the `shapely.geometry` module—points, multipoints, linestrings, multilinestrings, linearrings, multipolygons, polygons, and geometrycollections. Apart from representing these geometries, Shapely can be used to manipulate and analyze geometries through a number of methods and attributes.

Shapely has mainly the same classes and functions as OGR while dealing with geometries. The difference between Shapely and OGR is that Shapely has a more Pythonic and very intuitive interface, is better optimized, and has a well-developed documentation. With Shapely, you're writing pure Python, whereas with GEOS, you're writing C++ in Python. For **data munging**, a term used for data management and analysis, you're better off writing in pure Python rather than C++, which explains why these libraries were created.

For more information on Shapely, consult the documentation at `https://toblerity.org/shapely/manual.html`. This page also has detailed information on installing Shapely for different platforms and how to build Shapely from the source for compatibility with other modules that depend on GEOS. This refers to the fact that installing Shapely will require you to upgrade NumPy and GEOS if these are already installed.

Installing Shapely

Shapely can be installed using `pip` install, `conda`, and Anaconda3:

```
>> pip install shapely
>> conda install -c scitools shapely
```

Windows users can also get the wheels at `http://www.lfd.uci.edu/~gohlke/pythonlibs/#shapely`. A wheel is a built-package format for Python, containing a ZIP format archive with a specially formatted filename and the `.whl` extension. Shapely 1.6 requires a Python version higher than 2.6 and a GEOS version higher or equal to 3.3.

Also look at `https://pypi.python.org/pypi/Shapely` for more information on installing and using Shapely.

Fiona

Fiona is the API of OGR. It can be used for reading and writing data formats. The main reason for using it instead of OGR is that it's closer to Python than OGR as well as more dependable and less error-prone. It makes use of two markup languages, WKT and WKB, for representing spatial information with regards to vector data. As such, it can be combined well with other Python libraries such as Shapely, you would use Fiona for input and output, and Shapely for creating and manipulating geospatial data.

While Fiona is Python compatible and our recommendation, users should also be aware of some of the disadvantages. It is more dependable than OGR because it uses Python objects for copying vector data instead of C pointers, which also means that they use more memory, which affects the performance.

Installing Fiona

You can use `pip` install, `conda`, or Anaconda3 to install Fiona:

```
>> conda install -c conda-forge fiona
>> conda install -c conda-forge/label/broken fiona
>> pip install fiona
```

Fiona requires Python 2.6, 2.7, 3.3, or 3.4 and GDAL/OGR 1.8+. Fiona depends on the modules `six`, `cligj`, `munch`, `argparse`, and `ordereddict` (the two latter modules are standard in Python 2.7+).

Consult Fiona's readme page for more download info `https://toblerity.org/fiona/README.html`.

Python shapefile library (pyshp)

 The **Python shapefile library** (**pyshp**) is a pure Python library and is used to read and write shapefiles. The `pyshp` library's sole purpose is to work with shapefiles—it only uses the Python standard library. You cannot use it for geometric operations. If you're only working with shapefiles, this one-file-only library is simpler than using GDAL.

Installing pyshp

You can use `pip` install, `conda`, and Anaconda3 to install `pyshp`:

```
>> pip install pyshp
>> conda install pyshp
```

More documentation is available at PyPi: `https://pypi.python.org/pypi/pyshp/1.2.3`

The source code for `pyshp` is available at `https://github.com/GeospatialPython/pyshp`.

pyproj

The `pyproj` is a Python package that performs cartographic transformations and geodetic computations. It is a Cython wrapper to provide Python interfaces to PROJ.4 functions, meaning you can access an existing library of C code in Python.

PROJ.4 is a projection library that transforms data among many coordinate systems and is also available through GDAL and OGR. The reason that PROJ.4 is still popular and widely used is two-fold:

- Firstly, because it supports so many different coordinate systems
- Secondly, because of the routes it provides to do this—Rasterio and GeoPandas, two Python libraries covered next, both use `pyproj` and thus PROJ.4 functionality under the hood

The difference between using PROJ.4 separately instead of using it with a package such as GDAL is that it enables you to re-project individual points, and packages using PROJ.4 do not offer this functionality.

The `pyproj` package offers two classes—the `Proj` class and the `Geod` class. The `Proj` class performs cartographic computations, while the `Geod` class performs geodetic computations.

Installing pyproj

Installation of `pyproj` can be done with `pip` install, `conda`, and Anaconda3:

```
>> conda install -c conda-forge pyproj
>> pip install pyproj
```

The following link contains more information on `pyproj`: `https://jswhit.github.io/pyproj/`

You can find more about PROJ.4 at `http://proj4.org/`.

Rasterio

Rasterio is a GDAL and NumPy-based Python library for raster data, written with the Python developer in mind instead of C, using Python language types, protocols, and idioms. Rasterio aims to make GIS data more accessible to Python programmers and helps GIS analysts learn important Python standards. Rasterio relies on concepts of Python rather than GIS.

Rasterio is an open source project from the satellite team of Mapbox, a provider of custom online maps for websites and applications. The name of this library should be pronounced as *raster-i-o* rather than *ras-te-rio*. Rasterio came into being as a result of a project called the **Mapbox Cloudless Atlas**, which aimed to create a pretty-looking basemap from satellite imagery.

One of the software requirements was to use open source software and a high-level language with handy multi-dimensional array syntax. Although GDAL offers proven algorithms and drivers, developing with GDAL's Python bindings feels a lot like C++.

Therefore, Rasterio was designed to be a Python package at the top, with extension modules (using Cython) in the middle, and a GDAL shared library on the bottom. Other requirements for the raster library were being able to read and write NumPy ndarrays to and from data files, use Python types, protocols, and idioms instead of C or C++ to free programmers from having to code in two languages.

For georeferencing, Rasterio follows the lead of `pyproj`. There are a couple of capabilities added on top of reading and writing, one of them being a features module. Reprojection of geospatial data can be done with the `rasterio.warp` module.

Rasterio's project homepage can be found here: `https://github.com/mapbox/rasterio`

Rasterio dependencies

As stated earlier, Rasterio uses GDAL, meaning it's one of its dependencies. Python package dependencies are `affine`, `cligj`, `click`, `enum34`, and `numpy`.

The documentation for Rasterio can be found here: `https://mapbox.github.io/rasterio/`

Installation of Rasterio

To install Rasterio on a Windows machine, you need to download the `rasterio` and GDAL binaries for your system and run:

```
>> pip install -U pip
>> pip install GDAL-1.11.2-cp27-none-win32.whl
>> pip install rasterio-0.24.0-cp27-none-win32.whl
```

Using `conda`, you can install `rasterio` this way:

```
>> conda config --add channels conda-forge # this enables the conda-forge
channel
>> conda install rasterio
```

`conda-forge` is an additional channel from which packages may be installed.

Detailed installation instructions for different platforms are available here: `https://mapbox.github.io/rasterio/installation.html`

GeoPandas

GeoPandas is a Python library for working with vector data. It is based on the `pandas` library that is part of the SciPy stack. SciPy is a popular library for data inspection and analysis, but unfortunately, it cannot read spatial data. GeoPandas was created to fill this gap, taking `pandas` data objects as a starting point. The library also adds functionality from geographical Python packages.

GeoPandas offers two data objects—a GeoSeries object that is based on a `pandas` Series object and a GeoDataFrame, based on a `pandas` DataFrame object, but adding a geometry column for each row. Both GeoSeries and GeoDataFrame objects can be used for spatial data processing, similar to spatial databases. Read and write functionality is provided for almost every vector data format. Also, because both Series and DataFrame objects are subclasses from pandas data objects, you can use the same properties to select or subset data, for example `.loc` or `.iloc`.

GeoPandas is a library that employs the capabilities of newer tools, such as Jupyter Notebooks, pretty well, whereas GDAL enables you to interact with data records inside of vector and raster datasets through Python code. GeoPandas takes a more visual approach by loading all records into a GeoDataFrame so that you can see them all together on your screen. The same goes for plotting data. These functionalities were lacking in Python 2 as developers were dependent on IDEs without extensive data visualization capabilities which are now available with Jupyter Notebooks.

GeoPandas installation

There are various ways to install GeoPandas. You can use `pip` install, `conda` install, Anaconda3, or GitHub. Using a terminal window, you can install it as follows:

```
>> pip install geopandas
>> conda install -c conda-forge geopandas
```

Detailed installation info is available here: `http://geopandas.org/install.html`

GeoPandas is also available through PyPi: `https://pypi.python.org/pypi/geopandas/0.3.0`

GeoPandas is also available through Anaconda Cloud: `https://anaconda.org/IOOS/geopandas`

GeoPandas dependencies

GeoPandas depends on the following Python libraries, `pandas`, Shapely, Fiona, `pyproj`, NumPy, and `six`. These are either updated or installed when you install `GeoPandas`.

The `Geopandas` documentation is available at `http://geopandas.org`.

How it all works together

We've provided an overview of the most important open source packages for processing and analyzing geospatial data. The question then becomes when to use a certain package and why. GDAL, OGR, and GEOS are indispensable for geospatial processing and analyzing, but were not written in Python, and so they require Python binaries for Python developers. Fiona, Shapely, and `pyproj` were written to solve these problems, as well as the newer Rasterio library. For a more Pythonic approach, these newer packages are preferable to the older C++ packages with Python binaries (although they're used under the hood).

However, it's good to know the origins and history of all of these packages as they're all so widely used (and for good reason). The next chapter, which will be discussing geospatial databases, will build on information from this chapter. Chapter 5, *Vector Data Analysis*, and Chapter 6, *Raster Data Processing*, will specifically deal with the libraries discussed here, getting deeper into the details of both raster and vector data processing using these libraries.

At this point, you should have a global overview of the most important packages for processing and analyzing, their history, and how they relate to each other. You should have an idea of what options are available for a certain use case and why one package is preferable over another. However, as is often the way in programming, there might be multiple solutions for one particular problem. For example, when dealing with shapefiles, you could use `pyshp`, GDAL, Shapely, or GeoPandas, depending on your preference and the problem at hand.

Summary

In this chapter, we introduced the major code libraries used to process and analyze geospatial data. You learned the characteristics of each library, how they are related or are distinct to each other, how to install them, where to find additional documentation, and typical use cases. GDAL is a major library that includes two separate libraries, OGR and GDAL. Many other libraries and software applications use GDAL functionality under the hood, examples are Fiona and Rasterio, which were both covered in this chapter. These were created to make it easier to work with GDAL and OGR in a more Pythonic way.

The next chapter will introduce spatial databases. These are used for data storage and analysis, with examples being SpatiaLite and PostGIS. You will also learn how to use different Python libraries to connect to these databases.

3
Introduction to Geospatial Databases

In the previous chapters, you learned how to set up your Python environment and learned about the different libraries available for working with geospatial data using Python. In this chapter, you will start working with data.

Databases provide one of the most popular ways to store large amounts of data, and one of the most popular open source databases is PostgreSQL. PostGIS extends PostgreSQL, adding geographic objects and the ability to query records spatially. When PostgreSQL and PostGIS are combined, they create a powerful geospatial data repository.

Geospatial databases improve on basic relational database queries by allowing you to query your data by location or by location to other features in the database. You can also perform geospatial operations such as measurements of features, distances between features, and converting between projections. Another feature of geospatial databases is the ability to create new geometries from existing features from a buffer, union, or clip operation.

This chapter will cover the basics of geospatial databases. In this chapter, you will learn:

- How to install PostgreSQL and PostGIS
- How to install and use `pyscopg2` to connect to the database
- How to add data to a database
- How to perform basic spatial queries
- How to query length and area
- How to query for points within a polygon

In `Chapter 7`, *Geoprocessing with Geodatabases*, we will come back to geospatial databases and you will learn more advanced operations and how to display your data.

Installing PostgreSQL and PostGIS on Windows

You can install PostGIS by installing PostgreSQL and then install PostGIS afterwards, or you can install PostgreSQL and then use Stack Builder, which comes with PostgreSQL, afterwards to add PostGIS. Using Stack Builder allows you to download the desired PostgreSQL version and with a single-click also get the correct PostGIS version.

 When I installed PostgreSQL 10, Stack Builder did not include PostGIS. By the time of publication, this should have been added. Screenshots may show a different PostGIS version because I used an old copy of PostgreSQL to show how Stack Builder would work. You can download PostgreSQL from `https://www.postgresql.org/download/`.

As we proceed, I will walk you through installing PostgreSQL and then using Stack Builder to add PostGIS and a database. After downloading the executable, run it by double-clicking it. You will see the wizard as follows:

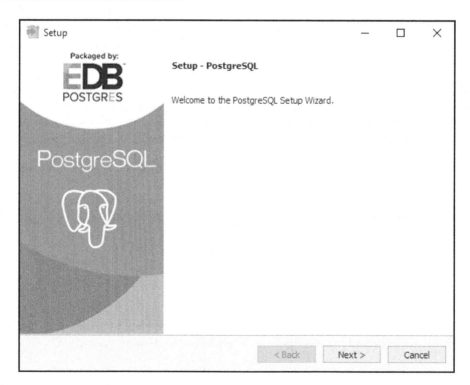

You can choose where to install PostgreSQL, but it is probably best to leave it as the default unless you have a specific reason to locate it elsewhere:

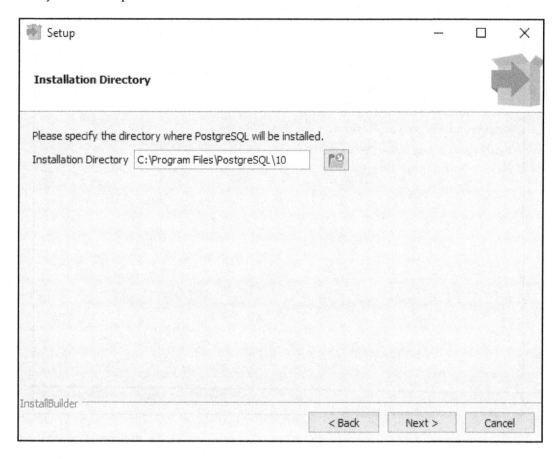

Again, it is probably best to store the data in the default location, which is the same root folder as the PostgreSQL installation:

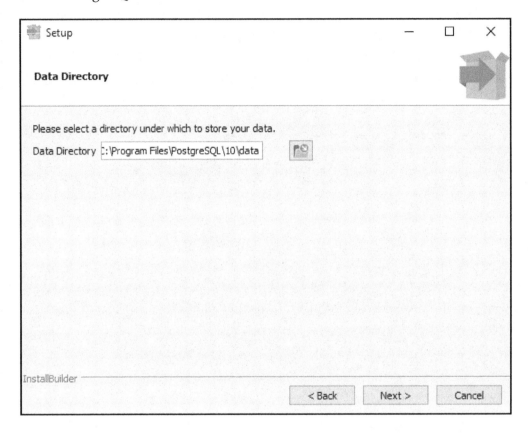

Select the port in which you would like to run PostgreSQL. Applications will expect to find PostgreSQL on this port, so change it at your own risk. More advanced users can reconfigure port channels in the `.config` file after installation:

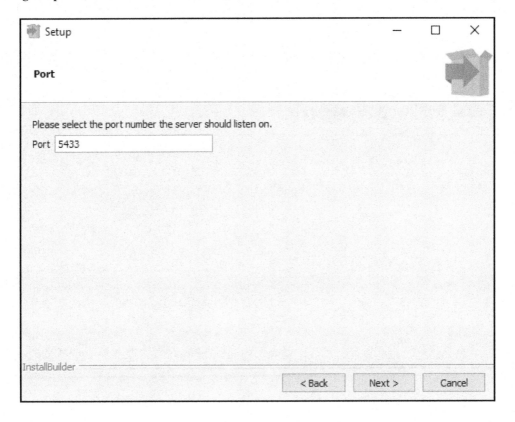

Choose your **Locale**, or select the default. I have selected **English, United States**:

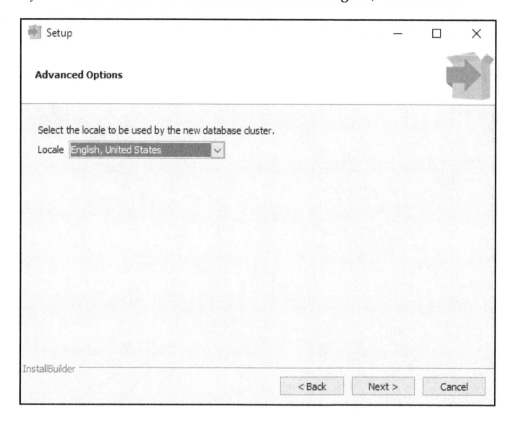

This is where you are presented with the option to launch Stack Builder, and from there, you can install PostGIS. Check the box to begin the installation. The installation should only take a few minutes on a newer system:

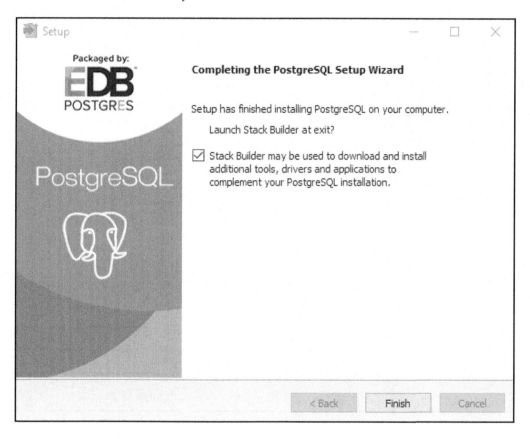

The PostgreSQL installation has been completed and Stack Builder should now be open. Under **Spatial Extensions**, select the proper version of PostGIS 32 or 64-bit. Notice that it is a bundle and includes other packages such as `pgRouting`:

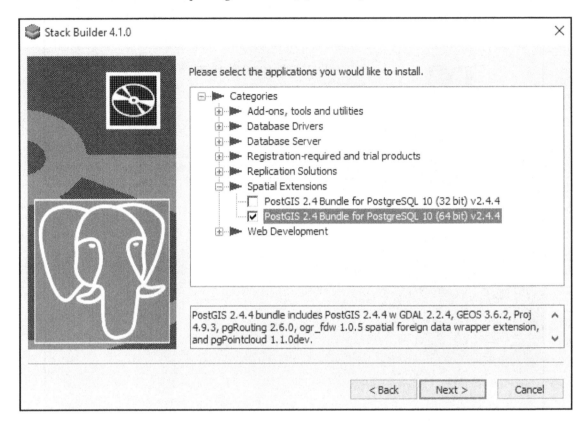

Now, the install wizard for PostGIS will launch. You have to agree to the terms of the license:

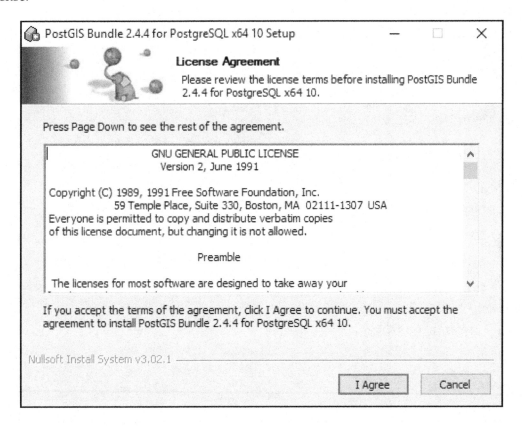

You can create a database at any time and this chapter will show you how to, however, it is best to check the **Create spatial database** box and take care of it now. If you do, your database will be set up and ready to use once PostGIS is installed:

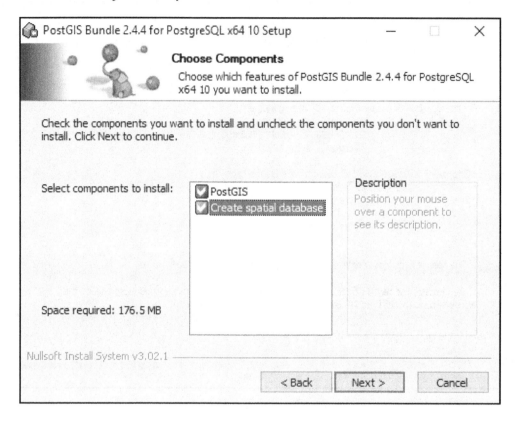

PostGIS will try to install where PostgreSQL was installed:

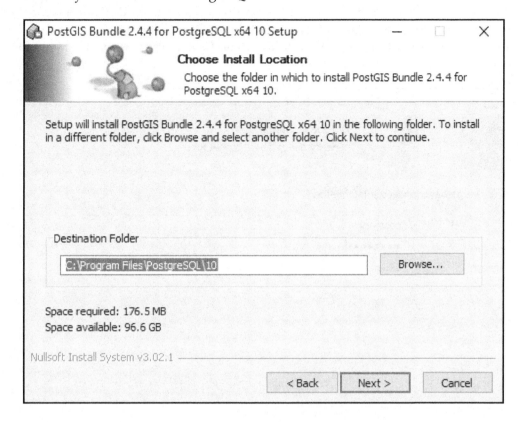

Enter the username, password, and port for the database. The examples in this chapter will use `postgres` (username) and `postgres` (password). If you select a different username and password combination, remember it. In production, it is best not to use default usernames and passwords as they are well-known and will make you an easy target for hackers:

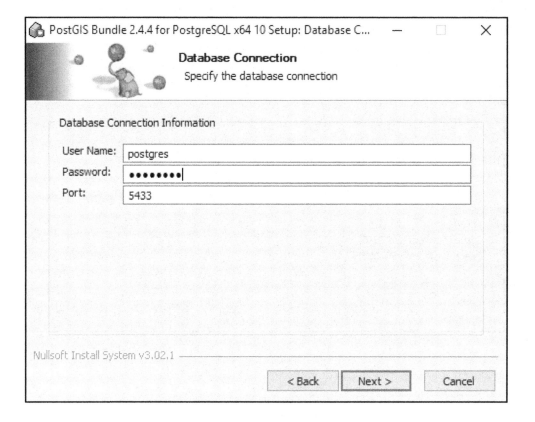

Enter the name for the database. The examples we will be looking at will use `pythonspatial` as the database name. You will only use the name for the initial connection. The SQL queries in the example will use the table name:

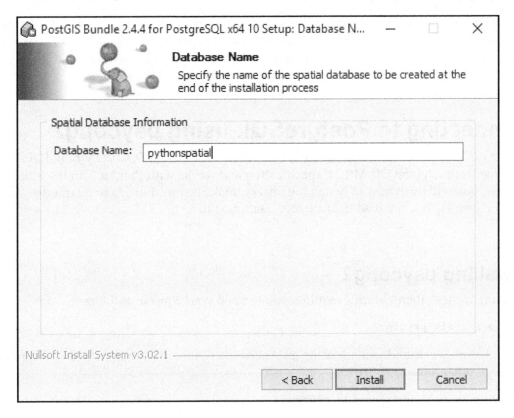

Installing PostgreSQL and PostGIS on Mac

To install PostgreSQL and PostGIS on a Mac, you can use `Postgres.app`. You can download the file from `http://postgresapp.com/`. After the file has downloaded, move it to the `applications` folder and double-click it. Click **Initialize**. You will have a server on `localhost:5432`. The username and database name is the same as your Mac user. There is no password.

You should then be able to use the `psql` commands to create a new database and enable PostGIS.

Working with PostgreSQL and PostGIS using Python

To connect and manipulate your PostgreSQL database in Python, you will need a library to assist you. psyscopg2 is that library. It provides a wrapper around the official libpq client library. In this section, we will cover how to install the library, how to connect to the database, and how to add a table and perform basic geospatial queries.

Connecting to PostgreSQL using psycopg2

pscycopg2 is the most popular library for working with PostgreSQL in Python. It fully implements the Python DB API 2.0 specification and works with Python 3. In the following sections, you will learn how to install the library, make connections, execute queries, and read the results. You can read the full documentation here: http://initd.org/psycopg/docs/

Installing psycopg2

Installing most Python libraries requires you to open your console and type:

```
pip install psycopg2
```

If that doesn't work, and you are using an Anaconda Python distribution, you can run the conda command, using:

```
conda install -c anaconda psycopg2
```

While most Python libraries can be downloaded and installed using:

```
python setup.py install
```

Since psycopg2 is more advanced than that and requires you to have a C compiler, Python header files, libpq header files, and the pg_config program. If you need to install psycopg2 from the source, the link to the instructions is in the following hint box.

To install `psycopg2` from the source, the instructions are located at: http://initd.org/psycopg/docs/install.html#install-from-source

Connecting to the database and creating a table

You should have created a database when you installed PostGIS. For the examples mentioned as follows, we will use this database.

If you did not create a database during the installation of PostGIS, you can do so using your terminal (command prompt in Windows) and the commands as follows:

```
createdb -U postgres pythonspatial
psql -U postgres -d pythonspatial -c "CREATE EXTENSION postgis;"
```

You may need to modify your path. On Windows, the command to do so is shown as follows:

```
set PATH=%PATH%;C:\Program Files\PostgreSQL\10\bin
```

To connect to your database, use the following code:

```
import psycopg2

connection =
psycopg2.connect(database="pythonspatial",user="postgres",
password="postgres")

cursor = connection.cursor()

cursor.execute("CREATE TABLE art_pieces (id SERIAL PRIMARY KEY,
code VARCHAR(255), location GEOMETRY)")

connection.commit()
```

The code mentioned earlier starts by importing `psycopg2`. It then makes a `connection` by using the `connect()` function and passing the parameters for the database name, the `user`, and the `password`. It then creates a `cursor` which allows you to communicate with the database. You can use the `execute()` method of the `cursor` to create the table passing SQL statements as strings.

The code executes an SQL command which creates a table named `art_pieces` with an `id` of type `SERIAL` and makes it a `PRIMARY KEY`, `code` as type `VARCHAR` and a length of `255`, and the `location` as the `GEOMETRY` type. The `SERIAL PRIMARY KEY` tells PostgreSQL that we want an auto-incremented unique identifier. You can also use the `BIGSERIAL` type. The other type that is different is the `location` of the `GEOMETRY` type. This is the column that will hold the geo portion of our records.

Lastly, you `commit()` to make sure the changes are saved. You can also `close()` when you are finished, but we will continue further.

Adding data to the table

In the previous section, we created a table. In this section, you will grab data from an open data site and put it on your table so that you can query it in the next section.

Most cities have open data websites and portals. The City of Albuquerque has several ArcServer endpoints with spatial data. The following code will use the `requests` Python library to grab public art data and then use `psycopg2` to send it to the PostgreSQL database, `pythonspatial`:

```
import requests

url='http://coagisweb.cabq.gov/arcgis/rest/services/public/PublicAr
t/MapServer/0/query'

params={"where":"1=1","outFields":"*","outSR":"4326","f":"json"}

r=requests.get(url,params=params)

data=r.json()

data["features"][0]
```

The code which we mentioned earlier imports `requests`, then, using the URL to the ArcServer endpoint, it grabs the results of a query asking for all of the data (`where:1=1`) and all of the fields (`outFields:*`) in **World Geodetic System (WGS) 84** (`outSR:4326`), and returns it as a JSON (`f:json`).

 ArcServer is a GIS Server made by the **Environmental Systems Research Institute (ESRI)**. It provides a way to serve GIS data using an API and returning JSON. Many government agencies will have an Open Data Portal that utilizes an ArcServer to deliver the data.

The results are loaded into the `data` variable. Each record is in the array features (`data["features"][n]`). A single record, `data["features"][0]`, is shown as follows:

```
{'attributes': {'ADDRESS': '4440 Osuna NE',
 'ARTIST': 'David Anderson',
 'ART_CODE': '101',
 'IMAGE_URL':
'http://www.flickr.com/photos/abqpublicart/6831137393/',
 'JPG_URL':
'http://farm8.staticflickr.com/7153/6831137393_fa38634fd7_m.jpg',
 'LOCATION': 'Osuna Median bet.Jefferson/ W.Frontage Rd',
 'OBJECTID': 951737,
 'TITLE': 'Almond Blossom/Astronomy',
 'TYPE': 'public sculpture',
 'X': -106.5918383,
 'Y': 35.1555,
 'YEAR': '1986'},
 'geometry': {'x': -106.59183830022498, 'y': 35.155500000061544}}
```

With the `data`, you will iterate through the array of `features`, inserting the ART_CODE as `code` and creating a **well-known text (WKT)** representation of each point.

> To learn more about WKT, you can read its Wikipedia entry at: https://en.wikipedia.org/wiki/Well-known_text

The following code shows you how to insert the data:

```
for a in data["features"]:
    code=a["attributes"]["ART_CODE"]
    wkt="POINT("+str(a["geometry"]["x"])+" "+str(a["geometry"]
["y"])+")"
    if a["geometry"]["x"]=='NaN':
        pass
    else:
        cursor.execute("INSERT INTO art_pieces (code, location)
VALUES ({},
        ST_GeomFromText('{}'))".format(code, wkt))
connection.commit()
```

The preceding code iterates through each feature. It assigns ART_CODE to `code`, then constructs the WKT (`Point(-106.5918 35.1555)`), and assigns it to `wkt`. The code uses ART_CODE to show how to load other properties into the database.

Data is almost never clean and perfect. This data is no exception. So that it doesn't crash when the x coordinate is missing, I have added an `if, else` statement to skip over missing data. This concept is known as **error handling**, and it is a best practice when constructing `requests`. The `else` statement is where the data gets inserted. Using `cursor.execute()`, you can construct the SQL query.

The query inserts `art_pieces` into the database along with the `code` and `location` fields with values. The first value, for `code`, is a placeholder `{}`. The second value, for `location`, is geometry which we stored as WKT. Because of this, it is inserted using the `ST_GeomFromText()` function and a placeholder `{}`.

The `format()` method is where you pass the variables to fill the placeholders—code, wkt. The following code shows what the query will look like when the placeholders are filled in:

```
INSERT INTO art_pieces (code, location) VALUES (101,
ST_GeomFromText('Point(-106.5918 35.1555)'))
```

In the previously mentioned code, you created the WKT as a concatenated string. This can be accomplished in a cleaner and more Pythonic fashion by using the Shapely library.

Shapely

Shapely can be installed using:

```
pip install shapely
```

Or with `conda`:

```
conda install -c scitools shapely
```

Shapely makes the task of creating and working with geometries easier and makes your code cleaner. In the previous code, you concatenated a string to create a WKT representation of a point. Using Shapely, you can create a point and then convert it to WKT. The following code shows you how:

```
from shapely.geometry import Point, MultiPoint

thepoints=[]

for a in data["features"]:
    code=a["attributes"]["ART_CODE"]
    p=Point(float(a["geometry"]["x"]),float(a["geometry"]["y"]))
    thepoints.append(p)
    if a["geometry"]["x"]=='NaN':
```

```
        pass
    else:
        cursor.execute("INSERT INTO art_pieces (code, location)
VALUES ('{}',
        ST_GeomFromText('{}'))".format(code, p.wkt))
connection.commit()
```

The previous code imports `Point` and `MultiPoint` from `shapely.geometry`. The code is the same as the previous version until the line in bold. To create a point, you use `Point(x,y)` in Shapely. It put all of the points in an array called `thepoints` to draw them in a Jupyter Notebook, for which an image is follows. Lastly, the SQL statement passes `p.wkt` to `ST_GeomFromText()`.

In a Jupyter Notebook, you can print Shapely geometry just by typing the name of the variable holding the geometry and it will draw the end. The public `art` points are in the variable `thepoints`. A `MultiPoint` can be created using an array of points, and printing them draws the following image:

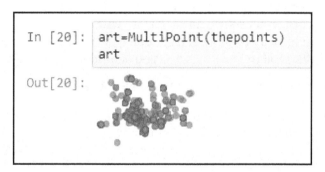

Querying the data

You created a table, added columns for code and location, and populated it using data from another source. Now, you will learn how to query the data and get it out of the database.

While there are spatial SQL queries available to you, you can always just select the data as if it were a non-spatially enabled database so that you can use it as follows:

```
SELECT * FROM table
```

The following code shows the generic `SELECT` all query and the results:

```
cursor.execute("SELECT * from art_pieces")
data=cursor.fetchall()
data
```

The result should look as follows:

```
[(1, '101', '010100000025FFBFADE0A55AC06A658B6CE7934140'),
(2, '102', '0101000000CC4E16E181AA5AC0D99F67B3EA8B4140'),
........,]
```

The first number, 1,2,n, is the id (the SERIAL PRIMARY KEY). Next, is the code. The geometry is the last column. The string of what appears to be random numbers and letters is a **well-known binary (WKB)** in hex.

To convert the WKB, you use shapely. The following code walks you through converting the WKB to a shapely Point, and then printing the WKT:

```
from shapely.wkb import loads
aPoint=loads(data[0][2],hex=True)
aPoint.wkt
```

The previous code imports the loads() method from shapely.wkb. You must add the hex parameter and make it equal to True or you will receive an error. To get the geography column of the first record, you can use data[0][2] with [0] as the record and [2] as the column. Now that you have a shapely Point, you can verify it by using type(aPoint), you can print it as a WKT using aPoint.wkt. You should see the result as follows:

POINT (-106.591838300225 35.15550000006154)

If you want PostgreSQL to return the data in WKB without hex, you can do so using ST_AsBinary(). The following code shows you how:

```
cursor.execute("SELECT id,code,ST_AsBinary(location) from
art_pieces")
data=cursor.fetchall()
data[0][2]
from shapely.wkb import loads
pNoHex=loads(bytes(data[0][2]))
pNoHex.wkt
```

The previous code wraps the location in ST_AsBinary(). To load the result into a shapely Point, you have to use bytes(). Then, you can see the WKT using pNoHex.wkt. You should see the same point as in the previous example.

Binary may come in handy, but you can also query the data and get the geometry back as a WKT:

```
cursor.execute("SELECT code, ST_AsText(location) from art_pieces")
data = cursor.fetchone()
```

The previous code uses `ST_AsText(geometry column)` to return the data as a WKT. You can return a column that contains geometry at any time by using `ST_AsText()`. Instead of `fetchall()`, the code uses `fetchone()` to grab a single record. You should see a single record as follows:

```
('101', 'POINT(-106.591838300225 35.1555000000615)')
```

You can load WKT into a `shapely Point` using `loads()`, but you need to import it first, just like you did earlier with WKB:

```
from shapely.wkt import loads
pb=loads(data[1])
pb.coords[:]
```

The previous code import `loads` from `shapely`—but this time using `shapely.wkt`, not `wkb`. Otherwise, you load the data the same way as in the previous examples. You can see the coordinates of the `shapely Point` using `pb.coords[:]`, or you can see them individually using `pb.x` and `pb.y`.

The result of `pb.coords[:]` will be a coordinate pair, which is shown as follows:

```
[(-106.591838300225, 35.1555000000615)]
```

Changing the CRS

The data in the database is using **World Geodetic System 84 (WGS 84)**, latitude and longitude. What if you need the data out in **European Petroleum Survey Group (EPSG) 3857**? You can change the spatial reference in your query using `ST_Transform()`. The following code shows you how by using PostGIS functions:

```
cursor.execute("SELECT
UpdateGeometrySRID('art_pieces','location',4326)")
cursor.execute("SELECT
Find_SRID('public','art_pieces','location')")
cursor.fetchall()
```

The previous code makes two queries to the database:

- Firstly, it assigns a spatial reference system identifier to the geometry column in the table using `UpdateGeomtrySRID()`. This needs to be done because the points were put in the table without any reference to an `SRID`. So when we try to get the results back using a different coordinate reference system, the database will not know how to transform our coordinates.

- Secondly, the code queries the database to tell us what the SRID is on the geometry column in the table using Find_SRID(). If you do not have a properly added geometry column, the function will fail.

Now that you have an SRID set on the column in the table, you can query the data and transform it:

```
cursor.execute("SELECT code, ST_AsTexT(ST_Transform(location,3857))
from art_pieces")
cursor.fetchone()
```

The previous code is a basic select code and location, as text, from art_pieces, but now there is an ST_Transform method. This method takes the column with geometry and the SRID you want the data sent back in. Now, the piece of art at (-106.59, 35.155) is returned using 3857, and shown as follows with the transformed coordinates:

```
('101', 'POINT(-11865749.1623 4185033.1034)')
```

Buffer

A spatial database allows you to store spatial data, but you can also perform operations on the data and get different geometries back. The most common of these operations would be a buffer. You have a table of points, but using ST_Buffer(), you can have the database return a polygon around the point with a specified radius. The following code shows you how:

```
cursor.execute("SELECT
ST_AsText(ST_Buffer(a.location,25.00,'quad_segs=2')) from pieces a
WHERE a.code='101'")

cursor.fetchall()
```

The previous code grabs a record from the table where the art code field equals 101, and selects a buffer with a radius of 25 around the location. The result will be a polygon, which is shown as follows:

 When using geography, if the buffer is large, falls between two UTM zones, or crosses the dateline, it may behave unexpectedly.

```
'POLYGON((-106.591563918525 35.1555036055616,-106.591568334295
35.1554595740463,-106.59158312469
35.1554170960907,...,-106.591570047094
```

```
35.155547498531,-106.591563918525 35.1555036055616))'
```

If you load the polygon into `shapely` using the following code, a Jupyter Notebook will draw the polygon:

```
from shapely.geometry import Polygon
from shapely.wkt import loads
buff=loads(data[0][0])
buff
```

The buffer returned from `ST_Buffer` as a `shapely` polygon is shown as follows:

You can also pass a parameter to `ST_Buffer` for the number of segments you used to draw a quarter of a circle. If you divide the circle into four quadrants, the `quad_segs` parameter will draw that many segments in each quadrant. A `quad_seg` value of 1 will draw a rotated square, which is shown as follows:

Whereas a `quad_seg` value of 2 would draw an octagon which is shown as follows:

Distance and near

In the previous section, you had the database buffer a point and return the polygon. In this section, you will learn how to query the database for the distance between two points, and you will query the database and have it return records based on the distance from a specified point.

The PostGIS function for distance is ST_Distance(a,b). You can pass a and b as geometry or geography. As geography, the result will be returned in meters. The following code will get the distance between two points in the database:

```
cursor.execute("SELECT
ST_Distance(a.location::geography,b.location::geography) FROM
art_pieces a, art_pieces b where a.name='101' AND b.name='102'")
dist=cursor.fetchall()
dist
```

The previous code executes the SQL query for ST_Distance(), passing the location column of a and b which are records, where the code equals 101 and 102. ::geography is how you cast a geometry to a geography in PostGIS. How far are they from each other? They are 9,560.45428363 meters apart.

To convert this to miles use: dist[0][0]*0.00062137, which makes them 5.940 miles apart.

In the previous example, you used two points from the database, but you can also pass a hard-coded point as in the following code:

```
cursor.execute("SELECT ST_Distance(a.location::geography,
                ST_GeometryFromText('POINT(-106.5
35.1)')::geography)
                FROM art_pieces a where a.name='101'")

cursor.fetchall()
```

The previous code is the same query, but this time you switch out point b (code=102) with a hard-coded WKT point. The results of the query should state that the points are 10,391.40637117 meters apart.

And, as in previous examples, you can also use `shapely` to pass the WKT of the point, as in the following code:

```
from shapely.geometry import Point
p=Point(-106.5,35.1)
cursor.execute("SELECT ST_Distance(a.location::geography,
                ST_GeometryFromText('{}')::geography)
                FROM art_pieces a where
a.name='101'".format(p.wkt))
cursor.fetchall()
```

The previous code creates the point in `shapely` and then uses `format(p.wkt)` to pass the WKT to the `{}` placeholder.

You can get the distance between two points, but what if you want the distance of more than one point from another? To do that, you can remove the `a.location` and just use `location` as the first point. The following code will return five points and their distances from the specified point:

```
cursor.execute("SELECT code, ST_Distance(location::geography,
                ST_GeometryFromText('POINT(-106.591838300225
                35.1555000000615)')::geography)
                as d from art_pieces LIMIT 5")
cursor.fetchall()
```

The results should look like the data showing the distance in meters:

```
[('101', 0.0),
 ('102', 9560.45428362),
 ('104', 4741.8711304),
 ('105', 9871.8424894),
 ('106', 7907.8263995)]
```

The database returned the first five points in the table with their code and distance from the specified point. If you remove the `LIMIT`, you will get all of the points.

By adding an `ORDER BY` clause and the k-nearest neighbor operator, you can extend this query to get the closest five points to the specified point. Look at the following code:

```
cursor.execute("SELECT code, ST_Distance(location::geography,
                ST_GeometryFromText('POINT(-106.591838300225
                35.1555000000615)')::geography) as d from
art_pieces
                ORDER BY location<-
                >ST_GeometryFromText('POINT(-106.591838300225
                35.1555000000615)') LIMIT 5")
```

```
cursor.fetchall()
```

The key element in the previous code is the symbol <->. This is the k-nearest neighbor operator. It returns the distance between two geometries. Using ORDER BY location <-> ST_GeometryFromText(), you are specifying two geometries. Because you set a LIMIT of 5, the database will return the 5 closest points to the one specified—including the point of origin. The results should look like the following points:

```
[('101', 0.0),
 ('614', 1398.08905864),
 ('492', 2384.97632735),
 ('570', 3473.81914218),
 ('147', 3485.71207698)]
```

Notice that the code value is not 101-106 or the first five from the database, and that the distance increases from 0.0. The closest point, code 101, is the point you specified in the query, so it is 0.0 meters away.

Lines in the database

The first section of this chapter focused on point operations. Now, we will turn our attention to lines. For the following examples, you will create a new table and insert three lines. The following code will accomplish that:

```
from shapely.geometry import LineString
from shapely.geometry import MultiLineString

connection =
psycopg2.connect(database="pythonspatial",user="postgres",
    password="postgres")

cursor = c.cursor()
cursor.execute("CREATE TABLE lines (id SERIAL PRIMARY KEY, location
GEOMETRY)")
thelines=[]
thelines.append(LineString([(-106.635585,35.086972),(-106.621294,35
.124997)]))
thelines.append(LineString([(-106.498309,35.140108),(-106.497010,35
.069488)]))
thelines.append(LineString([(-106.663878,35.106459),(-106.586506,35
.103979)]))

mls=MultiLineString([[((-106.635585,35.086972),(-106.621294,35.12499
7)),((-106.498309,35.140108),(-106.497010,35.069488)),((-106.663878
,35.106459),(-106.586506,35.103979))]])
```

```
for a in thelines:
    cursor.execute("INSERT INTO lines (location) VALUES
            (ST_GeomFromText('{}'))".format(a.wkt))
connection.commit()
```

The previous code should be familiar. It starts by connecting to the Python spatial database, gets a `cursor`, and then creates a table with an `id` and a location of the `geometry` type. You should import `shapely LineString` and `MultiLine`, `Multiline` is so you can print the lines in the Jupyter notebook. You should create an array of `lines` and then loop through them, inserting each into the table using the `cursor`. You can then `commit()` the changes.

To see that the lines have been added to the database, you can execute the following code:

```
cursor.execute("SELECT id, ST_AsTexT(location) from lines")
data=cursor.fetchall()
data
```

The previous code executes a basic select statement on the new table. There should be three records in the result set, as follows:

```
[(1, 'LINESTRING(-106.635585 35.086972,-106.621294 35.124997)'),
 (2, 'LINESTRING(-106.498309 35.140108,-106.49701 35.069488)'),
 (3, 'LINESTRING(-106.663878 35.106459,-106.586506 35.103979)')]
```

If you print the `mls` variable (the variable holding a multilinestring in the earlier code) you can see the lines which are shown in the following image:

Now that you have a database table with a few lines, you can proceed to measure them and find out if they intersect.

Length of a line

Points have no length and if they intersect, they have the same coordinates. Lines, however, have a length and can intersect at a point not specified in the table, between two of the points used to create the line.
The following code will return the length of all of the `lines`:

```
cu.execute("SELECT id, ST_Length(location::geography) FROM lines ")
cu.fetchall()
```

The previous code uses the ST_Length function. The function will accept both geometry and geography. In this example, ::geography was used to convert the geometry so meters would be returned.

The results are as follows:

```
[(1, 4415.21026808109),
 (2, 7835.65405408195),
 (3, 7059.45840502359)]
```

You can add an ORDER BY clause to the previous query and the database will return the lines from shortest to longest. The following code adds the clause:

```
cu.execute("SELECT id, ST_Length(location::geography)
           FROM lines ORDER BY ST_Length(location::geography)")
cu.fetchall()
```

Adding ORDER BY will return the records, swapping the position of 2 and 3, as follows:

```
[(1, 4415.21026808109),
 (3, 7059.45840502359),
 (2, 7835.65405408195)]
```

Intersecting lines

You know the length of the lines, and by drawing the lines in a Jupyter Notebook, you know that lines 1 and lines 3 intersect. In PostGIS, you can use the ST_Intersects() function, passing either geometries or geographies. The database will return either true or false.

The following code will execute the query on lines 1 and lines 3 and return True:

```
cu.execute("SELECT
ST_Intersects(l.location::geography,ll.location::geometry)
           FROM lines l, lines ll WHERE l.id=1 AND ll.id=3")
cu.fetchall()
```

The previous code will return True, because lines 1 and lines 3 intersect. But where do they intersect? Using ST_Intersection() will return to the point where the two lines meet:

```
cu.execute("SELECT ST_AsText(ST_Intersection(l.location::geography,
           ll.location::geometry)) FROM lines l, lines ll
           WHERE l.id=1 AND ll.id=3")
cu.fetchall()
```

By switching from `ST_Intersects` to `ST_Intersection`, you get a point of contact between the two `lines`. The point is as follows:

```
[('POINT(-106.628684465508 35.1053370957485)',)]
```

Polygons in the database

You can also store polygons using PostGIS. The following code will create a new table with a single polygon:

```python
from shapely.geometry import Polygon

connection =
psycopg2.connect(database="pythonspatial",user="postgres",
password="postgres")
cursor = conectionn.cursor()
cursor.execute("CREATE TABLE poly (id SERIAL PRIMARY KEY, location
GEOMETRY)")
a=Polygon([(-106.936763,35.958191),(-106.944385,35.239293),
          (-106.452396,35.281908),(-106.407844,35.948708)])
cursor.execute("INSERT INTO poly (location)
            VALUES (ST_GeomFromText('{}'))".format(a.wkt))
connection.commit()
```

The previous code is almost identical to the `Point` and `Line` examples. Make the database connection and then get a `cursor`. Use `execute()` to create the table. Import `shapely`, construct your geometry and insert it into the table. Lastly, `commit()` the changes.

The previous examples selected everything from the database and drew the geometry in the Jupyter Notebook. The following code will skip those steps and instead return to the area of the polygon:

```python
cur.execute("SELECT id, ST_Area(location::geography) from poly")
cur.fetchall()
```

Using `ST_Area()` and the geometry cast to geography, the previous code should return the following value in meters squared:

```
[(1, 3550790242.52023)]
```

Now that you know there is a polygon in the table, you can learn how to search for a point within a polygon.

Point in polygon

One of the most common problems is trying to determine whether a point is in the polygon. To solve this problem with PostGIS, you can use `ST_Contains` or `ST_Intersects`.

`St_Contains` takes two geometries and determines whether the first contains the second.

The order matters—*a* contains *b*, which is the opposite of `ST_Within`, which uses the order *b*, *a*.

By using contains, no part of geometry *b* can be outside of geometry *a*. The following code solves a **point in polygon (PIP)** problem:

```
isin=Point(-106.558743,35.318618)
cur.execute("SELECT
ST_Contains(polygon.location,ST_GeomFromText('{}'))
            FROM poly polygon WHERE
polygon.id=1".format(isin.wkt))
cur.fetchall()
```

The previous code creates a point and then uses `ST_Contains(polygon,point)` and returns `True`. The point is in the polygon. You can use `ST_Contains` with any other valid geometry. Just remember, it must contain the entire geometry to be true.

Another method to determine whether a point is in a polygon is by using `ST_Intersects`. `ST_Intersects` will return true if the point, or any other geometry, overlaps, touches, or is within the polygon. `ST_Intersects` can take either a geometry or a geography.

The following code will perform a PIP using `ST_Intersects`:

```
isin=Point(-106.558743,35.318618)
cur.execute("SELECT
ST_Intersects(ST_GeomFromText('{}')::geography,polygon.location::ge
ometry) FROM poly polygon WHERE polygon.id=1".format(isin.wkt))
cur.fetchall()
```

The previous code only differs from the `ST_Contains` example by the function that was used and that geometry was used. It also returns `True`. When using a polygon and a line, `ST_Intersects` will return true if any part of the line touches or is within the polygon. This differs from `ST_Contains`.

Using ST_Intersection, you can get the geometry that represents the intersection. In the lines example earlier, it was a point. In the case of a polygon and a line, which I will show later on, it will be a line. The following code uses ST_Intersection to get the LineString that intersects with the polygon:

```
isin=LineString([(-106.55,35.31),(-106.40,35.94)])
cur.execute("SELECT
ST_AsText(ST_Intersection(polygon.location,ST_GeomFromText('{}')))
FROM poly polygon WHERE polygon.id=1".format(isin.wkt))
cur.fetchall()
```

The previous code is almost identical to the preceding example, except we used intersection versus intersects. The result is the LINESTRING:

```
[('LINESTRING(-106.55 35.31,-106.411712640251 35.8908069109443)',)]
```

Summary

This chapter covered the installation of PostgreSQL and PostGIS as well as psycogp2 and Shapely. Then, we gave a brief overview of the major functions used when working with a spatial database. You should now be familiar with connecting to the database, executing queries to insert data, and how to get your data out. Furthermore, we covered functions that return new geometries, distances, and areas of geometry. Understanding how these functions work should allow you to read the PostGIS documents and be comfortable with forming the SQL statement for that function.

In the next chapter, you will learn about the major data types in GIS and how to use Python code libraries to read and write geospatial data. You will learn how to convert between data types, and how to upload and download data from geospatial databases and remote data sources.

4
Data Types, Storage, and Conversion

This chapter will focus on the many different data types that exist within GIS and will provide an overview of the major data types in GIS and how to use the previously covered Python code libraries to read and write geospatial data. Apart from reading and writing different geospatial data types, you'll learn how to use these libraries to perform file conversion between different data types and how to download data from geospatial databases and remote sources.

The following vector and raster data types will be covered in this chapter:

- Shapefiles
- GeoJSON
- KML
- GeoPackages
- GeoTIFF

The following file actions will also be covered, using Python geospatial data libraries covered in Chapter 2, *Introduction to Geospatial Code Libraries*:

- Opening existing files
- Reading and displaying different attributes (spatial and non-spatial)
- Creating and writing new geospatial data in different formats
- Converting one file format to another
- Downloading geospatial data

We'll provide an overview of the most used GIS data types before we head over to write some code for reading and writing them. Next, we will use some examples to explain how to use various Python libraries for reading, writing, downloading, and converting geospatial data. We'll start with an explanation of what geospatial data represents and the difference between vector and raster data.

Raster and vector data

Before diving into some of the most used GIS data types, a little background is required about what type of information geographical data represents. Earlier in this book, the distinction between raster and vector data was mentioned. All GIS data is comprised of one or the other, but a combination of both vectors and rasters is also possible. When deciding on which data type to use, consider the scale and type of geographical information represented by the data, which in turn determines what Python data libraries to use. As is illustrated in the following examples, the choice for a certain Python library can also depend on personal preference, and there may be various ways to do the same task.

In the geospatial world, raster data comes in the form of aerial imagery or satellite data, where each pixel has an associated value that corresponds to a different color or shade. Raster data is used for large continuous areas, such as differentiating between different temperature zones across various parts of the world. Other popular applications are elevation, vegetation, and precipitation mapping.

Rasters can also be used as input for creating vector maps, where, for example, objects such as roads and buildings can be distinguished (an example being the standard map view when navigating to Google Maps). Vector data itself consists of points, lines, and polygons to distinguish features in a geographical space, such as administrative boundaries. These are built up from individual points that have spatial relationships with each other that are described in an associated data model. Vectors maintain the same sharpness the more you zoom-in, while raster data will look more coarse-grained.

Now that you know what geographical data represents, let's discuss the most used geospatial data formats for vector and raster data.

Shapefiles

The shapefile is probably the most often-used data format for geographical vector data today. This file format was developed by Esri, based on a mostly open specification for data interoperability among Esri and other GIS software products. Although many other file formats have been introduced in an attempt to replace the shapefile, it remains a widely-used file format. These days, many third-party programming modules in Python exist for reading and writing shapefiles.

Although the name *shapefile* might suggest that there's only one file associated with it, a single shapefile requires in fact at least three files that need to be stored in the same directory in order to work correctly:

- A `.shp` file with the feature geometry itself
- A `.shx` file featuring a positional index of the feature geometry to allow seeking forwards and backwards quickly
- A `.dbf` file with columnar attributes for each shape

Shapefiles have their own structure. The main file (`.shp`) contains the geometry data, consisting of a single fixed-length header, followed by one or more variable-length records.

GeoJSON

GeoJSON is a JSON-based file format that has become popular in a short time. GeoJSON uses the **JavaScript Object Notation (JSON)** open data standard for storing geographical features as key-value pairs. The files are easily readable, can be created using a simple text editor, and are now common in spatial databases, open data platforms, as well as commercial GIS software. You would use GeoJSON for various types of geospatial vector data, such as points, lines, and polygons. GeoJSON uses either `.json` or `.geojson` as the filename extension. This means that a filename doesn't have to be `.geojson` in order to be a GeoJSON file.

KML

Keyhole Markup Language (KML), referring to the company that developed the format. It can be used to store geographic data which can be visualized using a host of applications such as Google Earth, Esri ArcGIS Explorer, Adobe Photoshop, and AutoCAD. KML is based on XML, using a tag-based structure with nested elements and attributes. KML files are often distributed in KMZ files, which are zipped KML files with a `.kmz` extension. For its reference system, KML uses longitude, latitude, and altitude coordinates, defined by the **World Geodetic System of 1984 (WGS84)**.

GeoPackage

An **Open Geospatial Consortium (OGC) GeoPackage (GPKG)** is an open data format for geographic information systems that support both vector and raster data. The format was defined by OGC and published in 2014, after which it has seen wide support from various government, commercial, and open source organizations. The GeoPackage data format was developed with the mobile user in mind—it was designed to be as efficient as possible, with all information contained in a single file. This makes it easy to rapidly share them on cloud storage and USB drives, and it is used in mobile applications that are disconnected. A GeoPackage file is built up as an extended SQLite 3 database file (`*.gpkg`) that combines data and metadata tables.

Raster data formats

These are some of the most popular raster data formats used for geographical information today:

- **ECW (Enhanced Compressed Wavelet)**: ECW is a compressed image format typically for aerial and satellite imagery. This GIS file type is known for its high compression ratios while still maintaining quality contrast in images.
- **Esri grid**: A file format for adding attribute data to a raster file. Esri grid files are available as integer and floating point grids.
- **GeoTIFF (Geographic Tagged Image File Format)**: An industry image standard file for GIS and satellite remote sensing applications. Almost all GIS and image processing software packages have GeoTIFF compatibility.

- **JPEG 2000**: An open source compressed raster format that allows both lossy and lossless compression. JPEG 2000 typically have a JP2 file extension. JPEG 2000 can achieve a compression ratio of 20:1, which is similar to the MrSID format.
- **MrSID (Multi-Resolution Seamless Image Database)**: A compressed wavelet format that allows for both lossy and lossless compression. LizardTech's proprietary MrSID format is commonly used for orthoimages in need of compression. MrSID images have an extension of SID and are accompanied with a world file with the file extension SDW.

Reading and writing vector data with GeoPandas

It's time for some hands-on exercises. We'll start with reading and writing some vector data in the form of GeoJSON using the GeoPandas library, which is the application used to demonstrate all examples is Jupyter Notebook, which comes preinstalled with Anaconda3. If you've installed all geospatial Python libraries from Chapter 2, *Introduction to Geospatial Code Libraries*, you're good to go. If not, do this first. You might decide to create virtual environments for different combinations of Python libraries because of different dependencies and versioning. Open up a new Jupyter Notebook and a browser window and head over to http://www.naturalearthdata.com/downloads/ and download the Natural Earth quick start kit at a convenient location. We'll examine some of that data for the rest of this chapter, along with some other geographical data files.

First, type the following code in a Jupyter Notebook with access to the GeoPandas library and run the following code:

```
In: import geopandas as gpd
    df = gpd.read_file(r'C:\data\gdal\NE\10m_cultural
    \ne_10m_admin_0_boundary_lines_land.shp')
    df.head()
```

The output looks as follows:

Out[1]:		featurecla	name	comment	adm0_usa	adm0_left	adm0_right	adm0_a3_l	adm0_a3_r	sov_a3_l	sov_a3_r	type	labelrank	scalerank	min_zoom	mir
	0	Indefinite (please verify)	None	None	1	Canada	United States of America	CAN	USA	Wat	US1	Water Indicator	2	1	2.0	
	1	International boundary (verify)	None	None	1	Sweden	Norway	SWE	NOR	SWE	NOR	Water Indicator	2	1	0.0	
	2	International boundary (verify)	None	None	1	Denmark	Germany	DNK	DEU	DN1	DEU	Water Indicator	5	1	0.0	
	3	International boundary (verify)	None	None	1	Singapore	Malaysia	SGP	MYS	SGP	MYS	Water Indicator	3	1	0.0	
	4	International boundary (verify)	None	None	1	Uruguay	Argentina	URY	ARG	URY	ARG	Water Indicator	2	1	0.0	

The code does the following—the first line imports the GeoPandas library and shortens its name, saving space whenever we reference it later. The second line reads the data on disk, in this case, a shapefile with land boundary lines. It is assigned to a dataframe variable, which refers to a `pandas` dataframe, namely a 2D object comparable to an Excel table with rows and columns. The data structures of GeoPandas mimic are subclasses from those of `pandas` and are named differently—the `pandas` dataframe in GeoPandas is called a **GeoDataFrame**. The third line prints the attribute table, which is limited to the first five rows. After running the code, a separate cell's output will list the attribute data from the referenced shapefile. You'll notice that the FID column has no name and that a `geometry` column has been added as the last column.

This is not the only command to read data, as you can also read data from a PostGIS database, by using the `read_postgis()` command. Next, we'll plot the data inside our Jupyter Notebook:

```
In: %matplotlib inline
    df.plot(color='black')
```

The output of the previous code is as follows:

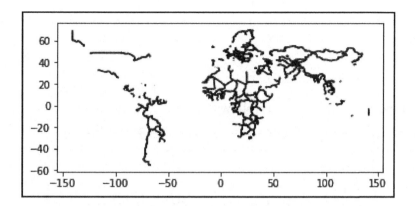

The first line is a so-called magic command, only to be used inside a Jupyter Notebook, and tells it to use the plotting capabilities of the `matplotlib` library inside a cell of the Jupyter Notebook app. This way, you can plot map data directly as opposed to working with an IDE. The second line states that we want the dataframe plotted, in `black` (the default color is blue). The output resembles a world map with only land borders, which are visible as black lines.

Next, we'll investigate some of the attributes of GeoPandas data objects:

```
In: df.geom_type.head()

Out:  0 LineString
      1 LineString
      2 MultiLineString
      3 LineString
      4 LineString
      dtype: object
```

This tells us that the first five entries in our attribute table are made of line strings and multiline strings. For printing all entries, use the same line of code, without `.head()`:

```
In: df.crs

Out: {'init': 'epsg:4326'}
```

The `crs` attribute refers to the **coordinate reference system (CRS)** of the dataframe, in this case, `epsg:4326`, a code defined by the **International Association of Oil and Gas Producers (IOGP)**. Go to `www.spatialreference.org` for more information on EPSG. The CRS offers essential information about your spatial dataset. EPSG 4326 is also known as WGS 1984, a standard coordinate system for the Earth.

You can change the CRS as follows to a Mercator projection, showing a more vertically stretched image:

```
In: merc = df.to_crs({'init': 'epsg:3395'})
    merc.plot(color='black')
```

The output of the previous code is as follows:

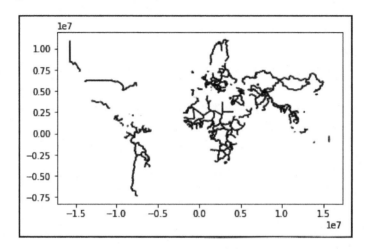

Suppose we want to convert the shapefile data of our dataframe into json. GeoPandas does this in one line of code, and the output is listed in a new cell:

```
In: df.to_json()
```

This previous command converted the data to a new format but did not write it to a new file. Writing your dataframe to a new geojson file can be done like this:

```
In: df.to_file(driver='GeoJSON',filename=r'C:\data\world.geojson')
```

Don't be confused by JSON file extensions—a JSON file with spatial data is a GeoJSON file, even though there's also a separate .geojson file extension.

For file conversion, GeoPandas relies on the Fiona library. To list all available drivers (a software component that lets the operating system and a device communicate with each other), use the following command:

```
In: import fiona; fiona.supported_drivers
```

Reading and writing vector data with OGR

Now, let's turn to OGR for reading and writing a vector so that you can compare both OGR and GeoPandas functionality for performing the same kind of tasks. To follow the instructions that are mentioned as we proceed, you can download the MTBS wildfire data from: `https://edcintl.cr.usgs.gov/downloads/sciweb1/shared/MTBS_Fire/data/composite_data/fod_pt_shapefile/mtbs_fod_pts_data.zip` and store them on your PC. The file that will be analyzed here is the `mtbs_fod_pts_20170501` shapefile's attribute table, which has 20,340 rows and 30 columns.

We'll start with the `ogrinfo` command which works in a terminal window and can be used for describing vector data. These are not Python commands, but we'll include them here as you can easily run them in a Jupyter Notebook with a simple prefix (adding an exclamation mark before the used command). Take, for instance, the following command, which is similar to the Fiona driver command:

```
In: !ogrinfo --formats
```

This command lists the available formats that `ogrinfo` can access, by using the general option `--formats`. The results also tells us whether GDAL/OGR can only read/open the format, or whether it can also write new layers in that format. As you can see from the output, there are many supported file formats with OGR. Looking at Esri shapefiles in the list, the addition of (rw+v) means OGR supports read, write, update (meaning create), and virtual formats for Esri shapefiles:

```
In: !ogrinfo -so "pts" mtbs_fod_pts_20170501
```

The previous command lists the summary information about all the layers in a data source, which in this case is all the shapefiles in the folder called "pts". The addition of -so stands for summary option. You can see that this command lists similar information as we saw with GeoPandas, such as the CRS. The same line of code, but without the -so addition will print all features and attributes, and takes some time to process. This is comparable to creating a GeoDataFrame in GeoPandas, but all attribute info is printed per feature on a new line instead of preserving the tabular form:

```
In: !ogrinfo "pts" mtbs_fod_pts_20170501
```

If we want to convert this shapefile into a GeoJSON file, we will use the following command:

```
In: !ogr2ogr -f "GeoJSON" "C:\data\output.json"
    "C:\data\mtbs_fod_pts_data\mtbs_fod_pts_20170501.shp"
```

The $-f$ prefix stands for the format, followed by the output driver name, the output file name, and the location and the input file. You might receive error warnings doing file conversions, for example when a bad feature is encountered, but an output file will be written anyway.

OGR has also read and write capabilities for KML files. Download this KML sample file (https://developers.google.com/kml/documentation/KML_Samples.kml) with the following code and run the following code to read its contents:

```
In:    !ogrinfo "C:\Users\UserName\Downloads\KML_Samples.kml" -summary

Out:   Had to open data source read-only.INFO: Open of
       `C:\Users\UserName\Downloads\KML_Samples.kml' using driver
       `KML' successful.
         1: Placemarks (3D Point)
         2: Highlighted Icon (3D Point)
         3: Paths (3D Line String)
         4: Google Campus (3D Polygon)
         5: Extruded Polygon (3D Polygon)
         6: Absolute and Relative (3D Polygon)
```

For a more Pythonic approach for OGR, let's see some examples of how you can read and write data with OGR.

The following code lists all 30 field names of our wildfire shapefile using OGR:

```
In: from osgeo import ogr
    source = ogr.Open(r"C:\data\mtbs_fod_pts_data\
    mtbs_fod_pts_20170501.shp")
    layer = source.GetLayer()
    schema = []
    ldefn = layer.GetLayerDefn()
    for n in range(ldefn.GetFieldCount()):
        fdefn = ldefn.GetFieldDefn(n)
        schema.append(fdefn.name)
    print(schema)

Out: ['FIRE_ID', 'FIRENAME', 'ASMNT_TYPE', 'PRE_ID', 'POST_ID', 'ND_T',
    'IG_T', 'LOW_T',
    'MOD_T', 'HIGH_T', 'FIRE_YEAR', 'FIRE_MON', 'FIRE_DAY', 'LAT',
    'LONG', 'WRS_PATH',
    'WRS_ROW', 'P_ACRES', 'R_ACRES', 'STATE', 'ADMIN', 'MTBS_ZONE',
    'GACC',
    'HUC4_CODE','HUC4_NAME', 'Version', 'RevCode', 'RelDate',
    'Fire_Type']
```

As you can see from the preceding code, this is a little more involved than using GeoPandas, where you can directly load all attribute data into one GeoDataFrame using little code. With OGR, you need to iterate over the individual features which need to be referenced from a layer definition and appended to an empty list. But first, you need to use the `GetLayer` function— this is because OGR has its own data model that does not adapt itself automatically to the file format it reads.

Now that we have all the field names, we can iterate over the individual features, for instance, for the state field:

```
In: from osgeo import ogr
    import os
    shapefile = r"C:\data\mtbs_fod_pts_data\mtbs_fod_pts_20170501.shp"
    driver = ogr.GetDriverByName("ESRI Shapefile")
    dataSource = driver.Open(shapefile, 0)
    layer = dataSource.GetLayer()
    for feature in layer:
        print(feature.GetField("STATE"))
```

Judging from the output of the last cell, there are apparently many features, but exactly how many? The total feature count can be printed as follows:

```
In: import os
    from osgeo import ogr
    daShapefile = r"C:\data\mtbs_fod_pts_data\
    mtbs_fod_pts_20170501.shp"
    driver = ogr.GetDriverByName("ESRI Shapefile")
    dataSource = driver.Open(daShapefile, 0)
    layer = dataSource.GetLayer()
    featureCount = layer.GetFeatureCount()
    print("Number of features in %s: %d" %
    (os.path.basename(daShapefile), featureCount))

Out: Number of features in mtbs_fod_pts_20170501.shp: 20340
```

As we've seen previously, the CRS is essential information about your spatial data. You can print this information in two ways—from the layer and the geometry of the layer. In the following code, two spatial reference variables will print the same output, as it should be (only the output of the first option is listed here to save space):

```
In: from osgeo import ogr, osr
    driver = ogr.GetDriverByName('ESRI Shapefile')
    dataset = driver.Open(r"C:\data\mtbs_fod_pts_data\
    mtbs_fod_pts_20170501.shp")
    # Option 1: from Layer
    layer = dataset.GetLayer()
```

```
spatialRef = layer.GetSpatialRef()
print(spatialRef)
# Option 2: from Geometry
feature = layer.GetNextFeature()
geom = feature.GetGeometryRef()
spatialRef2 = geom.GetSpatialReference()
print(spatialRef2)
```

```
Out: GEOGCS["GCS_North_American_1983",
       DATUM["North_American_Datum_1983",
       SPHEROID["GRS_1980",6378137.0,298.257222101]],
       PRIMEM["Greenwich",0.0],
       UNIT["Degree",0.0174532925199433]]
```

We can check if we're dealing with points and print the *x* and *y* values of all individual features as well as their centroids as follows:

```
In: from osgeo import ogr
    import os
    shapefile = r"C:\data\mtbs_fod_pts_data\mtbs_fod_pts_20170501.shp"
    driver = ogr.GetDriverByName("ESRI Shapefile")
    dataSource = driver.Open(shapefile, 0)
    layer = dataSource.GetLayer()
    for feature in layer:
        geom = feature.GetGeometryRef()
    print(geom.Centroid().ExportToWkt())
```

Reading and writing raster data with Rasterio

After covering how to read and write various vector data formats in Python, we'll now do the same for raster data. We'll start with the Rasterio library and have a look at how we can read and write raster data. Open up a new Jupyter Notebook where you have access to the Rasterio library and type the following code:

```
In: import rasterio
    dataset = rasterio.open(r"C:\data\gdal\NE\50m_raster\NE1_50M_SR_W
    \NE1_50M_SR_W.tif")
```

This imports the `rasterio` library and opens a GeoTIFF file. We can now perform some simple data description commands, such as printing the number of image bands.

Raster images contain either a single or multiple bands. All bands are contained in a single file, with each band covering the same area. When the image is read by your computer, these bands are overlayed on top of each other so that you'll see one single image. Each band contains a 2D array with rows and columns of data. Each data cell of each array contains a numeric value that corresponds to a color value (or elevation value, which is also possible). If a raster image has multiple bands, each band corresponds to a segment of the electromagnetic spectrum that was collected by a sensor. Users can display one or multiple bands, combining different bands together to make their own color composites. Chapter 9, *ArcGIS API for Python and ArcGIS Online* features some examples of these color composites when discussing displaying raster data using the ArcGIS API for Python.

In this case, there are three different bands:

```
In: dataset.count
Out: 3
```

A `dataset` band is an array of values representing the partial distribution of a single variable in a 2D space. The number of columns is returned by the `width` attribute:

```
In: dataset.width
Out: 10800
```

The number of rows is returned by the `height` attribute:

```
In:   dataset.height
Out: 5400
```

The following code returns the spatial bounding box in meters, so you can calculate the area it covers:

```
In:   dataset.bounds
Out: BoundingBox(left=-179.99999999999997, bottom=-89.99999999998201,
     right=179.99999999996405, top=90.0)
```

The CRS of the dataset can be printed as follows:

```
In:   dataset.crs
Out: CRS({'init': 'epsg:4326'})
```

You can access and return a NumPy ndarray with the raster array for a raster band as follows:

```
In:    band1 = dataset.read(1)
       band1
Out:   array([[124, 124, 124, ..., 124, 124, 124], ...
```

If you want to visualize the image, use the following code:

```
In: %matplotlib inline
    from matplotlib import pyplot
    pyplot.imshow(dataset.read(1))
    pyplot.show()
```

The output map will look like this:

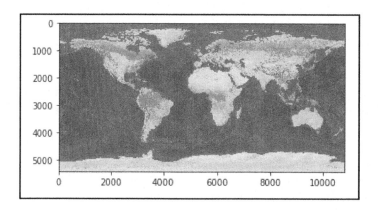

Reading and writing raster data using GDAL

Here are some commands for reading and writing raster data with GDAL:

```
In: !gdalinfo --formats
```

This command lists all supported file formats in GDAL. For a summary including the CRS, use !gdalinfo without any prefixes:

```
In: !gdalinfo "C:\data\gdal\NE\50m_raster\NE1_50M_SR_W
    \NE1_50M_SR_W.tif"

Out: Driver: GTiff/GeoTIFF
     Files: C:\data\gdal\NE\50m_raster\NE1_50M_SR_W\NE1_50M_SR_W.tif
     Size is 10800, 5400
```

```
Coordinate System is:
GEOGCS["WGS 84",
DATUM["WGS_1984", ...
```

You can convert a GeoTIFF to a JPEG file as follows:

```
In: !gdal_translate -of JPEG
    "C:\data\gdal\NE\50m_raster\NE1_50M_SR_W\NE1_50M_SR_W.tif"
    NE1_50M_SR_W.jpg

Out: Input file size is 10800, 5400
    0...10...20...30...40...50...60...70...80...90...100 - done.
```

The output, NE1_50M_SR_W.jpg, will look like this:

Now, let's open a GeoPackage using GDAL. GeoPackages can be either vector or raster-based, but in this case, we'll open a raster-based one, which becomes clear from the following output. For reading and writing GeoPackages, we need GDAL version 2.2.2, so the following example won't work for lower version numbers. Download the following GeoPackage file (http://www.geopackage.org/data/gdal_sample_v1.2_no_extensions.gpkg) and reference it as follows:

```
In: !gdalinfo
    "C:\Users\UserName\Downloads\gdal_sample_v1.2_no_extensions.gpkg"

Out: Driver: GPKG/GeoPackageFiles:
    C:\Users\UserName\Downloads\gdal_sample_v1.2_no_extensions.gpkg
    Size is 512, 512
    Coordinate System is''
    ...
```

The GDAL **Web Map Service** (**WMS**) driver allows for interacting with online web mapping services. You can use it to download various geospatial datasets, subsets, or information about available datasets directly from a command prompt (or in this case, a Jupyter Notebook) without using a browser to navigate to a website and download data manually. There are many different options, so refer to the online documentation for more information. The following example requires GDAL version 2.0 or higher. The following command uses the URL of a **REpresentational State Transfer** (**REST**) definition for an ArcGIS MapServer and returns the information about the requested image service, such as the amount of bands, band names, CRS, corner coordinates, and more:

```
In: !gdalinfo http://server.arcgisonline.com/ArcGIS/rest/services/
    World_Imagery/MapServer?f=json&pretty=true
```

Note that you added some information to the URL of the image service, in this case, `f=json&pretty=true`. This means the requested file format by the user is `pretty json`, which is a nicely formatted `json` that is easier to read for humans.

Summary

This chapter provided an overview of major data types in GIS. After explaining the difference between vector and raster data, the following vector and raster data types were covered—Esri shapefiles, GeoJSON, KML, GeoPackages, and GeoTIFF files. Next, we explained how to use some of the earlier described Python code libraries to read and write geospatial data. The following geospatial Python libraries for reading and writing raster and vector data were covered in particular—GeoPandas, OGR, GDAL, and Rasterio. Apart from reading and writing different geospatial data types, you learned how to use these libraries to perform file conversion between different data types and how to upload and download data from geospatial databases and remote sources.

The next chapter will cover geospatial analysis and processing. Python libraries covered are OGR, Shapely and GeoPandas. The reader will learn how to use these libraries and write scripts for geospatial analysis, using real-world examples.

5
Vector Data Analysis

This chapter will cover geospatial analysis and processing of vector data. The following three Python libraries will be covered—Shapely, OGR, and GeoPandas. The reader will learn how to use these Python libraries to perform geospatial analysis, including the writing of basic and advanced analysis scripts.

Each library is covered separately, with an overview of its data structures, methods, and classes where appropriate. We'll discuss the best use cases for each library and how to use them together for geospatial workflows. Short example scripts illustrate how to perform the basic geographical analysis. The GeoPandas library enables more complex functionality for doing data science tasks and incorporating geospatial analysis.

In this chapter, we'll cover the following topics:

- Reading and writing vector data
- Creating and manipulating vector data
- Visualizing (plotting) vector data on a map
- Working with map projections and reproject data
- Performing spatial operations such as spatial joins
- Working with vector geometries and attribute data in tabular form
- Analyzing the results to answer questions, such as how many wildfires are there in area x?

After this chapter, you'll have a solid foundation to start working with geospatial vector data. You'll know the characteristics and use cases of all three geospatial libraries, and know how to do basic vector data processing and analysis.

OGR Simple Features Library

OGR Simple Features Library (part of the **Geospatial Data Abstraction Library (GDAL)**) offers a set of tools for dealing with vector data. Although both GDAL and OGR are now more integrated than they used to be, we can still divide GDAL between a vector part (OGR) and a raster part (GDAL). While OGR was written in C++ and the documentation is also in C++, with Python bindings we can access all of GDAL's functionality using Python.

We can distinguish the following components of OGR:

- OGR batch commands for describing and processing vector data
- `ogrmerge`, an instant Python script for merging multiple vector data files
- The OGR library itself

We'll briefly cover these components first, before moving on to some examples of how to use all three.

OGR batch commands

OGR offers a series of batch commands that can be used to describe and convert existing geospatial vector data. We've already mentioned two of them, `ogrinfo` and `ogr2ogr`, in `Chapter 4`, *Data Types, Storage, and Conversion*:

- `ogrinfo` can be used for doing all sorts of reporting on vector data, such as listing supported vector formats, available layers, and summary details, and can be combined with SQL-query syntax to select features from a dataset.
- `ogr2ogr` is for doing vector data translations, such as converting vector files between different formats, converting multiple layers into a new data source, and reproject vector data and filter features based on location. It can also be used with SQL-query syntax just like `ogrinfo`.

These are very powerful commands that let you do a lot of work. It is recommended you familiarize yourself with these commands when working with vector data. We'll get to some examples shortly.

Additionally, two other batch commands exist for creating vector tiles, `ogrtindex` and `ogr2vrt`. The difference between the two is that the second one is more broadly usable than the first. The second command needs to be imported from an online script as it is not distributed with recent GDAL versions.

ogrmerge

Along with the installation of GDAL comes a set of Python scripts that can be used for specialized geospatial tasks. These scripts can be run directly from a Jupyter Notebook or terminal, along with a specified dataset. You can find all of the scripts inside of the `scripts` directory of your local `gdal` file folder, which on a Windows machine might be similar to the following path:

```
C:\Users\Username\Anaconda3\pkgs\gdal-2.2.2-py36_1\scripts
```

As you can see from the list of Python scripts in this folder, almost all of them are for GDAL rather than OGR. All of these Python scripts can be run from a Jupyter Notebook or a terminal. Using a Jupyter Notebook, you can use the magic command `%run` to execute your Python script, whereas using a terminal you'd use `python` followed by the name of the script and the input/output data files.

Magic commands are commands that extend the core Python language and can only be used in the Jupyter Notebook application. They offer useful shortcuts, for example, inserting code from an external script, and executing Python code from `.py` files on disc or `shell` commands. A full list of magic commands can be printed with the following command in an empty cell, `%lsmagic`.

The following example uses `ogrmerge.py`, a Python script available with GDAL version 2.2.2 and higher. Running this script from a Jupyter Notebook, it takes all shapefiles in a single folder from the Earth dataset and merges them into a single GeoPackage file called `merged.gpkg`:

```
In: %run "C:\Users\Eric\Anaconda3\pkgs\gdal-2.2.2-
    py36_1\Scripts\ogrmerge.py" -f GPKG -o
    merged.gpkg "C:\data\gdal\NE\10m_cultural\*.shp"
```

Please note that in order to run one of the Python scripts in the GDAL directory correctly, you need to reference their file location if it's located in a different folder than the one where you're running the script, which is likely to be the case if you're working with the Jupyter Notebook application.

The OGR library and Python bindings

The OGR library, combined with its Python bindings, forms the most important part for working with vector data in Python. With it, you can create points, lines, and polygons, and perform spatial operations on these elements. For example, you can calculate the area of a geometry, overlay different data on top of each other, and use proximity tools such as buffers. Additionally, just as with ogrinfo and ogr2ogr, the OGR library offers tools to read vector data files, iterate over individual elements, and select and reproject data.

OGR's main modules and classes

The OGR library consists of two main modules—ogr and osr. Both are sub-modules inside of the osgeo module. The ogr sub-module deals with vector geometry, while osr is all about projections. In the *Reading and writing vector data with OGR* section in Chapter 4, *Data Types, Storage, and Conversion*, we already saw some examples of how to make use of both.

OGR offers the following seven classes:

- Geometry
- Spatial Reference
- Feature
- Feature Class Definition
- Layer
- Dataset
- Drivers

The class names are mostly self-explanatory, but it's good to have an overview of how OGR is structured. In the following examples, we'll see how to access and make use of these classes. OGR's modules, classes, and functions are documented on the GDAL website (www.gdal.org/python) but offer no code examples, which makes it hard to get started. What's good to know at this point is that other Python libraries fill in the gap and offer a more user-friendly way to deal with GDAL's capabilities (such as Fiona and GeoPandas). Also, both ogrinfo and ogr2ogr might be preferable over using Python in some use cases, for example, when reprojecting vector data.

Let's look at a few OGR examples.

Creating polygon geometry with OGR

OGR lets you write vector geometries such as points, lines, mulitipoints, multilinestrings, multipolygons and geometry collections. You can give these geometry values in coordinates or meters if you plan to project them later. All geometries you create follow the same procedure, separate points are defined and then strung together as lines or polygons. You define separate entities in numbers, encode them in **well-known binary (WKB)**, and the final polygon is translated to **well-known text (WKT)**. A Jupyter Notebook will return the coordinates of the polygon but won't plot it automatically, for this, we'll use Shapely later in this chapter:

```
In: from osgeo import ogr
    r = ogr.Geometry(ogr.wkbLinearRing)
    r.AddPoint(1,1)
    r.AddPoint(5,1)
    r.AddPoint(5,5)
    r.AddPoint(1,5)
    r.AddPoint(1,1)
    poly = ogr.Geometry(ogr.wkbPolygon)
    poly.AddGeometry(r)
    print(poly.ExportToWkt())
Out: POLYGON ((1 1 0,5 1 0,5 5 0,1 5 0,1 1 0))
```

Creating polygon geometry from GeoJSON

You can also create a geometry by passing in GeoJSON to OGR, which saves space compared to the first example:

```
In: from osgeo import ogr
    geojson = """{"type":"Polygon","coordinates":[[[1,1],[5,1],
    [5,5],[1,5], [1,1]]]}"""
    polygon = ogr.CreateGeometryFromJson(geojson)
    print(polygon)
Out: POLYGON ((1 1,5 1,5 5,1 5,1 1))
```

Basic geometric operations

Here are some basic geometric operations we can perform on our polygon. We create the area, centroid, boundary, convex hull, buffer, and check if a polygon contains a certain point:

```
# 1 create area
In: print("The area of our polygon is %d" % polygon.Area())
Out: The area of our polygon is 16
```

```
# 2 calculate centroid of polygon
In: cen = polygon.Centroid()
print(cen)
Out: POINT (3 3)

# 3 Get the boundary
In: b = polygon.GetBoundary()
print(b)
Out: LINESTRING (1 1,5 1,5 5,1 5,1 1)

# 4 convex hull does the same in this case as boundary, as our
polygon is a square:
In: ch = polygon.ConvexHull()
print(ch)
Out: POLYGON ((1 1,1 5,5 5,5 1,1 1))

# 5 buffer. A buffer value of 0 (zero) returns the same values as
boundary and convex hull in this example:
In: buffer = polygon.Buffer(0)
print(buffer)
Out: POLYGON ((1 1,1 5,5 5,5 1,1 1))

# 6 check if a point is inside our polygon
In: point = ogr.Geometry(ogr.wkbPoint)
point.AddPoint(10, 10)
polygon.Contains(point)
Out: False
```

Writing polygon data to a newly created shapefile

Our current polygon only exists in memory. We can create a new shapefile and write the polygon geometry we created earlier to this shapefile. The script consists of the following steps:

1. Import the modules and set the spatial reference (in this case, **World Geodetic System 1984 (WGS1984)**).
2. Create the shapefile, then the layer using polygon geometry. Next, the geometry is put inside a feature and the feature in a layer. Notice that the script directly references the polygon from the earlier example.
3. The catch is to use the right geometry type in the first line of code, which in this case should be `wkbPolygon`.
4. The polygon geometry from our earlier example is referenced in this step and put into the shapefile.
5. The shapefile is added as a layer in this step.

Take a look at the following code:

```
In:  import osgeo.ogr, osgeo.osr
     # 1 set the spatial reference
     spatialReference = osgeo.osr.SpatialReference()
     spatialReference.ImportFromProj4('+proj=longlat +ellps=WGS84
     +datum=WGS84 +no_defs')
     # 2 create a new shapefile
     driver = osgeo.ogr.GetDriverByName('ESRI Shapefile')
     shapeData = driver.CreateDataSource('my_polygon.shp')

     # 3 create the layer
     layer = shapeData.CreateLayer('polygon_layer',
spatialReference,
     osgeo.ogr.wkbPolygon)
     layerDefinition = layer.GetLayerDefn()

     # 4 geometry is put inside feature
     featureIndex = 0
     feature = osgeo.ogr.Feature(layerDefinition)
     feature.SetGeometry(polygon)
     feature.SetFID(featureIndex)

     # 5 feature is put into layer
     layer.CreateFeature(feature)
```

We can use `ogrInfo` to see if the file has been created correctly:

```
In: !ogrinfo my_polygon.shp
Out: INFO: Open of `my_polygon.shp'
     using driver `ESRI Shapefile' successful.
     1: my_polygon (Polygon)
```

Using a spatial filter to select features

This example uses the Natural Earth Dataset introduced in Chapter 4, *Data Types, Storage, and Conversion*, under the *Reading and writing vector data with GeoPandas* section. We'll use latitude-longitude coordinates to create a spatial filter in the form of a bounding box. This box selects only the data inside of this box. This is a way to work with a subset of our data. We'll use OGR's `SpatialFilterRec` method, which takes four values—`minx`, `miny`, `maxx` and `maxy`, to create a bounding box. Our (random) example is to select the cities in our bounding box (which shows the state of Texas, as well as parts of Oklahoma and Mexico). To filter our results even further, we only want the cities in the US. This means we have to filter our search results with an extra `if/else` statement in our `for` loop.

The website www.mapsofworld.com gives the following four values for our example code: −102 (minx), 26 (miny), −94 (maxx), and 36 (maxy) for the state of Texas. Here is the script:

```
In: # import the modules
    from osgeo import ogr
    import os
    # reference the shapefile and specify driver type
    shapefile =
    r"C:\data\gdal\NE\10m_cultural\ne_10m_populated_places.shp"
    driver = ogr.GetDriverByName("ESRI Shapefile")
    # open the data source with driver, zero means open in read-only
    mode
    dataSource = driver.Open(shapefile, 0)
    # use the GetLayer() function for referencing the layer that holds
    the data
    layer = dataSource.GetLayer()
    # pass in the coordinates for the data frame to the
    SetSpatialFilterRect() function. This filter creates a rectangular
    extent and selects the features
      inside the extent
      layer.SetSpatialFilterRect(-102, 26, -94, 36)
      for feature in layer:
      # select only the cities inside of the USA
      # we can do this through a SQL query:
      # we skip the cities that are not in the USA,
      # and print the names of the cities that are
          if feature.GetField("ADM0NAME") != "United States of
    America":
              continue
          else:
              print(feature.GetField("NAME"))
```

```
Out:    Ardmore
        McAlester
        Bryan
        San Marcos
        Longview
        ...
```

Shapely and Fiona

The Shapely and Fiona libraries have been introduced in `Chapter 2`, *Introduction to Geospatial Code Libraries*, in the sections *Shapely* and *Fiona*. It makes sense to cover both of them together, as Shapely depends on other libraries for reading and writing files and Fiona fits the bill. As we'll see in the examples, we can use Fiona to open and read files and then pass geometry data to Shapely objects.

Shapely objects and classes

The Shapely library is used for creating and manipulating 2D vector data without the need for a spatial database. Not only does it do away with a database, it also does away with projections and data formats, focusing on geometry only. The strength of Shapely is that it uses easily-readable syntax to create a variety of geometries that can be used for geometric operations.

With the aid of other Python packages, these geometries and the results of geometric operations can be written to a vector file format and projected if necessary—we'll cover examples combing `pyproj` and Fiona with Shapely's capabilities. An example of a workflow incorporating Shapely might be where you'd read vector geometries out of a shapefile using Fiona, and then use Shapely to simplify or clean up existing geometries, in case things might line up correctly internally or in combination with other geometries. The cleaned-up geometries can be used as input for other workflows, for example, for creating a thematic map or performing data science.

The Shapely library uses a set of classes that are implementations of three fundamental types of geometric objects—points, curves, and surfaces. If you are familiar with geospatial data and their geometries, they will sound familiar. If you're not, use the examples to get familiar with them:

Geometric object name	Class name
Point	Point
Curve	LineString, LinearRing
Surface	Polygon
Collection of points	MultiPoint
Collection of curves	MultiLineString
Collection of surfaces	MultiPolygon

Shapely methods for geospatial analysis

Topological relationships are implemented as methods on geometric objects (for example, contains, touches, and more). Shapely also provides analysis methods that return new geometric objects (intersections, unions, and more). Creative use of the buffering method provides ways to clean shapes. Interoperation with other software is provided through well-known formats (WKT and WKB), NumPy + Python arrays, and the Python Geo Interface.

Fiona's data model

Although Fiona is OGR's Python wrapper, Fiona uses a data model that differs from OGR. While OGR uses data sources, layers and features, Fiona uses the term records for accessing geographic features stored in vector data. These are based on GeoJSON features—reading a shapefile with Fiona, you reference a record through one of its keys, using a Python dictionary object. A record has an ID, geometry, and property key.

Let's look at a few Shapely and Fiona code examples.

Creating geometries with Shapely

Just like OGR, you can use Shapely to create geometries. Jupyter Notebook will plot the geometries after you've created them, as opposed to OGR. You don't have to use extra plot statements to do this, just repeat the variable name used to store the geometries:

```
In:    from shapely.geometry import Polygon
       p1 = Polygon(((1, 2), (5, 3), (5, 7), (1, 9), (1, 2)))
       p2 = Polygon(((6,6), (7,6), (10,4), (11,8), (6,6)))
       p1
       # A new command line is required for printing the second polygon:
In:    p2

       # Point takes tuples as well as positional coordinate values
In:    from shapely.geometry import Point
       point = Point(2.0, 2.0)
       q = Point((2.0, 2.0))
       q

       # line geometry
In:    from shapely.geometry import LineString
       line = LineString([(0, 0), (10,10)])
       line

       # linear rings
In:    from shapely.geometry.polygon import LinearRing
       ring = LinearRing([(0,0), (3,3), (3,0)])
       ring

       # collection of points
In:    from shapely.geometry import MultiPoint
       points = MultiPoint([(0.0, 0.0), (3.0, 3.0)])
       points

       # collection of lines
In:    from shapely.geometry import MultiLineString
       coords = [((0, 0), (1, 1)), ((-1, 0), (1, 0))]
       coords

       # collection of polygons
In:    from shapely.geometry import MultiPolygon
       polygons = MultiPolygon([p1, p2,])
       polygons
```

Applying geometrical methods with Shapely

In a similar way to OGR, you can apply geometrical methods, using the polygon from the earlier example:

```
In:     print(p1.area)
        print(p1.bounds)
        print(p1.length)
        print(p1.geom_type)

Out:    22.0
        (1.0, 2.0, 5.0, 9.0)
        19.59524158061724
        Polygon
```

Reading JSON geometries with Shapely

Although Shapely does not read or write data files, you can access geometries from outside of the library, for instance, by feeding it vector data written in `json`. The following script creates a polygon in `json` that is read into Shapely in line. Next, the mapping command returns a new, independent geometry with coordinates copied from the context:

```
In:     import json
        from shapely.geometry import mapping, shape
        p = shape(json.loads('{"type": "Polygon", "coordinates":
        [[[1,1], [1,3 ], [3,3]]]}'))
        print(json.dumps(mapping(p)))
        p.area

Out:    {"type": "Polygon", "coordinates": [[[1.0, 1.0], [1.0, 3.0],
        [3.0, 3.0], [1.0, 1.0]]]}
        2.0             # result of p.area
```

Reading data with Fiona

The following code reads a file from our Natural Earth dataset and prints its dictionary keys:

```
In:     import fiona
        c = fiona.open(r"C:\data\gdal\NE\
        110m_cultural\ne_110m_admin_1_states_provinces.shp")
        rec = next(iter(c))
        rec.keys()
```

```
Out:  dict_keys(['type', 'id', 'geometry', 'properties'])
```

Using the data pretty-print (`pprint`) library that is part of Python's standard library, we can print the corresponding values to the keys of the first feature from our dataset:

```
In:   import pprint
      pprint.pprint(rec['type'])
      pprint.pprint(rec['id'])
      pprint.pprint(rec['properties'])
      pprint.pprint(rec['geometry'])

Out:  'Feature'
      '0'
      OrderedDict([('adm1_code', 'USA-3514'),
                  ('diss_me', 3514),
                  ('iso_3166_2', 'US-MN'),
                  ('wikipedia',
          'http://en.wikipedia.org/wiki/Minnesota'),
                  ('iso_a2', 'US'),
                  ('adm0_sr', 1),
                  ('name', 'Minnesota'), ....
```

Use the following methods on the data file object for printing the following information:

```
In:   print(len(c))         # prints total amount of features
      print(c.driver)       # prints driver name
      print(c.crs)          # prints coordinate reference system of data
file

Out:  51
      ESRI Shapefile
      {'init': 'epsg:4326'}
```

Accessing vector geometry in shapefiles using Shapely and Fiona

Using Fiona, you can open a shapefile and access attribute data, such as geometries. For example, our Natural Earth dataset contains a shapefile with all of the states in the US with their vector geometries. Use the following code to open the shapefile and get all of the vector geometry of the first feature (starting from index number 0):

```
In:   import pprint, fiona
      with fiona.open\
      (r"C:\data\gdal\NE\110m_cultural\ne_110m_admin_1_states_provinc
      es.shp") as src:
```

```
pprint.pprint(src[0])
```

We can use the `shape` method and pass in all of the coordinates from Minnesota:

```
In:    from shapely.geometry import shape
       minnesota = {'type': 'Polygon', 'coordinates':
       [[(-89.61369767938538, 47.81925202085796), (-89.72800594761503,
       47.641976019880644), (-89.84283098016755, 47.464725857119504),
       (-89.95765601272012, 47.286907253603175),....]]}
```

Next, we plot the geometry with Shapely:

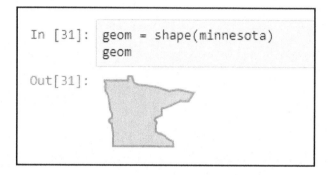

A note on plotting separate shapefile geometries in Python:

As you may have noticed from the prefacing text, referencing separate geometry elements such as a state from shapefiles and plotting them with Python isn't that straightforward. Luckily, there are many code examples available for professionals to solve this problem. Have a look at the following options that are freely available for Python users, to see how you could approach plotting shapefile vector geometries in Python, if you decide to work directly with shapefiles instead of converting to the GeoJSON format:

- Use NumPy arrays and `matplotlib`: You can use NumPy arrays to squeeze all of the coordinates in a one-dimensional array and plot these next.
- Use Shapely and create a new dictionary from an existing shapefile: If you know how to reorganize an existing collection of dictionaries, it is possible to create a new dictionary out of an existing shapefile that uses the name of a geographical area as a key, with the geometry data of that area as values. Next, you can use Shapely to pass in elements of these dictionaries and plot them in Python.
- Use `pyshp` and `matplotlib`: The `pyshp` library can be used to read in geometry information that can then be plotted with `matplotlib`.

- Use GeoPandas and `matplotlib`: The GeoPandas library can be used together to read in shapefiles. Not only can you plot vector data using matplotlib's capabilities, but you can also read in attribute tables as `pandas` dataframes.

GeoPandas

GeoPandas has been introduced in the *GeoPandas* section of `Chapter 2`, *Introduction to Geospatial Code Libraries*, where its data structures and methods have also been covered.

Geospatial analysis with GeoPandas

GeoPandas was created to offer data to scientists who want to work with spatial data similar to `pandas`, and this means giving access to geospatial attribute data through data structures not available through `pandas`. Combine this with a set of geometric operations, data overlay capabilities, geocoding and plotting capabilities and you have an idea of this library's capabilities. In the examples mentioned as we proceed, we'll cover GeoPandas' plotting methods, explain how to access and subset spatial data, and provide a typical workflow for doing geospatial analysis with GeoPandas, where data processing is an important condition for being able to analyze and interpret the data correctly.

Let's have a look at a few code examples of GeoPandas.

Selecting and plotting geometry data with GeoPandas and Matplotlib

The following script combines `pandas` dataframe methods on GeoPandas GeoDataFrame objects. Together, you can easily subset data and plot separate feature geometries. We start with importing the module, the magic command for plotting data inside a Juypter Notebook and input data, which is a shapefile with all US state boundaries:

```
In: import geopandas as gpd
    %matplotlib inline
    df = gpd.read_file\
  (r"C:\data\gdal\NE\110m_cultural\ne_110m_admin_1_states_provinces.shp" )
    df
```

Some simple data inspection methods—`type(df)` returns the object type, which is a GeoPandas `GeoDataFrame`, which takes in the same methods as `pandas` dataframes. The `shape` method returns a tuple with rows and column amounts, while `df.columns` returns the column names as a list item:

```
In:         type(df)
Out:        geopandas.geodataframe.GeoDataFrame

In:         df.shape
Out:        (51, 61)

In:         df.columns
Out:        Index(['adm1_code', 'diss_me', 'iso_3166_2', 'wikipedia', ...
```

We can subset separate rows of our `GeoDataFrame` using `pandas`, `.loc` and `.iloc` methods. We access the first feature's attributes, as follows:

```
In:         df.loc[0]

Out:        adm1_code       USA-3514
            diss_me         3514
            iso_3166_2      US-MN
            Wikipedia       http://en.wikipedia.org/wiki/Minnesota
            iso_a2          US
            adm0_sr         1
            name            Minnesota
            ...                ...
```

Now, we'll plot some state data. First, we'll get a list of all of the state names as we need the state names and their row numbers next:

```
In:     df['name']

Out:    0       Minnesota
        1       Montana
        2       North Dakota
        3       Hawaii
        4       Idaho
        5       Washington
        ...        ...
```

Separate rows can be referenced by `name` instead of row number using `.loc` and a value. Repeating the `name` value returns all columns and attribute data:

```
In:     california = df.loc[df['name'] == "California"]
        california
```

You can plot the geometry of this variable as follows:

```
In:     california.plot(figsize=(7,7))
```

Here is what the graph looks like:

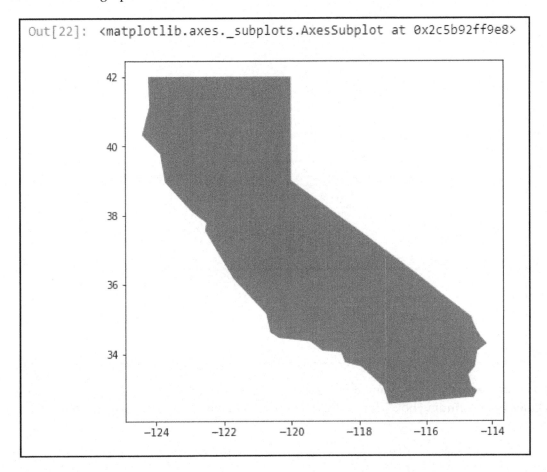

```
Out[22]:   <matplotlib.axes._subplots.AxesSubplot at 0x2c5b92ff9e8>
```

You can plot multiple items by using the `.iloc` function and pass it a list of row numbers; in this case, the row numbers correspond to Washington, California, Nevada, and Oregon, respectively:

```
In:    multipl = df.iloc[[5,7,9,11]]
       multipl.plot(cmap="Set1", figsize=(7,7))
```

The output graph will look like this:

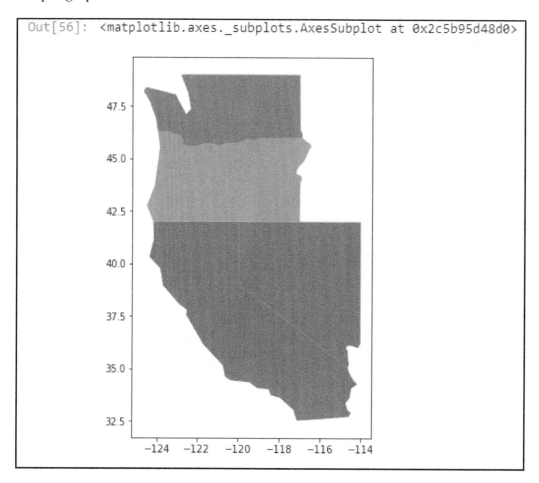

```
Out[56]:   <matplotlib.axes._subplots.AxesSubplot at 0x2c5b95d48d0>
```

The same results can be obtained using the `.cx` method on the `GeoDataFrame`, passing in values for a bounding box. This method uses the following syntax: `df.cx[xmin:xmax, ymin:ymax]`:

```
In:   exp = df.cx[-124:-118,30:50]
      exp.plot(cmap="Set1", figsize=(7,7))
```

Mapping wildfire data with GeoPandas

The following script can be used to create a choropleth map that shows the total wildfires in the US from 1984-2015, based on total count per state. We can use the MTBS with fire data that was introduced in Chapter 4, *Data Types, Storage, and Conversion*, which gives us point data of all of the wildfire occurrences from 1984-2015. We can use the state field of the wildfire data to map the wildfire occurrences by state. But, we choose here to overlay the data on a separate shapefile with state geometries, to illustrate the use of a spatial join. Next, we'll count the total wildfires per state and map the results. GeoPandas can be used to accomplish all of these tasks.

We start with importing the module:

```
In:    import geopandas
```

Next, we import the shapefile with all of the state boundaries:

```
In:    states =
       geopandas.read_file(r"C:\data\gdal\NE\110m_cultural\ne_110m_admin_
       1_states_provinces.shp")
```

The attribute table of the file can be displayed as a `pandas` dataframe by repeating the variable name:

```
In:    states
```

We can see all of the state names listed in the **name** column. We will need this column later. The vector data can be plotted inside our Jupyter Notebook, using the magic command and the `plot` method from `matplotlib`. As the default maps look quite small, we'll pass in some values using the `figsize` option to make it look bigger:

```
In: %matplotlib inline
    states.plot(figsize=(10,10))
```

You'll see the following map:

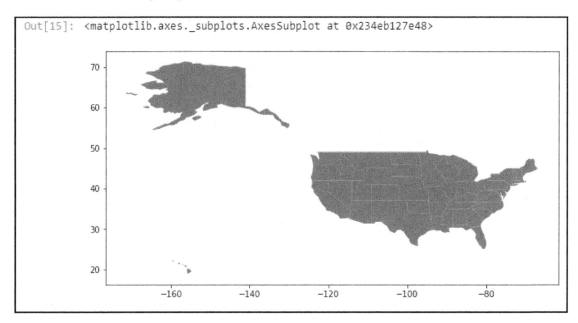

```
Out[15]:  <matplotlib.axes._subplots.AxesSubplot at 0x234eb127e48>
```

The same procedure is repeated for our wildfire data. Using large values for the `figsize` option gives a large map showing the location of the wildfires:

```
In: fires =
    geopandas.read_file(r"C:\data\mtbs_fod_pts_data\mtbs_fod_pts_201705
    01.shp")
    fires
In: fires.plot(markersize=1, figsize=(17,17))
```

The map looks something like this:

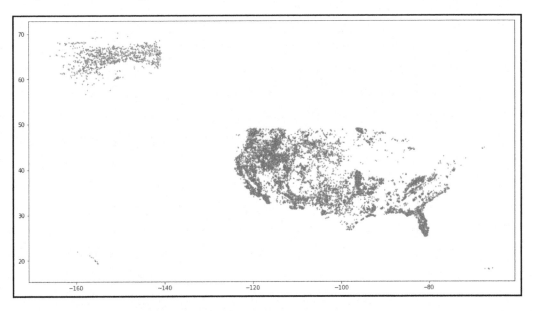

Have a look at the column called **MTBS Zone** in the `fires GeoDataFrame`, and verify that this dataset does not include all of the state names to reference the data. However, we have a geometry column that we can use to join both of the datasets. Before we can do this, we have to make sure that the data uses the same map projection. We can verify this as follows:

```
In:    fires.crs
Out:   {'init': 'epsg:4269'}

In:    states.crs
Out:   {'init': 'epsg:4326'}
```

There are two map projections, but both need to have the same CRS in order to line up correctly. We can reproject the `fires` shapefile to WGS84 as follows:

```
In: fires = fires.to_crs({'init': 'epsg:4326'})
```

Now, we're ready to perform a spatial join, using the `sjoin` method, indicating we want to know if the `fires` geometries are within the state geometries:

```
In: state_fires =
    geopandas.sjoin(fires,states[['name','geometry']].copy(),op='within'
)
    state_fires
```

The new `state_fires` GeoDataFrame has a column added to the outer right called **name**, showing the state where each fire is located:

Fire_Type	geometry	index_right	name
WF	POINT (-141.851 65.29600000000001)	50	Alaska
WF	POINT (-162.314 67.75700000000001)	50	Alaska
WF	POINT (-141.217 65.05)	50	Alaska
WF	POINT (-146.817 62.698)	50	Alaska
WF	POINT (-156.362 64.077)	50	Alaska
WF	POINT (-143.9 64.137)	50	Alaska
WF	POINT (-144.441 64.545)	50	Alaska

We can now count the total amount of wildfires per state. The result is a `pandas` series object showing the state name and total count. To start with the highest counts, we'll use the `sort_values` method:

```
In:    counts_per_state = state_fires.groupby('name').size()
       counts_per_state.sort_values(axis=0, ascending=False)
```

`Florida`, `California`, and `Idaho` are the three states with the most wildfires during 1984-2015, according to our data:

```
Out[54]:  name
          Florida        3635
          California     1577
          Idaho          1278
          Kansas         1124
          Alaska         1062
          Texas          1011
          Arizona         836
```

These values can be fed into the original shapefile as a new field, showing total wildfire count per state:

```
In: states =
    states.merge(counts_per_state.reset_index(name='number_of_fires'))
    states.head()
```

The `head` method prints the first five entries in the `states` shapefile, with a new field added to the right end of the table. Finally, a choropleth map for wildfire count per state can be created and plotted as follows:

```
In: ax = states.plot(column='number_of_fires', figsize=(15, 6),
    cmap='OrRd', legend=True)
```

The output will look something like this:

Compare this to another color scheme applied to the same results, doing away with the light colors for the lower values:

```
In: ax = states.plot(column='number_of_fires', figsize=(15, 6),
    cmap='Accent', legend=True)
```

Here is what the map looks like:

Use the following code to fine-tune the map a little further, by adding a title and dropping the *x*-axis and *y*-axis:

```
In: import matplotlib.pyplot as plt
    f, ax = plt.subplots(1, figsize=(18,6))
    ax = states.plot(column='number_of_fires', cmap='Accent',
    legend=True, ax=ax)
    lims = plt.axis('equal')
    f.suptitle('US Wildfire count per state in 1984-2015')
    ax.set_axis_off()
    plt.show()
```

The output is as follows:

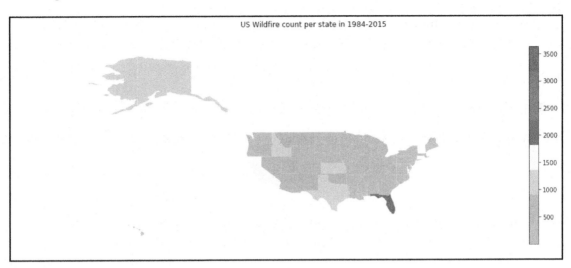

Why data inspection matters

When you're preparing your data, it's good to know the data you're dealing with. For example, listing statistics about your dataset that show you how many elements there are, and if there are any missing values. It's common that data has to be cleaned up before doing the analysis. Because the GeoPandas data objects are subclasses of pandas data objects, you can use their methods to do data inspection and cleaning. Take, for instance, the wildfire data shapefile we used earlier. By listing our dataframe object, it not only prints all of the attribute data, but also lists the total rows and columns, which is 20340 rows and 30 columns. The total amount of rows can also be printed this way:

```
In:        len(fires.index)

Out:       20340
```

This means there are 20340 individual wildfire cases in our input dataset. Now, compare this row value to the sum of the counts per state, after we've performed the spatial join:

```
In:        counts_per_state.sum()

Out:       20266
```

We notice that there are 74 less wildfires in our dataset after our spatial join. While at this point it's not clear what went wrong with our spatial join and why there are missing values, it's possible and recommended to check datasets before and after performing geometric operations, for example, checking for empty fields, non-values, or simply null-values:

```
In:         fires.empty    #checks if there are empty fields in the
                           dataframe

Out:     False
```

The same operation can also be done by specifying a column name:

```
In:         fires['geometry'].empty

Out:     False
```

Be aware of the fact that GeoPandas geometry columns use a combination of text and values, so checking for NaN or zero values doesn't make any sense.

Summary

This chapter covered three Python libraries for working with vector data—OGR, Shapely, and GeoPandas. In particular, we showed how to use all three for doing geospatial analysis and processing. Each library was covered separately, with their classes, methods, data structures and popular use cases. Short example scripts showed how to get started doing data processing and analysis. Taken as a whole, the reader now knows how to use each library separately, as well as how to combine all three for doing the following tasks:

- Reading and writing vector data
- Creating and manipulating vector data
- Plotting vector data
- Working with map projections
- Performing spatial operations
- Working with vector geometries and attribute data in tabular form
- Presenting and analyzing the data to answer questions with a spatial component

The next chapter discusses raster data processing and how to use the GDAL and Rasterio libraries. Using these libraries, the reader will learn how to perform raster-based geospatial search and analysis, and how to use geolocated text and images.

6

Raster Data Processing

Geographic information systems (GIS) are often comprised of points, lines, and polygons. These data types are called vector data. There is, however, another data type in GIS—rasters. In this chapter, you will learn the basics of working with raster data. You will learn how to:

- Use the **Geospatial Data Abstraction Library (GDAL)** to load and query rasters
- Use GDAL to modify and save rasters
- Use GDAL to create rasters
- Load rasters into PostgreSQL
- Perform queries on rasters using PostgreSQL

 Installing GDAL can be difficult. By using virtual environments and running Anaconda, you can simplify this process by using the GUI of the environment.

Raster operations using GDAL

The GDAL library allows you to read and write both vector and raster data. To install GDAL on Windows, you will need the appropriate binaries:

 You can download OSGeo4W, which contains the binaries, at: `https://trac.osgeo.org/osgeo4w/`

When you have the binaries, you can install `gdal` using `conda`, as follows:

```
conda install -c conda-forge gdal
```

In the following sections, you will learn how to load and work with a `.tif` file.

Using the GDAL library to load and query rasters

Now that you have `gdal` installed, import it using:

```
from osgeo import gdal
```

GDAL 2 is the most recent version. If you have an older version of `gdal` installed, you may need to import it using the following code:

```
import gdal
```

If this is the case, you may want to look into upgrading your version of `gdal`. Once you have `gdal` imported, you can open a raster image. First, let's get an image from the web. The Earth Data Analysis Center at the University of New Mexico maintains the **Resource Geographic Information System (RGIS)**. In it, you will find New Mexico GIS data. Browse to `http://rgis.unm.edu/` and from the **Get Data** link, Select `Shaded Relief`, `General`, and `New Mexico`. Then, download the `Color Shaded Relief of New Mexico (Georeferenced TIFF)` file.

When you extract the ZIP file, you will have several files. We are only interested in `nm_relief_color.tif`. The following code will open TIF using `gdal`:

```
nmtif = gdal.Open(r'C:\Desktop\ColorRelief\nm_relief_color.tif')
print(nmtif.GetMetadata())
```

The previous code opens TIF. It is very similar to opening any file in Python, except you used `gdal.Open` instead of the standard Python library `open`. The next line prints the metadata from the TIF, and the output is shown as follows:

```
{'AREA_OR_POINT': 'Area', 'TIFFTAG_DATETIME': '2002:12:18 8:10:06',
'TIFFTAG_RESOLUTIONUNIT': '2 (pixels/inch)', 'TIFFTAG_SOFTWARE': 'IMAGINE
TIFF Support\nCopyright 1991 - 1999 by ERDAS, Inc. All Rights
Reserved\n@(#)$RCSfile: etif.c $ $Revision: 1.9.3.3 $ $Date: 2002/07/29
15:51:11EDT $', 'TIFFTAG_XRESOLUTION': '96', 'TIFFTAG_YRESOLUTION': '96'}
```

The previous metadata gives you some basic information such as dates created and revised, the resolution, and pixels per inch. One characteristic of the data we are interested in is the projection. To find it, use the following code:

```
nmtif.GetProjection()
```

Using the `GetProjection` method on the TIF, you will see that we didn't find any. The output of the code is as follows:

```
'LOCAL_CS[" Geocoding information not available Projection Name = Unknown
Units = other GeoTIFF Units = other",UNIT["unknown",1]]'
```

If you open this TIF in QGIS, you will get a warning that the CRS is undefined and it will default to `epsg:4326`. I know that the image is projected and we can find this out by looking at the `nm_relief_color.tif.xml` file. If you scroll to the bottom, you will see the values under the XML tag `<cordsysn>`, as follows:

```
<cordsysn>
<geogcsn>GCS_North_American_1983</geogcsn>
<projcsn>NAD_1983_UTM_Zone_13N</projcsn>
</cordsysn>
```

If you look up the projection at `spatialreference.org`, you will find that it is EPSG:26913. We can use `gdal` to set the projection, as shown in the following code:

```
from osgeo import osr
p=osr.SpatialReference()
p.ImportFromEPSG(26913)
nmtif.SetProjection(p.ExportToWkt())
nmtif.GetProjection()
```

The previous code imports the `osr` library. It then uses the library to create a new `SpatialReference`. Next, it imports a known reference using `ImportFromEPSG` and passes `26913`. It then uses `SetProjection`, passing the WKT for EPSG:26913. Lastly, it calls `GetProjection` so that we can see that the code worked. The results are as follows:

```
'PROJCS["NAD83 / UTM zone
13N",GEOGCS["NAD83",DATUM["North_American_Datum_1983",SPHEROID["GRS
1980",6378137,298.257222101,AUTHORITY["EPSG","7019"]],TOWGS84[0,0,0,0,0,0,0
],AUTHORITY["EPSG","6269"]],PRIMEM["Greenwich",0,AUTHORITY["EPSG","8901"]],
UNIT["degree",0.0174532925199433,AUTHORITY["EPSG","9122"]],AUTHORITY["EPSG"
,"4269"]],PROJECTION["Transverse_Mercator"],PARAMETER["latitude_of_origin",
0],PARAMETER["central_meridian",-105],PARAMETER["scale_factor",0.9996],PARA
METER["false_easting",500000],PARAMETER["false_northing",0],UNIT["metre",1,
AUTHORITY["EPSG","9001"]],AXIS["Easting",EAST],AXIS["Northing",NORTH],AUTHO
RITY["EPSG","26913"]]'
```

The previous output is the WKT for EPSG:26913.

Open QGIS and the TIF will load with no warnings. I can add a copy of the Albuquerque streets to it and they will appear exactly where they should. Both sets of data are in EPSG:26913. The following image shows the TIF and the streets in the center of New Mexico-Albuquerque:

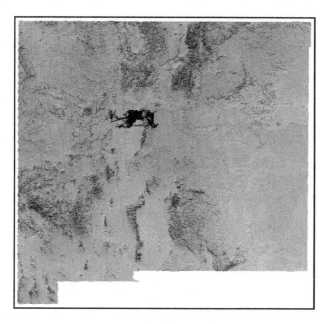

Tif of NM with Streets shapefile

Now that we have added a projection, we can save a new version of the TIF:

```
geoTiffDriver="GTiff"
driver=gdal.GetDriverByName(geoTiffDriver)
out=driver.CreateCopy("copy.tif",nmtif,strict=0)
```

To see that the new file has the spatial reference, use the following code:

```
out.GetProjection()
```

The previous code will output the **well-known text (WKT)** for EPSG:26913, as follows:

```
'PROJCS["NAD83 / UTM zone
13N",GEOGCS["NAD83",DATUM["North_American_Datum_1983",SPHEROID["GRS
1980",6378137,298.257222101,AUTHORITY["EPSG","7019"]],TOWGS84[0,0,0,0,0,0,0
],AUTHORITY["EPSG","6269"]],
PRIMEM["Greenwich",0,AUTHORITY["EPSG","8901"]],UNIT["degree",0.017453292519
9433,AUTHORITY["EPSG","9122"]],
AUTHORITY["EPSG","4269"]],PROJECTION["Transverse_Mercator"],PARAMETER["lati
```

```
tude_of_origin",0],PARAMETER["central_meridian",
-105],PARAMETER["scale_factor",0.9996],PARAMETER["false_easting",500000],PA
RAMETER["false_northing",0],UNIT["metre",1,
AUTHORITY["EPSG","9001"]],AXIS["Easting",EAST],AXIS["Northing",NORTH],AUTHO
RITY["EPSG","26913"]]'
```

A color raster dataset has three bands—red, green, and blue. You can get each of the bands individually using the following code:

```
nmtif.RasterCount
```

The previous code will return 3. Unlike an array, the bands are indexed 1-n, so a three band raster will have indexes 1, 2, and 3. You can grab a single band by passing the index to GetRasterBand(), which is shown in the following code:

```
band=nmtif.GetRasterBand(1)
```

Now that you have a raster band, you can perform queries on it and you can lookup values at positions. To find the value at a specified row and column, you can use the following code:

```
values=band.ReadAsArray()
```

Now, values is an array, so you can lookup values by index notation, as follows:

```
values[1100,1100]
```

The previous code will return a value of 216. In a single band array, this would be helpful, but in a colored image, you would most likely want to know the color at a location. This would require knowing the value of all three bands. You can do that by using the following code:

```
one= nmtif.GetRasterBand(1).ReadAsArray()
two = nmtif.GetRasterBand(2).ReadAsArray()
three= nmtif.GetRasterBand(3).ReadAsArray()
print(str(one[1100,1100])+","+
str(two[1100,1100])+","+str(three[1100,1100]))
```

The previous code returns the values—216, 189, 157. These are the RGB values of the pixel. These three values are composited—overlayed on each other, which, should be the color shown in the following image:

The color represented by the three bands at [1100,1100]

With a band, you have access to several methods for obtaining information about the band. You can get the mean and standard deviation of the values, as shown in the following code:

```
one=nmtif.GetRasterBand(1)
two=nmtif.GetRasterBand(2)
three=nmtif.GetRasterBand(3)
one.ComputeBandStats()
two.ComputeBandStats()
three.ComputeBandStats()
```

The output is shown as follows:

```
(225.05771967375847, 34.08382839593031)
(215.3145137636133, 37.83657996026153)
(195.34890652292185, 53.08308166590347)
```

You can also get the minimum and maximum values from a band, as shown in the following code:

```
print(str(one.GetMinimum())+","+str(one.GetMaximum()))
```

The result should be 0.0 and 255.0.

You can also get the description of the band. The following code shows you how to get and set the description:

```
two.GetDescription()    # returns 'band_2'
two.SetDescription("The Green Band")
two.GetDescription()    # returns "The Green Band"
```

The most obvious thing you may want to do with a raster dataset is to view the raster in Jupyter Notebook. There are several ways to load images in a Jupyter notebook, one being using HTML and an <img>. In the following code, you are shown how to plot the image using `matplotlib`:

```
import numpy as np
from matplotlib.pyplot import imshow
%matplotlib inline

data_array=nmtif.ReadAsArray()
x=np.array(data_array[0])
# x.shape ---> 6652,6300
w, h =6652, 6300
image = x.reshape(x.shape[0],x.shape[1])
imshow(image, cmap='gist_earth')
```

The previous code imports `numpy` and `matplotlib.pyploy.imshow`.

NumPy is a popular library for working with arrays. When dealing with rasters, which are arrays, you will benefit from having a strong understanding of the library. Packt published several books on NumPy such as *NumPy Cookbook, NumPy Beginners Guide,* and *Learning NumPy Array,* and this would be a good place to start learning more.

It then sets plotting an inline for this notebook. The code then reads in the TIF as an array. It then makes a `numpy` array from the first band.

Bands are indexed *1-n,* but once read in as an array, they become indexed at 0.

To isolate the first band, the code reshapes the array using the width and height. Using `x.shape`, you can get them both, and if you index, you can get each one individually. Lastly, using `imshow`, the code plots the image using the color map for `gist_earth`. The image will display in Jupyter as follows:

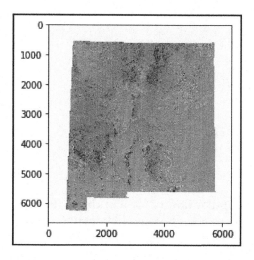

Tif in Jupyter using imshow

Now that you know how to load a raster and perform basic operations, you will learn how to create a raster in the following section.

Using GDAL to create rasters

In the previous section, you learned how to load a raster, perform basic queries, modify it, and save it out as a new file. In this section, you will learn how to create a raster.

A **raster** is an array of values. So to create one, you start by creating an array, as shown in the following code:

```
a_raster=np.array([
[10,10,1,10,10,10,10],
[1,1,1,50,10,10,50],
[10,1,1,51,10,10,50],
[1,1,1,1,50,10,50]])
```

The previous code creates a `numpy` array with four rows of seven columns. Now that you have the array of data, you will need to set some basic properties. The following code will assign the values to variables and then you will pass them to the raster in the following example:

```
coord=(-106.629773,35.105389)
w=10
h=10
name="BigI.tif"
```

The following code sets the lower-left corner, width, height, and name for the raster in the variable `coord`. It then sets the width and height in pixels. Lastly, it names the raster.

The next step is to create the raster by combining the data and properties. The following code will show you how:

```
d=gdal.GetDriverByName("GTiff")
output=d.Create(name,a_raster.shape[1],a_raster.shape[0],1,gdal.GDT_UInt16)
output.SetGeoTransform((coord[0],w,0,coord[1],0,h))
output.GetRasterBand(1).WriteArray(a_raster)
outsr=osr.SpatialReference()
outsr.ImportFromEPSG(4326)
output.SetProjection(outsr.ExportToWkt())
output.FlushCache()
```

The previous code assigns the `GeoTiff` driver to the variable `d`. Then, it uses the driver to create the raster. The create method takes five parameters—the `name`, size of `x`, size of `y`, the number of bands, and the data type. To get the size of `x` and `y`, you can access `a_raster.shape`, which will return (4,7). Indexing `a_raster.shape` will give you `x` and `y` individually.

`Create()` accepts several data types—starting with `GDT_`. Other data types include Unknown, Byte, UInt16, Int16, UInt32, Int32, Float32, Float64, CInt16, CInt32, CFloat32, and Cfloat64.

Next, the code sets the transformation from map to pixel coordinates using the upper-left corner coordinates and the rotation. The rotation is the width and height, and if it is a north up image, then the other parameters are 0.
To write the data to a band, the code selects the raster band—in this case, you used a single band specified when you called the `Create()` method, so passing 1 to `GetRasterBand()` and `WriteArray()` will take the `numpy` array.

Now, you will need to assign a spatial reference to the TIF. Create a spatial reference and assign it to `outsr`. Then, you can import a spatial reference from the EPSG code. Next, set the projection on the TIF by passing the WKT to the `SetProjection()` method.

The last step is to `FlushCache()`, which will write the file. If you are done with the TIF, you can set `output = None` to clear it. However, you will use it again in the following code snippet, so you will skip that step here.

To prove that the code worked, you can check the projection, as shown in the following code:

```
output.GetProjection()
```

And the output shows that the TIF is in EPSG:4326:

```
'GEOGCS["WGS 84",DATUM["WGS_1984",SPHEROID["WGS
84",6378137,298.257223563,AUTHORITY["EPSG","7030"]],AUTHORITY["EPSG","6326"
]],PRIMEM["Greenwich",0,AUTHORITY["EPSG","8901"]],UNIT["degree",0.017453292
5199433,AUTHORITY["EPSG","9122"]],AUTHORITY["EPSG","4326"]]'
```

You can display the TIF in Jupyter and see if it looks like you expected. The following code demonstrates how to plot the `image` and inspect your results:

```
data=output.ReadAsArray()
w, h =4, 7
image = data.reshape(w,h) #assuming X[0] is of shape (400,) .T
imshow(image, cmap='Blues') #enter bad color to get list
data
```

The previous code reads the raster as an array and assigns the width and height. It then creates an `image` variable, reshaping the array to the width and height. Lastly, it passes the image to `imshow()` and prints the `data` in the last line. If everything worked, you will see the following image:

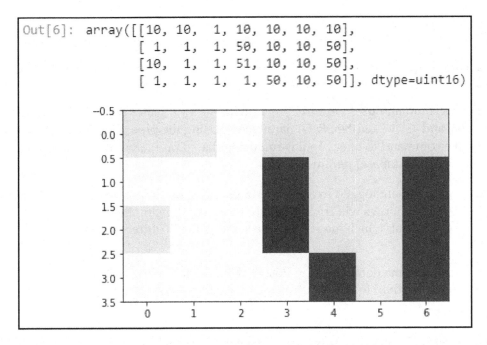

```
Out[6]: array([[10, 10,  1, 10, 10, 10, 10],
               [ 1,  1,  1, 50, 10, 10, 50],
               [10,  1,  1, 51, 10, 10, 50],
               [ 1,  1,  1,  1, 50, 10, 50]], dtype=uint16)
```

The array values and the raster created from them

The following section will teach you how to use PostgreSQL to work with rasters as an alternative or in conjunction with `gdal`.

Raster operations using PostgreSQL

In the first section of this chapter, you were able to load, display, and query rasters using `gdal`. In this section, you will learn how to load and query rasters using a spatial database—PostgreSQL. As you start to model your data, you will most likely hold it in a spatial database. You can leverage your database to perform the queries on your rasters.

Loading rasters into PostgreSQL

To load a raster into PostgreSQL, you can use the `raster2pgsql` binary. If it is not in your path, you may need to add it. You should be able to find the binary in your PostgreSQL install directory on Windows at `\PostgreSQL\10\bin`.

The following command should be executed from your operating system's command line. It will load the TIF you created earlier in this chapter into an existing PostgreSQL database:

```
>raster2pgsql -I -C -s 4326 C:\Users\Paul\Desktop\BigI.tif public.bigi |
psql -U postgres -d pythonspatial
```

The previous command uses `raster2pgsql` with the `-I` (creates an index), `-C` (adds raster constraints), and `-s 4326` (the SRID) parameters. Using the pipe operator on Windows, you send the command to `psql`. Psql is run using the `-U postgres` (username) and `-d pythonspatial` (database) parameters.

 If you are logged in as the Postgres user, you do not need the `-U`. Without it, Windows will try to log in to PostgreSQL using the logged in user account, which may not be the same as the PostgreSQL user.

Now that you have the data loaded in PostgreSQL, the following section will show you how you can use Python to query it.

Performing queries on rasters using PostgreSQL

With a raster loaded into PostgreSQL, you can query it using Python. The Python library for working with PostgreSQL is `psycopg2`. The following code will connect to the database where you loaded the TIF:

```
import psycopg2
connection = psycopg2.connect(database="pythonspatial",user="postgres",
password="postgres")
cursor = connection.cursor()
```

The previous code imports `psycopg2`. It then makes a connection passing the database name, username, and password. Lastly, it gets a `cursor` object so that you can execute queries.

To see the raster in PostgreSQL, you can execute a select all, as shown in the following code:

```
cursor.execute("SELECT * from bigi")
#Big I is the name of the intersection where I-25 and I-40 meet and split
Albuquerque in quadrants.
cursor.fetchall()
```

The previous code executes a select all statement and prints all the results. There are two columns in the table—rid and `rast`. Rid is the unique ID field for the raster. If you had tiled it when running `raster2pgsql`, there would be more rows. The `rast` column holds the raster data:

```
[(1,
 '01000001000000000000000244000000000000002440D8B969334EA85AC0D82D02637D8D4140
0000000000000000000000000000000000E61000000700040004000A0A010A0A0A0A010101320
A0A320A0101330A0A3201010101320A32')]
```

Querying raster metadata

Using PostgreSQL, you can perform various queries on your data. In this section, you will learn how to query the raster for basic metadata and properties. This section will present a few of the many PostgreSQL functions that are available.

You can query the data for a basic text summary. The following code shows you how to use the `ST_Summary()` function:

```
cursor.execute("select ST_Summary(rast) from bigi;")
cursor.fetchall()
```

The summary function takes the raster data column as a parameter and returns a string containing the size of the raster, the bounding box, the number of bands, and if there are no data values in any of the bands. The following is the output from the previous code:

```
[('Raster of 7x4 pixels has 1 band and extent of BOX(-106.629773
35.105389,-36.629773 75.105389)\n band 1 of pixtype 8BUI is in-db with no
NODATA value',)]
```

Parsing out the individual pieces of information from `ST_Summary` would be difficult. You can retrieve this information in a more machine-readable format by using the `ST_Metadata` function. You can use the following code to do so:

```
cursor.execute("select ST_MetaData(rast) from bigi")
cursor.fetchall()
```

The previous code queries the raster for the upper-left *X* value, the upper-left *Y* value, the width, the height, the scale of *X*, the scale of *Y*, the skew of *X*, the skew of *Y*, the SRID, and the number of bands in the raster. The output is shown as follows:

```
[('(-106.629773,35.105389,7,4,10,10,0,0,4326,1)',)]
```

The output allows you to select individual pieces of metadata by using index notation, which is a simpler solution to parsing the string provided by ST_Summary.

You can query for specific and individual attributes of the raster. To get the raster as a single polygon—instead of the two-point box described in the summary—you can use the following code:

```
cursor.execute("select ST_AsText(ST_Envelope(rast)) from bigi;")
cursor.fetchall()
```

The output of the previous code is the WKT for a vector-polygon-of the raster. It is shown as follows:

```
[('POLYGON((-106.629773 75.105389,-36.629773 75.105389,-36.629773
35.105389,-106.629773 35.105389,-106.629773 75.105389))',)]
```

The following code will query the height and width of the raster:

```
cursor.execute("select st_height(rast), st_Width(rast) from bigi;")
#st_width
cursor.fetchall()
```

As you may recall from earlier in the chapter, the raster is 4x7, as shown in the output:

```
[(4, 7)]
```

Another piece of metadata that may come in handy is the pixel size. The following code will show you how:

```
cursor.execute("select ST_PixelWidth(rast), ST_PixelHeight(rast) from
bigi;")
cursor.fetchall()
```

Using ST_PixelWidth and ST_PixelHeight, you will get the output as follows. This matches the height and width from when you created the raster earlier in the chapter:

```
[(10.0,10.0)]
```

You can query the raster for basic statistical information about the data within the cells for a specific band. ST_SummaryStats provides basic summary statistics for the data values. The following code shows you how to query:

```
cursor.execute("select ST_SummaryStats(rast) from bigi;")
cursor.fetchall()
```

The output of the previous code returns the count, sum, mean, standard deviation, min, and max for a raster band. You can pass the raster band by passing it as an integer in the second parameter, `ST_SummaryStats(rast,3)`. If you do not specify the band, the default is 1. The output is shown as follows:

```
[('(28,431,15.3928571428571,18.5902034218377,1,51)',)]
```

You can also query for a histogram of the values in the raster, as shown in the following code:

```
cursor.execute("SELECT ST_Histogram(rast,1) from bigi;")
cursor.fetchall()
```

The previous code uses `ST_Histogram` and passes the raster column and a band. You can pass the number of bins as the third parameter or you can let the function decide. The result is shown as follows:

```
[('(1,9.33333333333333,10,0.357142857142857)',),
 ('(9.33333333333333,17.6666666666667,12,0.428571428571429)',),
 ('(17.6666666666667,26,0,0)',),
 ('(26,34.3333333333333,0,0)',),
 ('(34.3333333333333,42.6666666666667,0,0)',),
 ('(42.6666666666667,51,6,0.214285714285714)',)]
```

The previous output is an array of bins. Each bin contains the minimum value, the maximum value, the count, and the percentage.

Queries returning geometry

The previous queries returned basic information about the raster and returned collections with the data. In PostgreSQL, there are a series of functions that return geometries from queries. This section will cover a few of those functions.

A raster is comprised of a matrix of cells and values. These cells become georeferenced pixels in our raster data. Using PostgreSQL, you can query your raster data for a specific cell and get the polygon representation of that cell back. The following code shows you how:

```
cursor.execute("select rid, ST_asText(ST_PixelAsPolygon(rast,7,2)) from bigi;")
cursor.fetchall()
```

Using `ST_PixelAsPolygons`, you can pass the raster column, the column, and the row of a cell and get back polygon geometry for that cell. By wrapping the query in `ST_AsText`, you get back the WKT representation of the polygon instead of the binary.

The following is the result:

```
[(1,
'POLYGON((-46.629773 45.105389,-36.629773 45.105389,-36.629773
55.105389,-46.629773 55.105389,-46.629773 45.105389))')]
```

The previous output returned the rid (raster ID) of the pixel. Since you did not tile the raster when loading it into PostgreSQL, all the queries will return a rid of 1.

The previous query returned a polygon, but you can use functions to return points. Using `ST_PixelAsPoints` and `ST_PixelAsCentroids`, you can retrieve a point for every pixel in the raster dataset.

Using `ST_PixelAsPoints`, you can retrieve a point geometry representing the upper-left corner of each pixel. The query also returns the x and y of the cell and the value. The following code will show you how:

```
cursor.execute("SELECT x, y, val, ST_AsText(geom) FROM (SELECT
(ST_PixelAsPoints(rast, 1)).* FROM bigi) as foo;")

cursor.fetchall()
```

The previous code has a two-part query. Starting after the FROM statement, the query selects the pixels as points for band 1. The first statement performs a select on the results and retrieves the point geometry, and the x, y, and value of the cell. `ST_PixelAsPoints`, by default, does not return data for cells with no values. You can pass the third parameter as false to return cells with no values.

The output of the previous query is an array with a row for each cell. Each row contains the x,y, value, and geometry. The results are shown as follows:

```
[(1, 1, 10.0, 'POINT(-106.629773 35.105389)'),
 (2, 1, 10.0, 'POINT(-96.629773 35.105389)'),
 (3, 1, 1.0, 'POINT(-86.629773 35.105389)'),
 (4, 1, 10.0, 'POINT(-76.629773 35.105389)'),
 (5, 1, 10.0, 'POINT(-66.629773 35.105389)'),
 (6, 1, 10.0, 'POINT(-56.629773 35.105389)'),
 (7, 1, 10.0, 'POINT(-46.629773 35.105389)'),
 (1, 2, 1.0, 'POINT(-106.629773 45.105389)'),
 (2, 2, 1.0, 'POINT(-96.629773 45.105389)'),
 (3, 2, 1.0, 'POINT(-86.629773 45.105389)'),
```

```
(4, 2, 50.0, 'POINT(-76.629773 45.105389)'),
(5, 2, 10.0, 'POINT(-66.629773 45.105389)'),
(6, 2, 10.0, 'POINT(-56.629773 45.105389)'),
(7, 2, 50.0, 'POINT(-46.629773 45.105389)'),
(1, 3, 10.0, 'POINT(-106.629773 55.105389)'),
(2, 3, 1.0, 'POINT(-96.629773 55.105389)'),
(3, 3, 1.0, 'POINT(-86.629773 55.105389)'),
(4, 3, 51.0, 'POINT(-76.629773 55.105389)'),
(5, 3, 10.0, 'POINT(-66.629773 55.105389)'),
(6, 3, 10.0, 'POINT(-56.629773 55.105389)'),
(7, 3, 50.0, 'POINT(-46.629773 55.105389)'),
(1, 4, 1.0, 'POINT(-106.629773 65.105389)'),
(2, 4, 1.0, 'POINT(-96.629773 65.105389)'),
(3, 4, 1.0, 'POINT(-86.629773 65.105389)'),
(4, 4, 1.0, 'POINT(-76.629773 65.105389)'),
(5, 4, 50.0, 'POINT(-66.629773 65.105389)'),
(6, 4, 10.0, 'POINT(-56.629773 65.105389)'),
(7, 4, 50.0, 'POINT(-46.629773 65.105389)')]
```

Using `ST_PixelAsCentroids`, you can get a point that represents the centroid of the pixel or cell. The query is identical to the previous example and is shown as follows:

```
cursor.execute("SELECT x, y, val, ST_AsText(geom) FROM (SELECT
(ST_PixelAsCentroids(rast, 1)).* FROM bigi) as foo;")

cursor.fetchall()
```

The previous query is in two parts. It first executes the `ST_PixelAsCentroids` function and then selects the x,y, value, and geometry from that result set. The output is shown as follows. Notice that the points are different than in the previous example:

```
[(1, 1, 10.0, 'POINT(-101.629773 40.105389)'),
 (2, 1, 10.0, 'POINT(-91.629773 40.105389)'),
 (3, 1, 1.0, 'POINT(-81.629773 40.105389)'),
 (4, 1, 10.0, 'POINT(-71.629773 40.105389)'),
 (5, 1, 10.0, 'POINT(-61.629773 40.105389)'),
 (6, 1, 10.0, 'POINT(-51.629773 40.105389)'),
 (7, 1, 10.0, 'POINT(-41.629773 40.105389)'),
 (1, 2, 1.0, 'POINT(-101.629773 50.105389)'),
 (2, 2, 1.0, 'POINT(-91.629773 50.105389)'),
 (3, 2, 1.0, 'POINT(-81.629773 50.105389)'),
 (4, 2, 50.0, 'POINT(-71.629773 50.105389)'),
 (5, 2, 10.0, 'POINT(-61.629773 50.105389)'),
 (6, 2, 10.0, 'POINT(-51.629773 50.105389)'),
 (7, 2, 50.0, 'POINT(-41.629773 50.105389)'),
 (1, 3, 10.0, 'POINT(-101.629773 60.105389)'),
 (2, 3, 1.0, 'POINT(-91.629773 60.105389)'),
```

```
(3, 3, 1.0, 'POINT(-81.629773 60.105389)'),
(4, 3, 51.0, 'POINT(-71.629773 60.105389)'),
(5, 3, 10.0, 'POINT(-61.629773 60.105389)'),
(6, 3, 10.0, 'POINT(-51.629773 60.105389)'),
(7, 3, 50.0, 'POINT(-41.629773 60.105389)'),
(1, 4, 1.0, 'POINT(-101.629773 70.105389)'),
(2, 4, 1.0, 'POINT(-91.629773 70.105389)'),
(3, 4, 1.0, 'POINT(-81.629773 70.105389)'),
(4, 4, 1.0, 'POINT(-71.629773 70.105389)'),
(5, 4, 50.0, 'POINT(-61.629773 70.105389)'),
(6, 4, 10.0, 'POINT(-51.629773 70.105389)'),
(7, 4, 50.0, 'POINT(-41.629773 70.105389)')]
```

The previously mentioned functions returned geometry for all of the pixels in the raster dataset. Both of these functions have a corresponding function which allows you to specify a single pixel.

Removing the plural from centroids and points will allow you to specify single pixels, but will not return the x, y, and value. The following code shows you how to query a single pixel as a centroid:

```
cursor.execute("SELECT ST_AsText(ST_PixelAsCentroid(rast,4,1)) FROM bigi;")
cursor.fetchall()
```

The previous code uses ST_PixelAsCentroid and passes the raster, row, and column. The result is a single centroid point geometry for the cell which has been specified. The output is shown as follows:

```
[('POINT(-71.629773 40.105389)',)]
```

Wrapping the query in ST_AsText resulted in the output being returned in WKT.

Queries returning values

The two previous sections returned information about the raster and geometries representing the raster data. This section will show you how to query your raster dataset for values.

To get the value of a specific cell, you use ST_Value, which is shown as follows:

```
cursor.execute("select ST_Value(rast,4,3) from bigi;")
cursor.fetchall()
```

The previous code passes the raster, the column, and row to ST_Value. Optionally, you can pass false if you want don't want to return any data values. The result of the previous query is shown as follows:

```
[(51.0,)]
```

The output is the value at the given cell.

If you want to search for all pixels with a given value, you can use ST_PixelOfValue, as follows:

```
cursor.execute("select ST_PixelOfValue(rast,1,50) from bigi;")
cursor.fetchall()
```

The previous code passes the band and the value to search for. The result of this query is an array of all (*x,y*) coordinates, where the value is 50. The output is shown as follows:

```
[('(4,2)',), ('(5,4)',), ('(7,2)',), ('(7,3)',), ('(7,4)',)]
```

For each of the coordinates shown earlier, the value is 50.

To summarize the occurrences of every value in the raster, you can query using ST_ValueCount, as follows:

```
cursor.execute("select ST_ValueCount(rast) from bigi;")
cursor.fetchall()
```

The previous code passes the raster column to ST_ValueCount. You can specify a raster band by passing the band as an integer as the second parameter—ST_ValueCount(raster,2) would be band 2. Otherwise, the default is band 1. The output is as follows:

```
[('(10,12)',), ('(1,10)',), ('(50,5)',), ('(51,1)',)]
```

The previous output contains the value and the count in the format of (value, count).

You can also query for the number of times a single value occurs in the data. The following code shows you how:

```
cursor.execute("select ST_ValueCount(rast,1,True,50) from bigi;")
cursor.fetchall()
```

Using ST_ValueCount and passing a search value (50), you will receive the number of times 50 occurs as a value in the raster, as follows:

```
[(5,)]
```

The previous output shows that 50 occurs 5 times in the raster dataset.

To return all the values in the raster data, you can use ST_DumpValues, as follows:

```
cursor.execute("select ST_DumpValues(rast,1) from bigi;")
cursor.fetchall()
```

The previous code passes the raster column and the band. The results are all the values in the raster as an array. The output is shown as follows:

```
[([[10.0, 10.0, 1.0, 10.0, 10.0, 10.0, 10.0],
  [1.0, 1.0, 1.0, 50.0, 10.0, 10.0, 50.0],
  [10.0, 1.0, 1.0, 51.0, 10.0, 10.0, 50.0],
  [1.0, 1.0, 1.0, 1.0, 50.0, 10.0, 50.0]],)]
```

Using the previous output, you can query individual cells using standard Python indexing notation.

The previous queries returned values from a specified cell or by using a specified value. The two queries that are to be followed will return values based on a point geometry.

Using ST_NearestValue, you can pass a point and get the closest pixel value to that point. If the raster data contained elevation values, you would be querying for the known elevation which is closest to the point. The following code shows you how:

```
cursor.execute("select ST_NearestValue(rast,( select ST_SetSRID(
ST_MakePoint(-71.629773,60.105389),4326))) from bigi;".format(p.wkt))

cursor.fetchall()
```

The previous code passes the raster column and a point to ST_NearestValue. Starting from the inside out, the point parameter used ST_MakePoint to make a point from coordinates. The function is wrapped in ST_SetSRID. ST_SetSRID takes two parameters—a point and a spatial reference. In this case, the point is ST_MakePoint, and the spatial reference is ESPG 4326. The result of the previous query is shown as follows:

```
[(51.0,)]
```

The value of 51 is the closest value to the point. The coordinates in the query are the centroid of the cell (4,3) from the earlier ST_PixelAsCentroids example. In that example, the value of that point was 51.

To retrieve more than one value near a given point, you can use ST_Neighborhood, as shown in the following code:

```
cursor.execute("select ST_Neighborhood(rast,(select ST_SetSRID(
ST_MakePoint(410314,3469015),26913)),1,1) from newmexicoraster;")

cursor.fetchall()
```

The ST_Neighborhood function takes the raster column, a point, and an x, y distance value. In the previous code, you used ST_MakePoint and ST_SetSRID to create the point. You then passed the point and the distances of 1 and 1 for the *x* and *y* distance parameter. This will return a 3x3 neighborhood, as shown in the following output:

```
[([[255.0, 255.0, 255.0], [255.0, 255.0, 255.0], [255.0, 255.0, 255.0]],)]
```

The previous output shows that the values of the surrounding neighborhood are all 255.

Finally, you can select vector geometry as a raster. When querying a vector table which contains Albuquerque Police Area Commands as polygons, the following code will extract a single area command as a raster:

```
cursor.execute("SELECT ST_AsPNG(ST_asRaster(geom,150,250,'8BUI')) from
areacommand where name like 'FOOTHILLS';")

c=cursor.fetchall()

with open('Foothills.png','wb') as f:
    f.write(c[0][0])
f.close()
```

The previous code is a select statement that selects a geometry from the areacommand table, where the name is FOOTHILLS. The geometry portion of the query is where you perform the raster conversion.
ST_AsRaster takes a geometry, the scale of x, the scale of y, and the type of pixels. The ST_AsRaster function is wrapped in the ST_AsPNG function. The result is a PNG file in memory view. Using standard Python file operations, the code opens a file, Foothills.png, in write binary mode, and then writes the memory view c[0][0] to disk. It then closes the file.

The output is shown in the following image:

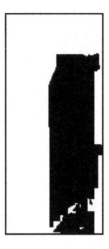

The image showing the foothills as a raster

Summary

In this chapter, you learned how to use GDAL and PostgreSQL to work with raster data.

First, you learned how to use the GDAL to load and query rasters. You also learned how to use GDAL to modify and save rasters. Then, you learned how to create your own raster data. You learned how to load raster data into PostgreSQL using the `raster2pgsql` tool. Once in PostgreSQL, you learned how to query for metadata, attributes, values, and geometry. You learned several common functions within PostgreSQL for raster data analysis.

While this chapter only scratched the surface of working with raster data, you should have enough knowledge now to know how to learn new techniques and methods for working with rasters. In the next chapter, you will learn how to work with vector data in PostgreSQL.

7
Geoprocessing with Geodatabases

In Chapter 3, *Introduction to Geospatial Databases*, you learned how to install PostGIS, create a table, add data, and perform basic spatial queries. In this chapter, you will learn how to work with geospatial databases to answer questions and make maps. This chapter will have you load crime data into tables. Once you have populated your geodatabase with real-world data, you will learn how to perform common crime analysis tasks. You will learn how to map queries, query by date ranges, and perform basic geoprocessing tasks such as buffers, point in polygon, and nearest neighbor. You will learn how to add widgets to your Jupyter Notebooks to allow queries to be interactive. Lastly, you will learn how to use Python to create charts from your geospatial queries. As a crime analyst, you will make maps, but not all GIS-related tasks are map-based. Analysts use GIS data to answer questions and create reports. Executives are often more familiar with charts and graphs.

In this chapter, you will learn:

- How to use spatial queries to perform geoprocessing tasks
- How to add triggers to your tables
- How to map your geospatial query results
- How to graph geospatial queries
- How to use Jupyter to interact with and connect widgets to your queries

A crime dashboard

To build an interactive **crime dashboard**, you will need to collect data to build a database. Then, you will query the data and add widgets to allow users to modify the queries without needing to code. Lastly, you will graph and map the query results.

Building a crime database

To build the components for a crime dashboard, we will use the City of Albuquerque's open data. Albuquerque has datasets for crime incidents, as well as area commands and `beats`. By combining the areas with `incidents`, you will be able to report on two geographic areas. You could then extend the analysis using neighborhood associations or any other boundary—Census blocks, groups, or tracts, and get demographic information as well.

> You can find links to the data on the main open data site located at: `http:/ /www.cabq.gov/abq-data/`. Scroll to the bottom of the page and look for the **Safety Data Sets** heading.

Creating the tables

We will need to create three tables to hold the crime data. We need a table for:

1. Area commands
2. Beats
3. Incidents

To create the tables, we need to import the required libraries:

```
import psycopg2
import requests
from shapely.geometry import Point,Polygon,MultiPolygon, mapping
import datetime
```

The precious code imports `psycopg2` for connecting to PostGIS, `requests` to make the call to the service so you can grab the data, `Point`, `Polygon`, and `MultiPolygon` from `shapely.geometry` to make converting the `GeoJSON` to objects easier, and `datetime` because the `incidents` have a `date` field.

In `Chapter 3`, *Introduction to Geospatial Databases*, you created a database named `pythonspatial` with a user called `postgres`. We will create the tables in that database. To populate the tables, we will copy some of the fields from the service. The layer page of the service has a list of fields at the bottom.

> The URL to the layer is linked to the root page of the service or the layer number. For incidents, the URL to the layer is: `http://coagisweb.cabq.gov/arcgis/rest/services/public/APD_Incidents/MapServer/0`.

Each of the fields has a type and length for the `incidents` layer as follows:

- `OBJECTID` (type: esriFieldTypeOID, alias: Object_ID)
- `Shape` (type: esriFieldTypeGeometry, alias: Geometry)
- `CV_BLOCK_ADD` (type: esriFieldTypeString, alias: Location, length: 72)
- `CVINC_TYPE` (type: esriFieldTypeString, alias: Description, length: 255)
- `date` (type: esriFieldTypeDate, alias: Date, length: 8)

 Supported operations: Query, Generate Renderer, Return updates.

Create the tables using the following code:

```
connection = psycopg2.connect(database="pythonspatial",user="postgres",
password="postgres")
cursor = connection.cursor()

cursor.execute("CREATE TABLE areacommand (id SERIAL PRIMARY KEY, name
VARCHAR(20), geom GEOMETRY)")

cursor.execute("CREATE TABLE beats (id SERIAL PRIMARY KEY, beat VARCHAR(6),
agency VARCHAR(3), areacomm VARCHAR(15),geom GEOMETRY)")

cursor.execute("CREATE TABLE incidents (id SERIAL PRIMARY KEY, address
VARCHAR(72), crimetype VARCHAR(255), date DATE,geom GEOMETRY)")

connection.commit()
```

The previous code starts by creating the connection and getting the `cursor`. It then creates the `areacommand` table, with a field for the `name` and a `GEOMETRY` field. In the **ArcServer** service, the area command field has a length of 20, so the code created a field called `name` as a `VARCHAR(20)`. The next two lines create the tables for `beats` and `incidents`, and lastly, the code commits, making the changes permanent.

Populating the data

With the tables in place, we need to grab the data and populate them. The following code will grab the area commands and insert them into our table:

```
url='http://coagisweb.cabq.gov/arcgis/rest/services/public/adminboundaries/
MapServer/8/query'
```

```
params={"where":"1=1","outFields":"*","outSR":"4326","f":"json"}
r=requests.get(url,params=params)
data=r.json()

for acmd in data['features']:
    polys=[]

    for ring in acmd['geometry']['rings']:
        polys.append(Polygon(ring))
    p=MultiPolygon(polys)
    name=acmd['attributes']['Area_Command']
    cursor.execute("INSERT INTO areacommand (name, geom) VALUES ('{}',
    ST_GeomFromText('{}'))".format(name, p.wkt))

connection.commit()
```

The previous code uses `requests` to query the URL passing parameters. The parameters just grab all the data (1=1), and grab all the fields (*) in reference 4326 and as json. The results are loaded in the variable data using the json() method.

 To learn about the **Environmental Systems Research Institute (ESRI)** ArcServer query parameters, see the API reference here: http://coagisweb.cabq.gov/arcgis/sdk/rest/index.html#/Query_Map_Service_Layer/02ss0000000r000000/

The next block of code is the `for` loop that will insert the data. The service returns json, and the data we need is stored in the features array. For each area command (acmd) in the features array (data['features']), we will grab the name and geometry.

The geometry is comprised of multiple rings—in this case, because our data is comprised of polygons. We need to loop through the rings. To do so, the code has another for loop that iterates through each ring, creates a polygon, and adds it to polys[]. When all the rings are collected as polygons, the code creates a single MultiPolygon with the name of the area command and inserts it into the table using cursor.execute().

The SQL is the basic insert command but uses a parameterized query and ST_GeometryFromText(). Do not get distracted by those additions. Build the query by using the base query as follows:

```
INSERT INTO table (field, field) VALUES (value,value)
```

To pass the values, the code uses .format(). It passes the string name and uses Shapely to convert the coordinates to WKT (p.wkt).

You will need to do the same thing for the `beats` table:

```
url='http://coagisweb.cabq.gov/arcgis/rest/services/public/adminboundaries/
MapServer/9/query'
params={"where":"1=1","outFields":"*","outSR":"4326","f":"json"}
r=requests.get(url,params=params)
data=r.json()

for acmd in data['features']:
    polys=[]
    for ring in acmd['geometry']['rings']:
        polys.append(Polygon(ring))
    p=MultiPolygon(polys)

    beat = acmd['attributes']['BEAT']
    agency = acmd['attributes']['AGENCY']
    areacomm = acmd['attributes']['AREA_COMMA']

    cursor.execute("INSERT INTO beats (beat, agency,areacomm,geom) VALUES
('{}','{}','{}',
    ST_GeomFromText('{}'))".format(beat,agency,areacomm,p.wkt))

connection.commit()
```

The previous code is the same as the code for area commands, only passing additional fields using multiple placeholders (`'{}'`).

Lastly, we need to add the `incidents`:

```
url='http://coagisweb.cabq.gov/arcgis/rest/services/public/APD_Incidents/Ma
pServer/0/query'
params={"where":"1=1","outFields":"*","outSR":"4326","f":"json"}
r=requests.get(url,params=params)
data=r.json()

for a in data["features"]:
    address=a["attributes"]["CV_BLOCK_ADD"]
    crimetype=a["attributes"]["CVINC_TYPE"]
    if a['attributes']['date'] is None:
        pass
    else:
        date = datetime.datetime.fromtimestamp(a['attributes']['date'] /
1e3).date()
    try:
        p=Point(float(a["geometry"]["x"]),float(a["geometry"]["y"]))
        cursor.execute("INSERT INTO incidents (address,crimetype,date,
geom) VALUES
```

```
            ('{}','{}','{}',
    ST_GeomFromText('{}'))".format(address,crimetype,str(date), p.wkt))

    except KeyError:
        pass
connection.commit()
```

The previous code grabs the data using `requests`. It then iterates through the `features`. This code block has some error checking because there are `features` with blank dates and some with no coordinates. The code passes if there is no `date` and uses a `try`, with the `catch` block accepting a `KeyError`, which will catch the missing coordinates.

Now that the data is loaded into the tables, we can start to query the data and present it in maps and charts.

Mapping queries

In `Chapter 3`, *Introduction to Geospatial Databases*, you queried the database and got text back. The `geometry` came back as **well-known text** (**WKT**). These are the results we asked for, but I cannot visualize geographic data by reading a list of coordinates. I need to see it on a map. In this section, you will use `ipyleaflet` and Jupyter to map the results of your queries.

To map the queries in Jupyter, you need to install `ipyleaflet`. You can do this using `pip` at your OS's command prompt:

pip install ipyleaflet

Then you may need to enable the extension, depending on your environment. At the command prompt, type:

jupyter nbextension enable --py --sys-prefix ipyleaflet

For the code, and examples of using `ipyleaflet`, you can view the GitHub repository at: `https://github.com/ellisonbg/ipyleaflet`

If you receive an error in your mapping, you may need to enable the `widgetsnbextension`:

jupyter nbextension enable --py --sys-prefix widgetsnbextension

If you have Jupyter running, you will need to restart it.

With `ipyleaflet` installed and enabled, you can map your queries:

```
import psycopg2
from shapely.geometry import Point,Polygon,MultiPolygon
from shapely.wkb import loads
from shapely.wkt import dumps, loads
import datetime
import json
from ipyleaflet import (
    Map, Marker,
    TileLayer, ImageOverlay,
    Polyline, Polygon, Rectangle, Circle, CircleMarker,
    GeoJSON
)
```

The previous code imports the libraries we need to query and map the data. Let's make the `connection` and get the `cursor`, as shown in the following code:

```
connection = psycopg2.connect(database="pythonspatial",user="postgres",
password="postgres")
cursor = connection.cursor()
```

In Chapter 3, *Introduction to Geospatial Databases*, the queries all used `ST_AsText()` to return `geometry`. Now that we will map the results, it will be easier if we have them returned as `GeoJSON`. In the following code, you will use `ST_AsGeoJSON()` to get the `geometry`:

```
cursor.execute("SELECT name, ST_AsGeoJSON(geom) from areacommand")
c=cursor.fetchall()
c[0]
```

The previous query grabs all the records in the `areacommand` table, with their `name` and `geometry` as `GeoJSON`, then prints the first record (`c[0]`). The result is as follows:

```
('FOOTHILLS',
'{"type":"MultiPolygon","coordinates":[[[[-106.519742762931,35.050529224122
7],[-106.519741401085,35.0505292211811],[-106.51973952181,35.0505292175042]
,[-106.518248463965,35.0505262104449],[-106.518299012166,35.0517336649125],
[-106.516932057477,35.0537380198153],....]]]}
```

 `ST_AsText` and `ST_AsGeoJSON` are two of the 17 ways to get `geometry` out of PostGIS. For a full list of available return types, see the PostGIS reference at: `https://postgis.net/docs/reference.html#Geometry_Accessors`

Now that you have some GeoJSON, it is time to create a map to display it. To make the leaflet map, use the following code:

```
center = [35.106196,-106.629515]
zoom = 10
map = Map(center=center, zoom=zoom)
map
```

The previous code defines the center of the map which, for Albuquerque, I always use the intersections of I-25 and I-40. This intersection splits the city into quadrants. The code then defines the zoom level—the higher the number, the closer the zoom. Lastly, it prints the map.

You will have a blank basemap with OpenStreetMap tiles. In Jupyter, when you add data to the map, you can scroll back to the original print of the map to see the data; you do not need to reprint the map every time.

The GeoJSON of the area commands is stored in variable c. For every item c[x], the GeoJSON is in position 1 (c[x][1]). The following code will iterate through c and add the GeoJSON to the map:

```
for x in c:
    layer=json.loads(x[1])
    layergeojson=GeoJSON(data=layer)
    map.add_layer(layergeojson)
```

The previous code assigns the GeoJSON to a layer using json.loads(). This will make the returned GeoJSON string a dictionary in Python. Next, the code calls the ipyleaflet GeoJSON() method on the layer, and passes it to the variable layergeojson. Finally, add_layer() is called on the map and passes layergeojson. There are other ways to draw maps in Jupyter; for example, you could plot them using Matplotlib, Plotly, or Bokeh. If you come from web mapping, you are probably already familiar with the Leaflet JavaScript library, which will make using ipyleaflet familiar. Also, ipyleaflet loads a basemap and provides interactivity.

If you scroll up to the map, you should see the screenshot as follows:

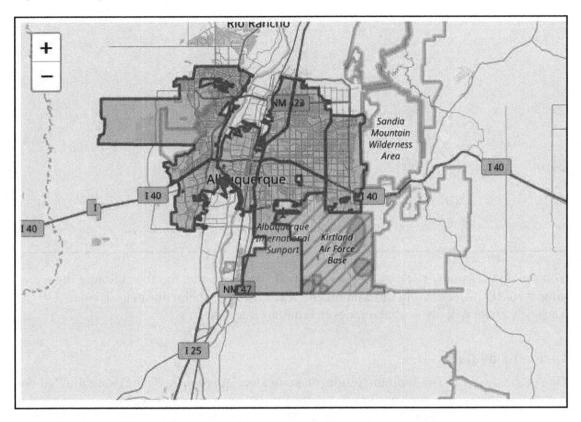

Changing the SQL query in cursor.execute(), you can map the beats:

```
cursor.execute("SELECT beat, ST_AsGeoJSON(geom) from beats")
c=cursor.fetchall()
for x in c:
    layer=json.loads(x[1])
    layergeojson=GeoJSON(data=layer)
    map.add_layer(layergeojson)
```

You should see the `beats` drawn as follows:

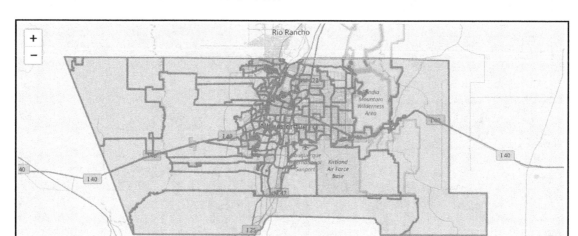

You can do the same for `incidents`, but we will hold on to that for now, because there are almost 30,000 `incidents` in the data set and it would overwhelm our map. To map `incidents`, we will use spatial queries to limit our selection.

Incidents by date

One of the ways you can limit the results of an incident query is by `date`. Using the Python `datetime` library, you can specify a `date`, then query `incidents` on that `date`, and get the `geometry` of the results as `GeoJSON` and add it to your map:

```
d=datetime.datetime.strptime('201781','%Y%m%d').date()
cursor.execute("SELECT address,crimetype,date,ST_AsGeoJSON(geom) from
incidents where date =
'{}' ".format(str(d)))
incidents_date=cursor.fetchall()
for x in incidents_date:
    layer=json.loads(x[3])
    layergeojson=GeoJSON(data=layer)
    map.add_layer(layergeojson)
```

The previous code specifies a `date` (YYYYMD) of August 1, 2017. It queries the `incidents` table we're using, where `date = d` and returns the `geometry` as `GeoJSON`. It then uses the `for` loop you used for area commands, and `beats` to map the `incidents`.

When you create a map in a Jupyter Notebook, further blocks of code will modify that map. You may need to scroll back up to your map to see the changes.

The map you created earlier will now look like the screenshot as follows:

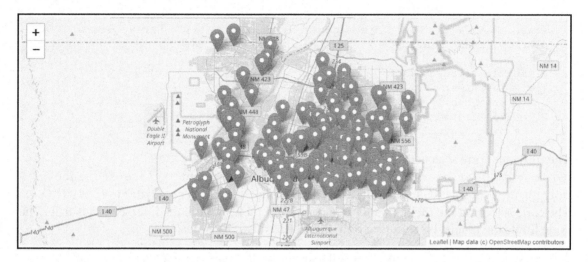

Besides specifying a specific `date`, you could get all the `incidents` where the `date` was greater than a specific day:

```
d=datetime.datetime.strptime('201781','%Y%m%d').date()
cursor.execute("SELECT address,crimetype,date,ST_AsGeoJSON(geom) from
incidents where date >
'{}' ".format(str(d)))
```

Or, you could query dates at an `interval` earlier than today and now:

```
cursor.execute("select * from incidents where date >= NOW() - interval '10
day'")
```

The previous code uses the `NOW()` method and a `10 day` interval. By specifying >=, you will get all the crimes that are 10 days old, and newer from the current day. I wrote this on November 24, 2017, so the results will be all `incidents` from November 14th until today.

Incidents in a polygon

Our crime database has a polygon area—area commands and `beats`—as well as incident points. To build a crime dashboard, we want to be able to map `incidents` within a specific area command or `beat`. We can do that by using `JOIN` and `ST_Intersects`. The following code shows you how:

```
cursor.execute("SELECT ST_AsGeoJSON(i.geom) FROM incidents i JOIN
areacommand acmd ON ST_Intersects(acmd.geom, i.geom) WHERE acmd.name
like'FOOTHILLS' and date >= NOW() - interval '10 day';")

crime=cursor.fetchall()
for x in crime:
    layer=json.loads(x[0])
    layergeojson=GeoJSON(data=layer)
    map.add_layer(layergeojson)
```

The previous code selects the `geometry` from `incidents` as `GeoJSON` (`ST_AsGeoJSON(i.geom)` from `incidents`), where the incident `ST_Intersects` the polygon area command, specifically where the name of the area command is `FOOTHILLS`. The code is joining the incident and area command tables where the intersection is true. The code limits the results by selecting only the last 10 days of crimes.

The code then iterates through the results and maps them as in the previous examples. You should see the screenshot as follows:

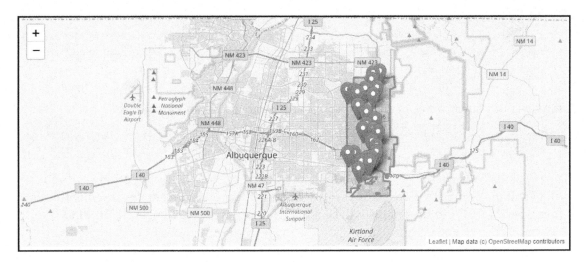

The preceding screenshot overlays the `incidents` on the `Foothills` area command. Notice all the `incidents` are within the polygon.

You can do the same thing for specific `beats` by changing the SQL query. The following code will map specific `beats`:

```
cursor.execute("SELECT ST_AsGeoJSON(geom) from beats where beats.beat in
('336','523','117','226','638','636')")

c=cursor.fetchall()
for x in c:
    layer=json.loads(x[0])
    layergeojson=GeoJSON(data=layer)
    map.add_layer(layergeojson)
```

The previous code uses an array of the `beats.beat` field. In Python, the array is `[]`, but in the SQL statement, use parentheses. The results are the specified `beats`. Then, the code maps them.

Using the same specified `beats`, we can select the `incidents` using a join on `ST_Intersects()` with the `beats`, and mapping the `incidents` as shown in the code:

```
cursor.execute("SELECT ST_AsGeoJSON(i.geom) FROM incidents i JOIN beats b
ON ST_Intersects(b.geom, i.geom) WHERE b.beat in
('336','523','117','226','638','636') and date >= NOW() - interval '10
day';")

crime=cursor.fetchall()
for x in crime:
    layer=json.loads(x[0])
    layergeojson=GeoJSON(data=layer)
    map.add_layer(layergeojson)
```

The previous code passes the `beats` array and filters again by the last 10 days. It then maps the `incidents`, as shown in the following screenshot:

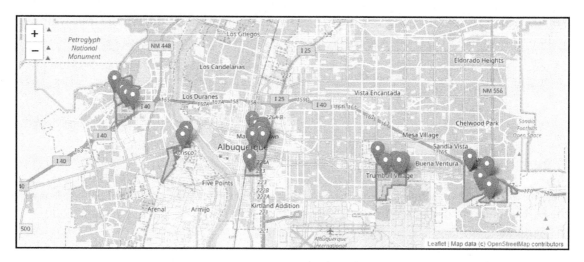

Buffers

You have mapped data from tables, but now you will map the results of a geoprocessing task—buffer.

To code a buffer example, we must first create a point. The following code will do that for us:

```
from shapely.geometry import mapping
p = Point([-106.578677,35.062485])
pgeojson=mapping(p)
player=GeoJSON(data=pgeojson)
map.add_layer(player)
```

The previous code creates a point using Shapely. It then converts it to `GeoJSON` using `shapely.geometry.mapping()`. The next two lines allow us to display it on the map.

PostGIS allows you to send data to the database and get data back, none of which has to be in a table. For example, examine the following code:

```
cursor.execute("SELECT
ST_AsGeoJSON(ST_Buffer(ST_GeomFromText('{}')::geography,1500));".format(p.w
kt))
buff=cursor.fetchall()
buffer=json.loads(buff[0][0])
```

```
bufferlayer=GeoJSON(data=buffer)
map.add_layer(bufferlayer)
```

The previous code uses `ST_Buffer()` to get a polygon back from PostGIS. `ST_Buffer()` can take a point geography and a radius in meters to return the polygon. The code wraps the result in `ST_AsGeoJSON` so we can map it. In this example, the result set is a single item, so we don't need the `for` loop. The code loads the result `buff[0][0]` and maps it.

The result of the previous code is shown in the following screenshot:

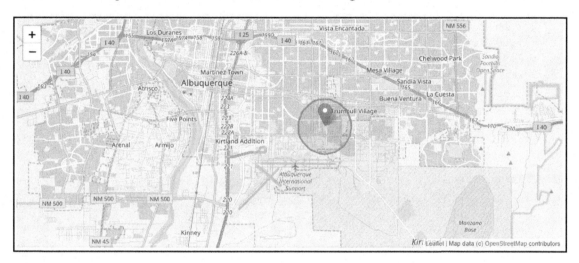

We now have a polygon that we can use to select `incidents` from. The following code will execute the same query as earlier, but instead of `ST_AsGeoJSON`, we will use `ST_AsText`. We are not mapping the polygon, but using it as a parameter for a point in the polygon operation:

```
cursor.execute("SELECT
ST_AsText(ST_Buffer(ST_GeomFromText('{}')::geography,1500));".format(p.wkt)
)
bufferwkt=cursor.fetchall()
b=loads(bufferwkt[0][0])
```

In the previous code, the query result is passed to a `shapely` polygon named b using `loads()`. Now, you can pass that polygon to another query using `ST_Intersects()`, as in the following code:

```
cursor.execute("SELECT ST_AsGeoJSON(incidents.geom) FROM incidents where
ST_Intersects(ST_GeomFromText('{}'), incidents.geom) and date >= NOW() -
interval '10 day';".format(b.wkt))
```

```
crime=cursor.fetchall()
for x in crime:
    layer=json.loads(x[0])
    layergeojson=GeoJSON(data=layer)
    map.add_layer(layergeojson)
```

The previous code selects the `incidents` as `GeoJSON`, where they intersect the `buffer` (`b.wkt`), and where they are within the last 10 days. The results are mapped. The following map shows the output of the previous code:

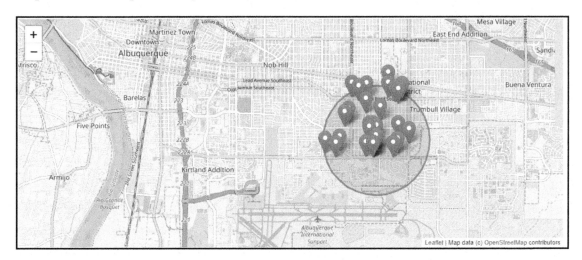

Nearest neighbor

Using a `buffer`, you can get all the `incidents` within a specified radius of the point of interest. But what if you only want the 5, 10, or 15 closest incidents? To do that, you can use the `<->` operator or k-nearest neighbor.

You can use the following code to select the 15 closest points to a specified point, `p`:

```
p = Point([-106.578677,35.062485])
cursor.execute("SELECT ST_AsGeoJSON(incidents.geom),
ST_Distance(incidents.geom::geography,ST_GeometryFromText('{}')::geography)
from incidents ORDER BY incidents.geom<->ST_GeometryFromText('{}') LIMIT
15".format(p.wkt,p.wkt))
c=cursor.fetchall()
for x in c:
    layer=json.loads(x[0])
    layergeojson=GeoJSON(data=layer)
    map.add_layer(layergeojson)
```

The previous code creates a point using Shapely, and uses it in the SQL query. The query selects the incident `geometry` as `GeoJSON`, and then calculates the distance of each incident from the specified point. The `ORDER BY` clause, `<->` operator, and limit clause make sure that we get the `15` nearest points in order of closeness.

The last block of code is our code for adding the results to the map. The results are shown in the following screenshot. The point in the center of the screenshot is the specified point:

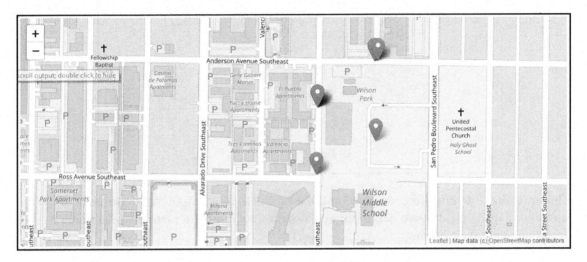

Now that you know how to map the results of your spatial queries, let's add interactive widgets to modify the queries and change the map without writing new code.

Interactive widgets

At the beginning of the chapter, you learned how to query and map `incidents` based on a `date`. In Jupyter, you can use interactive widgets to change values. The code will help us in how you can use `ipywidgets` to import `interact`, which will allow you to insert a `DatePicker` so that you can select a `date` to interact with the Notebook:

```
In [29]:  @widgets.interact(x=DatePicker())
          def theDate(x):

              return str(x)

                        x  11/22/2017

              '2017-11-22'
```

The previous code imports `interact` and the `DatePicker` widget. At its simplest, the previous screenshot shows a decorator and function to allow interactively selecting a `date` and displaying it as a string.

When the `DatePicker` changes, x (the `DatePicker`) is sent to the function `theDate(x)`, and x is printed as a string. The actual return value is `datetime.date`.

Using the `DatePicker` widget, you can pass a `date` value to an SQL query, and then map the results. When the `DatePicker` changes, you can erase the map and then display the new results. The following code will show you how:

```
from ipywidgets import interact, interactive, fixed,
interact_manual,DatePicker
import ipywidgets as widgets

@widgets.interact(x=DatePicker())
def theDate(x):

    if x:
        for l in map.layers[1:]:
        map.remove_layer(l)
    nohyphen=str(x).replace("-","")
    d=datetime.datetime.strptime(nohyphen,'%Y%m%d').date()
    cursor.execute("SELECT ST_AsGeoJSON(geom) from incidents where date
    = '{}' ".format(str(d)))
```

```
c=cursor.fetchall()

for x in c:
    layer=json.loads(x[0])
    layergeojson=GeoJSON(data=layer)
    map.add_layer(layergeojson)
return len(c)

else:
    pass
```

The previous code creates an interactive `DatePicker` widget. The code has an `if...else` statement because, on the first pass, x will be none. The `DatePicker` is not selected, so we `pass` on the first go around.

Next, the code grabs all the layers on the map, and removes them using `map.remove_layer()`, starting at the second (`[1:]`) layer. Why the second layer? Because the first layer on the map is the `TileLayer`—the basemap. We want that to stay, and only remove the markers that were added from the SQL query.

The code then strips the hyphens from the `date` string and converts it into a `datetime`. Once it is a `datetime`, you can pass it to the SQL query.

The next code block is the same block you have used throughout this chapter to add the query results to the map.

Selecting a `date` of November 2, 2017, is shown in the following screenshot:

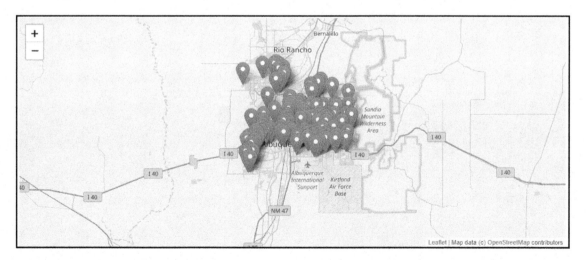

And when selecting November 8, 2017, the map is redrawn and shown in the following screenshot:

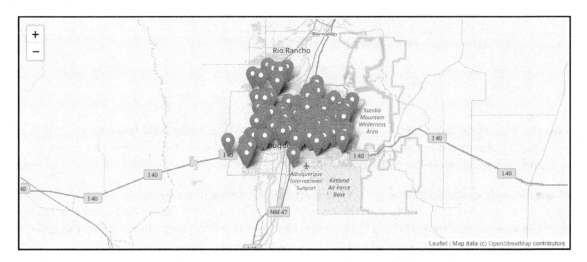

These screenshots were generated immediately following the reselection of a date. A user can use a DatePicker drop-down to requery the data in your PostGIS database.

In Jupyter, if you set the value of a variable to a string or an integer, you will get a number slider or a text box. In the following screenshot, the decorator has x="None", with None being a string. The text None is a placeholder to create the text box. This creates a text box with the word None in it:

```
In [34]: @widgets.interact(x="None")
         def areaCommand(x):

             if x:
                 for l in m.layers[1:]:
                     m.remove_layer(l)
                 cursor.execute("SELECT ST_AsGeoJSON(i.geom) FROM incidents i JOIN areacommand acmd ON ST_Intersects(acmd.geom, i.geom)
                 c=cursor.fetchall()

                 for x in c:
                     layer=json.loads(x[0])
                     layergeojson=GeoJSON(data=layer)
                     m.add_layer(layergeojson)
                 return c

             else:
                 pass
```

```
         x   None
```

```
         []
```

The code in the previous screenshot is presented as follows. The code will allow you to type the name of an area command, and then display the `incidents` within that area command:

```
@widgets.interact(x="None")
def areaCommand(x):
    if x:
        for l in map.layers[1:]:
            map.remove_layer(l)
        cursor.execute("SELECT ST_AsGeoJSON(i.geom) FROM incidents i
        JOIN areacommand acmd ON
        ST_Intersects(acmd.geom, i.geom) WHERE acmd.name like'{}' and
        date >= NOW() - interval '10
        day';".format(x))
        c=cursor.fetchall()

        for x in c:
            layer=json.loads(x[0])
            layergeojson=GeoJSON(data=layer)
            map.add_layer(layergeojson)
        return c
    else:
        pass
```

The previous code starts with the decorator and a string. This will draw the text box. The `areaCommand()` function acts exactly as the `date` example mentioned earlier, but passes a string to the SQL query. It returns the results of the query, and draws the `incidents` on the map.

The following screenshot shows the return values for NORTHWEST:

```
x  NORTHWEST

[('{"type":"Point","coordinates":[-106.711733243194,35.1098713550846]}',),),
 ('{"type":"Point","coordinates":[-106.655683824035,35.2060045419773]}',),),
 ('{"type":"Point","coordinates":[-106.686411508609,35.1829412107437]}',),),
 ('{"type":"Point","coordinates":[-106.703657979881,35.1493086826256]}',),),
 ('{"type":"Point","coordinates":[-106.697602558722,35.1246750028775]}',),),
 ('{"type":"Point","coordinates":[-106.655433125799,35.1933328155158]}',),),
 ('{"type":"Point","coordinates":[-106.729923405452,35.197342393655]}',),),
 ('{"type":"Point","coordinates":[-106.718105925956,35.1080088212142]}',),),
 ('{"type":"Point","coordinates":[-106.672925712103,35.1894973500514]}',),),
 ('{"type":"Point","coordinates":[-106.684048998701,35.1485500784539]}',),),
 ('{"type":"Point","coordinates":[-106.701263018333,35.1592793420069]}',),),
 ('{"type":"Point","coordinates":[-106.66188893686,35.1826722919749]}',),),
 ('{"type":"Point","coordinates":[-106.738651750264,35.0918937278029]}',),),
 ('{"type":"Point","coordinates":[-106.745559617831,35.1019894719585]}',),),
 ('{"type":"Point","coordinates":[-106.728399466573,35.1144476669129]}',),),
 ('{"type":"Point","coordinates":[-106.71886074256,35.1293708118017]}',),),
 ('{"type":"Point","coordinates":[-106.673288411391,35.1900456867706]}',),),
 ('{"type":"Point","coordinates":[-106.698024406681,35.1098242309646]}',),),
 ('{"type":"Point","coordinates":[-106.684583724467,35.1578885992953]}',),),
 ('{"type":"Point","coordinates":[-106.650876685625,35.1987252625439]}',),),
 ('{"type":"Point","coordinates":[-106.676428929709,35.1775339576113]}',),),
 ('{"type":"Point","coordinates":[-106.697637614578,35.150720281939]}',),),
```

The following screenshot shows the map when the user types NORTHWEST in the text box:

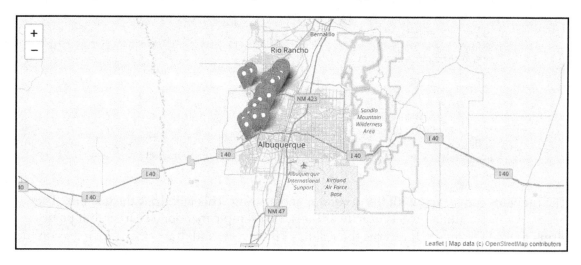

In this section, you have learned how to perform queries on your spatial data, and how to map the results. In the next section, you will learn how to chart the results of your queries.

Charts

Maps are a great data visualization tool, but sometimes a bar chart will do the trick. In this section, you will learn how to chart your data using `pandas.DataFrame`.

A `DataFrame` stores two-dimensional tabular data (think of a spreadsheet). Data frames can be loaded with data from many different sources and data structures, but what interests us is that it can load data from SQL queries.

The following code loads an SQL query into a `DataFrame`:

```
import pandas as pd
d=datetime.datetime.strptime('2017101','%Y%m%d').date()
cursor.execute("SELECT date, count(date) from incidents where date > '{}'
group by date".format(str(d)))
df=pd.DataFrame(cursor.fetchall(),columns=["date","count"])
df.head()
```

The previous code selects the `date`, and then counts the occurrence of each `date` in `incidents` where the `date` is greater than October 1, 2017. The `DataFrame` is then populated using `DataFrame` (SQL, columns). In this case, the code passes `cursor.fetchall()`, and `columns=["date","count"]`. The resulting five records are displayed using `df.head()`. You could use `df.tial()` to see the last five records, or `df` to see it all.

The following screenshot shows `df.head()`:

	date	count
0	2017-10-17	175
1	2017-10-08	216
2	2017-11-09	139
3	2017-11-03	113
4	2017-10-22	196

The preceding screenshot shows that on **2017-10-17**, there were **175** `incidents`.

You can plot a `DataFrame` by calling the `plot()` method from the `pandas` library. The following code will plot a bar chart of the `DataFrame df`:

```
df.sort_values(by='date').plot(x="date",y="count",kind='bar',figsize=(15,10
))
```

The previous code sorts the data frame by `date`. This is so that the dates are in chronological order in our bar chart. It then plots the data using a bar chart, with the *x*-axis being the `date`, and the *y*-axis is the `count`. I specified the figure size to make it fit on the screen. For smaller data sets, the default figure size tends to work well.

The following screenshot is the result of the `plot`:

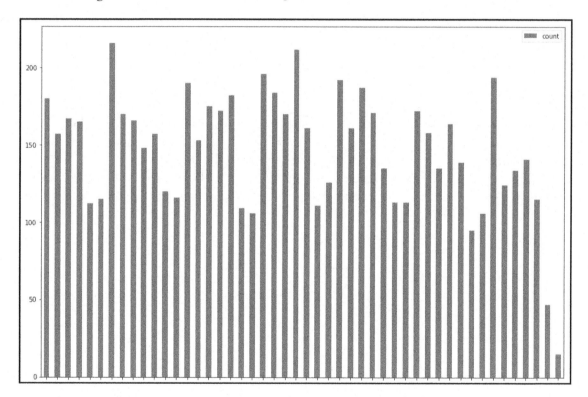

This chart shows us what a map cannot—that crimes seem to decrease on Friday and Saturday.

Let's walk through another example using `beats`. The following code will load crimes by beat:

```
cursor.execute("SELECT beats.beat, beats.agency, count(incidents.geom) as
crimes from beats left join incidents on
ST_Contains(beats.geom,incidents.geom) group by beats.beat, beats.agency")
area=pd.DataFrame(cursor.fetchall(),columns=["Area","Agency","Crimes"])
area.head()
```

The previous code selects the `beat`, `agency`, and count of `incidents` from the `beats` table. Notice the `left join`. The `left join` will give us `beats` that may have zero `incidents`. The join is based on an incident being in a `beat` polygon. We group by each field we selected.

The query is loaded into a `DataFrame`, and the `head()` is displayed. The result is in the screenshot as follows:

	Area	Agency	Crimes
0		APD	0
1		AVI	0
2	100	APD	0
3	111	APD	146
4	112	APD	120

Notice that we have `beats` with no crimes instead of missing beats. There are too many `beats` to scroll through, so let's chart the `DataFrame`. We will use the plot function again, passing an x, y, `kind`, and `figsize` as follows:

```
area.plot(x="Area",y="Crimes",kind='bar',figsize=(25,10))
```

The result of the plot is shown in the following screenshot:

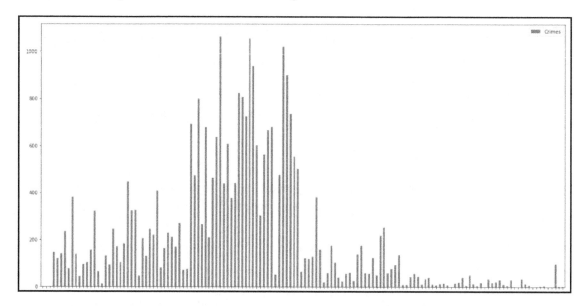

That is a lot of data to look through, but certain `beats` stand out as high crime. This is where data frames can help. You can query the `DataFrame` instead of requerying the database. The following code will plot the selection of `beats`:

```
area[(area['Crimes']>800)].plot(x='Area',y='Crimes',kind='bar')
```

The previous code passes an expression to the area. The expression selects records in the `DataFrame` column `Crimes`, where the value is over `800`; `Crimes` is the `count` column. The result is shown in the following screenshot:

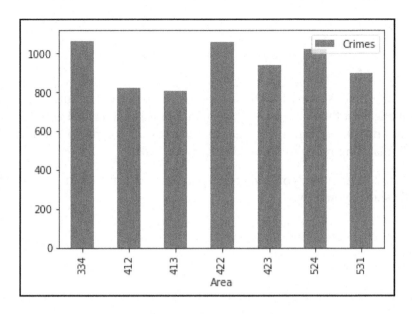

Loading your queries into a `DataFrame` will allow you to plot the data, but also to slice and query the data again without having to requery the database. You can also use the interactive widgets to allow users to modify the charts as you learned with the maps.

Triggers

In any database, when data is inserted, updated, or deleted, you can have the table launch a **trigger**. For example, if a user inserts a record, you could launch a trigger to make sure that the record meets some specified criteria—no null values. Spatial databases allow you to use the same triggers. You can create these in several languages, including Python and SQL. The following example will use `PL/pgsql`.

You create triggers using SQL expressions. The following code will create a trigger to prevent entering an incomplete incident:

```
query=('CREATE FUNCTION newcrime()'+'\n'
  'RETURNS trigger' +'\n'
  'AS $newcrime$' +'\n'
  'BEGIN' +'\n'
  'IF NEW.crimetype IS NULL THEN'+'\n'
  'RAISE EXCEPTION' +" '% Must Include Crime Type', NEW.address;"+'\n'
  'END IF;'+'\n'
  'RETURN NEW;'+'\n'
  'END;'+'\n'
```

```
'$newcrime$'+'\n'
'LANGUAGE \'plpgsql\';'
)
cursor.execute(query)
```

The previous code creates a new function named `newcrime()`. The function is an `if` statement that checks if the `NEW.crimetype` is null. If it is, the record is not added, and an exception is raised. The exception will state that `NEW.address` must include a crime type. The assumption is being made that the address is not null.

Now that you have a function, you can create a trigger that calls that function. The following code shows you how:

```
query=('CREATE TRIGGER newcrime BEFORE INSERT OR UPDATE ON incidents FOR
EACH ROW EXECUTE PROCEDURE newcrime()')
cursor.execute(query)
connection.commit()
```

The previous code executes the SQL statement that creates the trigger. It is created `BEFORE INSERT OR UPDATE`. To test the trigger, let's insert a point with no crime type. The following code will attempt to enter the incident:

```
p=Point([-106,35])
address="123 Sesame St"
cursor.execute("INSERT INTO incidents (address, geom) VALUES ('{}',
ST_GeomFromText('{}'))".format(address, p.wkt))
```

The previous code creates an incident with only an `address` and a `geom`. The result of executing the previous code is shown in the following screenshot:

```
-----------------------------------------------------------------
InternalError                          Traceback (most recent call last)
<ipython-input-61-e8f933e39904> in <module>()
      2 address="123 Sesame St"
      3
----> 4 cursor.execute("INSERT INTO incidents (address, geom) VALUES ('{}', ST_GeomFromText('{}'))".format(address, p.wkt))

InternalError: 123 Sesame St Must Include Crime Type
CONTEXT: PL/pgSQL function newcrime() line 4 at RAISE
```

In the previous screenshot, the **InternalError** states that **123 Sesame St Must Include Crime Type**. Our trigger successfully blocked bad data from being entered. To double-check, we can query for `"123 Sesame St."` The results are shown in the following screenshot:

```
In [66]:  cursor.execute("select * from incidents where address like '123 Sesame St'")
          cursor.fetchall()

Out[66]:  []
```

A trigger can be used to prevent bad data from being loaded for emailing or texting when changes have occurred. For example, you could allow users to enter polygons they are interested in, and their phone number. On a new incident being added to the database, you could see if it is within a polygon, and if so, text the phone number associated with the polygon.

To install other languages for triggers, open **Stack Builder** and add the add-on shown in the following screenshot:

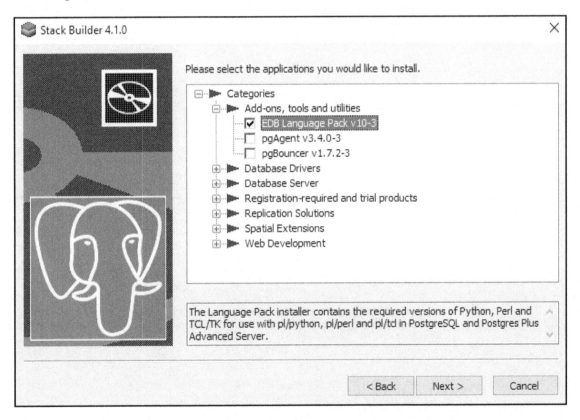

Summary

In this chapter, you learned how to use spatial queries to perform geoprocessing tasks. You also learned how to map and chart the results of your queries using `ipyleaflet` and data frames. You learned how to modify the maps and queries using interactive widgets in Jupyter. Lastly, you learned about how triggers work, and were shown a quick example of data checking using trigger.

In the next chapter, you will learn how to perform geoprocessing tasks using QGIS. You will learn how to use toolboxes that are already included in QGIS. You will learn how to write your own toolboxes that you can use and share with other QGIS users, and you will learn how to use QGIS to map the results. The results can be saved as a QGIS project, or as one of many spatial data formats from QGIS.

Automating QGIS Analysis

8

This book has introduced you to using Python from the command line, in a Jupyter Notebook, and in an IDE to perform geospatial tasks. While these three tools will allow you to accomplish your tasks, there are many times when work needs to be done using desktop GIS software.

QGIS, a popular open source GIS application, provides desktop GIS functionality with the ability to work in a Python console and the ability to write toolboxes and plugins using Python. In this chapter, you will learn how to manipulate desktop GIS data using Python and how to automate these tasks using toolboxes and plugins.

In this chapter, you will learn how to:

- Load and save layers
- Create layers from API data sources
- Add, edit, and delete features
- Select specific features
- Call geoprocessing functions
- Write geoprocessing toolboxes
- Write plugins

Working in the Python console

The QGIS Python console is a Python console. You can perform all of your normal Python tasks with the added benefit of having the QGIS libraries added. From the console, you can manipulate GIS data and display it on the screen, or not.

The Python console is located under the **Plugins** menu on the QGIS toolbar. You can also access it by pressing *Ctrl + Alt + P* on the keyboard. The console will usually open in the bottom of the main window. You can undock it by clicking on the title bar (where it says **Python Console**), holding down the mouse button, and dragging the window to another location on the screen or by clicking the window button at the top-right of the console:

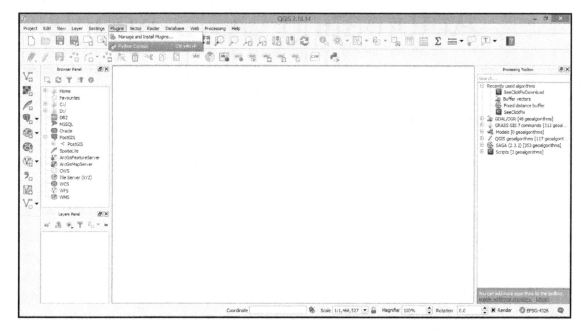

A screenshot of the Python console

The console has buttons for clearing the window, importing GIS and QGIS specific libraries, running the current command (you can press *Enter* instead of clicking this button), showing the editor, modifying options, and viewing the **Help** files. The editor launches a simplified text editor you can use for writing your Python code. It has a few benefits over the command line. You can use the editor to open existing Python files and run or edit them. When you write code in the console, you can save it to a file. In the console, you would need to select all, then copy and paste it into another file, removing all of the output. The editor also allows you to search for text, cut text, add or remove comments, and inspect objects.

Now that you understand the basics of the console and the editor, we can start writing some Python code.

Loading layers

One of the first things you will probably need to do is load some existing GIS data. You can open several different file formats. The method for doing this is the same. It is done by creating a `QgsVectorLayer` and passing a parameter for the data source, the layer name to be shown in the layers panel widget, and the provider name as shown in the following code:

```
import requests
import json
from qgis.core import *
from qgis.PyQt.QtGui import *
from qgis.PyQt.QtWidgets
import *
from qgis.PyQt.QtCore import *

streets =
QgsVectorLayer(r'C:\Users\Paul\Desktop\PythonBook\CHP8\Streets.shp',
"Streets","ogr")
scf = QgsVectorLayer(r'C:\Users\Paul\Desktop\PythonBook\CHP8\SCF.shp',
"SeeClickFix","ogr")
```

For most vector layers, you will use `"ogr"` as the provider. You can then add the layer to the map using the following code:

```
QgsMapLayerRegistry.instance().addMapLayers([scf,streets])
```

The previous code adds the layer to the map registry. Alternatively, you can do the previously mentioned code in a single line of code using `iface` as shown in the following code:

```
streets =
iface.addVectorLayer(r'C:\Users\Paul\Desktop\PythonBook\CHP8\Streets.shp',
"Streets","ogr")
scf =
iface.addVectorLayer(r'C:\Users\Paul\Desktop\PythonBook\CHP8\SCF.shp',
"SeeClickFix","ogr")
```

The previous code loads a vector layer and adds it to the registry in a single step. The following screenshot shows the layers added in QGIS and the names added to the layers panel:

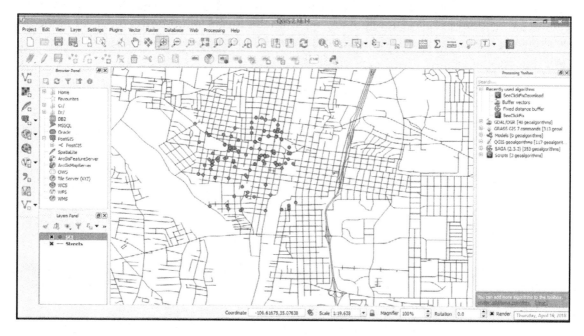

A screenshot of the layers loaded in QGIS

The registry holds a list of all of the layers in the map document. You can get a list of loaded layers by using the following code:

```
QgsMapLayerRegistry.instance().mapLayers()
```

The previous code should show that two layers, SeeClickFix and Streets, are loaded:

```
{u'SeeClickFix20171129100436571': <qgis._core.QgsVectorLayer object at
0x000000002257F8C8>, u'Streets20171129100433367':
<qgis._core.QgsVectorLayer object at 0x000000002257F268>}
```

You can remove a layer from the map by using removeMapLayer() and passing the id of the layer to remove. The id is the string from the result of calling mapLayers(). In this case, the id of the loaded layer is 'Steets20171129092415901'. The following code will remove the layer:

```
QgsMapLayerRegistry.instance().removeMapLayer('Streets20171129100433367')
```

The previous code passes the layer `id` to `removeMapLayer()`. Since the data was loaded in the `streets` variable, you can also pass `streets.id()` instead of typing the layer `id`, as shown in the following code:

```
QgsMapLayerRegistry.instance().removeMapLayer(streets.id())
```

Both methods will result in the layer being removed from the map.

Processing a layer

Once the layer is loaded, you will want to examine the layer and the features in the layer. For the layer, you will probably want to know the projection, the coordinate reference system, and how many features it has.

Layer properties

To find the coordinate reference system, you can use `crs()` on the layer as shown in the following code:

```
crs = scf.crs()
```

The previous code assigns the coordinate reference system to the variable `crs`. From here, you can inspect it by getting the descriptions shown in the following code:

```
crs.description()
```

The previous code will return the output as follows:

```
'WGS 84'
```

For a **well-known text (WKT)** representation of the coordinate reference system, you can use the `toWkt()` method:

```
crs.toWkt()
```

This will return the results as follows:

```
'GEOGCS["WGS 84",DATUM["WGS_1984",SPHEROID["WGS
84",6378137,298.257223563,AUTHORITY["EPSG","7030"]],AUTHORITY["EPSG","6326"
]],PRIMEM["Greenwich",0,AUTHORITY["EPSG","8901"]],UNIT["degree",0.017453292
5199433,AUTHORITY["EPSG","9122"]],AUTHORITY["EPSG","4326"]]'
```

You can get the bounding box of the layer by using the `extent()` method shown as follows:

```
extent = scf.extent()
```

You can then get a string of the extent using `toString()`, get the WKT using `asWktPolygon()`, or you can get each coordinate individually using `xMinimum()`, `xMaximum()`, `yMinimum()`, and `yMaximum()`. The methods and their output are shown as follows:

```
extent.toString()
u'-106.6649165999999980,35.0744279999999975 :
-106.6457526013259951,35.0916344666666973'

extent.asWktPolygon()
'POLYGON((-106.66491659999999797 35.0744279999999975, -106.6457526013259951
35.0744279999999975, -106.6457526013259951 35.09163446666669728,
-106.66491659999999797 35.09163446666669728, -106.66491659999999797
35.0744279999999975))'

extent.xMinimum()
-106.6649166

extent.xMaximum()
-106.645752601326

extent.yMinimum()
35.074428

extent.yMaximum()
35.0916344666667
```

To see the available methods on an object, use `dir(object)`.
To see the methods for the extent object, use `dir(extent)`.

You can get the number of features in the layer by using `pendingFeatureCount()`. The following code returns the feature count for the `SeeClickFix` layer:

```
scf.pendingFeatureCount()
```

The result is a long datatype and in this case, equals 126.

Feature properties

You can get the first feature using the code as follows:

```
item=scf.getFeatures().next()
```

The previous code uses `getFeatures().next()` to get the first feature and assigns it to the `item` variable. If you remove the `.next()`, you get a `QgsFeatureIterator`, which allows you to iterate through all of the features. For the following examples we will use a single feature.

To get the `geometry`, assign it to a variable as shown:

```
g = item.geometry()
```

To get the `type`, you can use the following code:

```
g.type()
0
```

The previous code returns `0` for points. Knowing that the features are points, we can see the coordinates using `asPoint()` as shown in the following code:

```
item.geometry().asPoint()
(-106.652,35.0912)

item.geometry().asPoint()[0]
-106.65153503418

item.geometry().asPoint()[1]
35.0912475585134
```

If we try the same code on the `streets` layer, we will get a type of `1` and the coordinates of the `Polyline` as shown in the following code:

```
street = streets.getFeatures().next().geometry().type()
1

street.geometry().asPolyline()
[(-106.729,35.1659), (-106.729,35.1659), (-106.729,35.1658),
(-106.729,35.1658), (-106.73,35.1658), (-106.73,35.1658),
(-106.73,35.1658), (-106.73,35.1658)]
```

To get information about the fields in the features, use `fields()` as shown in the following code:

```
item.fields().count()
4
```

You can get a field name and type by using `.name()` and `.typeName()` for each of the four fields. Using field 2, the following code will show you how to get the name and type:

```
item.fields()[2].name()
u'Type'
item.fields()[2].typeName()
u'String'
```

Knowing the name of the field, you can get the value of the field for the first record. Or, you could always use the numerical index as shown in the following code:

```
item["Type"]
u'Other'

item[0]
1572.0

item[1]
3368133L

item[2]
u'Other'

item[3]
u'Acknowledged'
```

Now that you know how to access the geometry and attributes of a feature, you can iterate through the features using `getFeatures()`. The following code will iterate through the features and `print` the `ID` of all of the records with a `Status` of `'Closed'`:

```
for f in scf.getFeatures():
    if f["Status"]=='Closed':
        print(f["ID"])
```

The previous code uses the `getFeatures()` to return an iterator. It then checks if the `Status` attribute is equal to `'Closed'` and then prints the attribute `ID` if it is. The output is shown as follows:

```
3888698
3906283
3906252
```

```
3882952
3904754
3904463
3904344
3904289
3903243
3903236
3902993
```

Drawing a layer from PostGIS

QGIS will allow you to load a PostgreSQL layer using the `QgsDataSourceURI` class and `QgsVectorLayer` (URI, name, provider (Postgres)). For this to work, QGIS needs to be compiled with Postgres support. In this section, you will use `psycopg2` as you learned in `Chapter 3`, *Introduction to Geospatial Databases*, and `Chapter 7`, *Geoprocessing with Geodatabases*. The method of adding features to a layer and a layer to the map in this section will be used later in this chapter when you learn how to write toolboxes.

Drawing points

Before you learn how to load the data from PostGIS, we will first cover how to draw multiple points, convert them to a feature, add them to a layer, then load the layer to the map. The following code will walk you through the process.

Start by creating a `memory` layer as shown in the code:

```
theLayer=QgsVectorLayer('Point?crs=epsg:4326','SomePoints','memory')
```

The previous code creates a vector layer and assigns it to the variable `theLayer`. The parameters are the type and coordinate reference system of the layer, the name for the layer panel, and we specified that it is a `memory` layer.

Next, you need to create the features:

```
from qgis.PyQt.QtCore import *
theFeatures=theLayer.dataProvider()
theFeatures.addAttributes([QgsField("ID", QVariant.Int),QgsField("Name",
Qvariant.String)])
```

The previous code imports `qgis.PyQtCore`. You need the library for the `QVariant`. First, you call the data provider for the layer and pass it to the features. Next, you add the attributes and their types to the features. In the following code, you create a `point` and add it to the features:

```
p=QgsFeature()
point=QgsPoint(-106.3463,34.9685)
p.setGeometry(QgsGeometry.fromPoint(point))
p.setAttributes([123,"Paul"])
theFeatures.addFeatures([p])
theLayer.updateExtents()
theLayer.updateFields()
```

The previous code creates a p variable and makes it a `QgsFeature`. It then creates a point p and passes longitude and latitude coordinates. The feature is assigned geometry from the `point`. Next, you assign the attributes to the feature. Now you have a feature with geometry and attributes. In the next line, you pass the feature to the features array using `addFeature()`. Lastly, you update the layer extents and fields.

Repeat the block of code a second time and assign the `point` different coordinates, `(-106.4540,34.9553)`, and then add the layer to the map as in the earlier section of this chapter, shown in the following code:

```
QgsMapLayerRegistry.instance().addMapLayers([theLayer])
```

You will now have a map with two points as shown in the following screenshot:

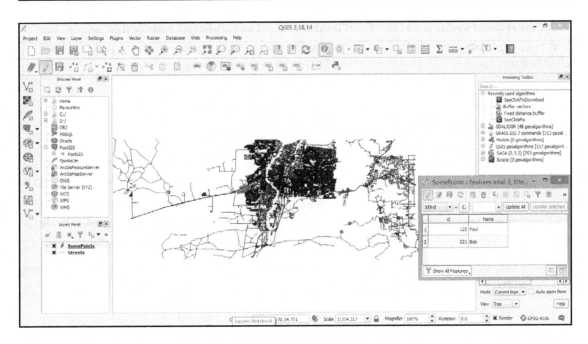

Two points with attributes loaded in QGIS from the Python console

You can see in the **Layers Panel** that the layer is named **SomePoints**. In the attribute table, you can see two fields, **ID** and **Name** for two features. Now that you know how to create features from geometry, add attributes, add the features to a layer, and display the layer on the map, we will add PostGIS to the mix and loop through the process mentioned earlier.

Drawing polygons from PostGIS

In this example, you will draw the Albuquerque Police Department Area Commands polygons from a PostGIS database. You will use the following code with an added PostGIS query, a loop to add all of the features, and a WKT function to draw the geometry instead of hard-coding the coordinates.

The first step is to connect to the PostGIS database. The following code is the same as you used in Chapter 3, *Introduction to Geospatial Databases*, and Chapter 7, *Geoprocessing With Geodatabases*:

```
import psycopg2
connection =
psycopg2.connect(database="pythonspatial",user="postgres",
password="postgres")
cursor = connection.cursor()
cursor.execute("SELECT name, ST_AsTexT(geom) from areacommand")
c=cursor.fetchall()
```

The previous code connects to PostGIS, grabs all of the Area Commands with their name and geometry, and assigns them to the c variable. Next, you will create the layer as in the earlier example. You will create a counter x and make it the ID field of the features:

```
APD=QgsVectorLayer('Polygon?crs=epsg:4326','AreaCommands','memory')
APDfeatures=APD.dataProvider()
APDfeatures.addAttributes([QgsField("ID",QVariant.Int),QgsField("Name",
QVariant.String)])
x=0
```

The previous code creates a polygon memory layer, creates the features, and adds attributes. Next, you will look through the cursor, creating geometry for each Area Command and adding attributes, then you update the layer's extents and fields:

```
for acmd in c:
    g=QgsGeometry()
    g=QgsGeometry.fromWkt(acmd[1])
    p=QgsFeature()
    print(acmd[0])
    p.setGeometry(g)
    x+=1
    p.setAttributes([x,str(acmd[0])])
    APDfeatures.addFeatures([p])
    APD.updateExtents()
    APD.updateFields()
```

The previous code is the same as in the points example in the previous section. The one major difference is that you are creating the polygon using QgsGeometry.fromWkt(wkt). The acmd[1] variable is the WKT MultiPolygon string from PostGIS.

Lastly, add the layer to the map as in the following code:

```
QgsMapLayerRegistry.instance().addMapLayers([APD])
```

The following code will render the screenshot as follows:

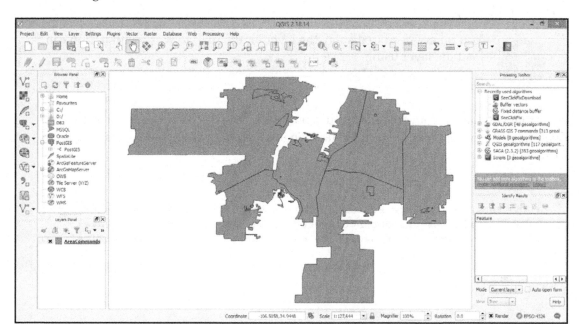

And there you have it, the Area Command polygons for the Albuquerque Police Department as a layer in QGIS. Next, you will learn how to add, edit, and delete features from a layer.

Adding, editing, and deleting features

In the previous examples, you created an empty layer and added fields, then added data and displayed it. There will be times when you will need to do that, more often than not, you will already have a layer and you will need to add data, edit data, or delete data from it. In this section, you will learn how to perform those tasks on existing data.

Adding features to an existing layer

To add data to a layer, you first need to load the layer. Start by loading a subset of some SeeClickFix data for Albuquerque as shown in the following code:

```
scf =
iface.addVectorLayer(r'C:\Users\Paul\Desktop\PythonBook\CHP8\SCF.shp',
"SeeClickFix","ogr")
```

The previous code loads and displays the layer on the map. It is the same code from the first section of this chapter.

> You do not need to display the layer on the map to work with it. You can load the layer using `scf = QgsVectorLayer("C:\Users\Paul\Desktop\PythonBook\CHP8\SCF .shp", "SeeClickFix","ogr")`.

Now that you have the layer loaded you can use `capabilitiesString()` to see what operations the provider allows on the data. The following code shows the results on the loaded layer:

```
scf.dataProvider().capabilitiesString()

u'Add Features, Delete Features, Change Attribute Values, Add Attributes,
Delete Attributes, Rename Attributes, Create Spatial Index, Create
Attribute Indexes, Fast Access to Features at ID, Change Geometries'
```

Since `Add Features` is a capability, you can add a new feature as shown in the following code:

```
feat = QgsFeature(scf.pendingFields())
feat.setAttribute('fid',911)
feat.setAttribute('ID',311)
feat.setAttribute('Type','Pothole')
feat.setAttribute('Status','Pending')
feat.setGeometry(QgsGeometry.fromPoint(QgsPoint(-106.65897,35.07743)))
scf.dataProvider().addFeatures([feat])
```

The previous code creates a feature and gets the fields from the loaded layer. It then sets each of the attributes. Next, it sets the geometry from a point. Lastly, the feature is added to the layer. When you call `addFeatures()` there are two return values you can assign to variables—the result and the feature. The result of `addFeature()` will be either true or false. The returned feature is a list of features. It may be convenient to hold the feature if you need to perform more operations with it.

> When automating the process, you can perform a capabilities check before trying to edit the layer.

The results are a new point and record in the attributes table as shown in the following screenshot:

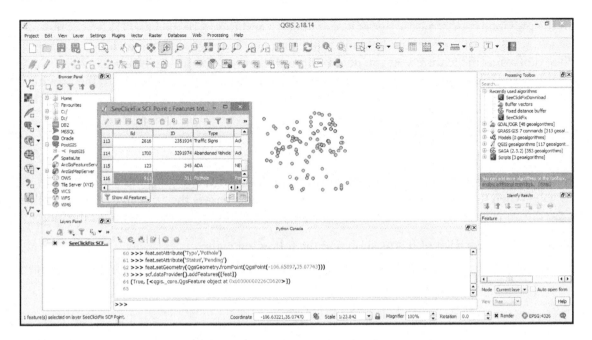

A feature added to the layer

You can simplify the previous code by passing all the attributes in a single line using a list. The following code shows you how:

```
feat.setAttributes([912,312,"Other","Closed"])
```

The previous code writes the attributes using a list and `setAttributes()` instead of the singular `setAttribute()`. If you want to remember the field names when reading your code later, the more verbose version is clearer. But if the efficiency of the code is your goal, the latter version is more appropriate.

What if we made a mistake, or have records we do not need? The next section will show you how to delete a feature.

Deleting features from an existing layer

Deleting features can be done in a single line of code following the format as shown:

```
LayerName.dataProvider().deleteFeatures([list of id])
```

In the previous code, you use `deleteFeatures()` and the `id` of the layer. The `id` is the `feature.id()`. It is a number held internally and not in a user assigned attribute. To get the `id` of a specific feature you can iterate through them as you learned earlier in this chapter. The following code shows you how to delete the feature we created in the previous section:

```
for x in scf.getFeatures():
    if x["ID"]==311:
        scf.dataProvider().deleteFeatures([x.id()])
```

The previous code iterates through the features in the layer looking for the one with the `ID` of 311. When it finds it, it uses `deleteFeatures()` and passes the `id` using `x.id()`. In this case the `id` was 216. If you know the `id` of the feature, you can delete it without the loop.

You can also pass a list of IDs as shown in the following code:

```
for x in scf.getFeatures():
    if x["Status"]=='Closed':
        key.append(x.id())
    scf.dataProvider().deleteFeatures(key)
```

The previous code iterates through the features in the layer looking for all of the `'Closed'` cases. When it finds one, it puts the `id` in the list `key`. Lastly, it calls `deleteFeatures()` and passes the list.

Editing features from an existing layer

You can now add and delete features, but sometimes you only need to change an attribute value. For example, an open case status to a closed case status. In this section, you will learn how to modify attributes.

Attributes are modified by calling `changeAttributeValues()`. The following code changes a single feature:

```
scf.dataProvider().changeAttributeValues({114:{0:123,1:345,2:"ADA",3:"NEW"}
})
```

The previous code calls `changeAttributeValues()` and passes a dictionary with the key being the feature `id` and the value being a dictionary of attributes—`{id:{0:value, 1:value, n:value}}`. The keys for the attributes dictionary are the field indexes. There are four fields in the features so the dictionary of attributes will have keys `0` through `3`. The following screenshot shows the change in the attribute table:

	fid	ID	Type	Status
108	1696	3293160	Abandoned Vehicle	Acknowledged
109	648	3740699	Abandoned Vehicle	Acknowledged
110	3399	1001379	Traffic Signs	Acknowledged
111	3400	1001367	Traffic Signs	Acknowledged
112	257	3890075	Other	Open
113	2616	2351934	Traffic Signs	Acknowledged
114	1700	3291974	Abandoned Vehicle	Acknowledged
115	123	345	ADA	NEW
116	911	311	Pothole	Pending

A single feature edited

The previous example assumes you already know the `id` of the feature you want to modify. It also assumes you want to modify all of the attribute values. The following code will modify several features but only a single attribute value in each—**Status**:

```
attributes={3:"Closed"}
for x in scf.getFeatures():
    if x["Type"]=='Other':
        scf.dataProvider().changeAttributeValues({x.id():attributes})
```

In the previous code, a dictionary is declared with a key of 3 (the 'Status' field) and a value of "Closed". The code then iterates through the features in the layer looking for a match. When it finds a match, it changes the attribute value, but this time only the value of the **Status** field. The results are reflected in the attributes table shown in the screenshot as follows:

	fid	ID	Type	Status
12	2496	2601540	Aggressive Dog	Acknowledged
13	7	3907467	Graffiti	Acknowledged
14	3151	1480264	Abandoned Vehicle	Acknowledged
15	3152	1477519	Traffic Pavement...	Closed
16	1058	3594249	Abandoned Vehicle	Acknowledged
17	1846	3187768	Abandoned Vehicle	Acknowledged
18	2763	2111716	Traffic Signs	Acknowledged
19	1978	3100358	Other	Open
20	1062	3592164	Abandoned Vehicle	Acknowledged
21	1979	3098768	Other	Open
22	277	3886704	Other	Open
23	1592	3358613	Other	Open

SeeClickFix SCF Point :: Features total: 116, filtered: 11...

Show All Features

All features of the Other type now have a status of Open

In the previous examples, you have been iterating through features and selecting them based on a condition. In the next section, you will learn how to highlight the selected features and how to use expressions to select instead of a condition.

Selecting features using expressions

Using expressions, you can iterate through features and evaluate the expression returning true(1) or false(0). Before we get into expressions, let's select and highlight a feature. Selecting a feature is accomplished by calling setSelectedFeatures() and passing a list of IDs. The following code will select a single feature:

```
from qgis.PyQt.QtGui import *
from qgis.PyQt.QtWidgets import *
iface.mapCanvas().setSelectionColor( QColor("red") )
scf.setSelectedFeatures([100])
```

The previous code, imports QtGUI, and Qt.Widgets. These are needed to set the color using QColor. The next line gets the map canvas and sets the section color to red. Lastly, the code selects the feature with an id of 100. It will now display red on the map.

The previous example assumes you want to select a single feature and that you know the id. That is rarely the case. More often than not you will want to select by some condition—or using an expression. Using QgsExpression() you can pass an expression string and evaluate it against features. The following code shows you how:

```
closed=[]
exp=QgsExpression("Type='Traffic Signs' and Status='Acknowledged'")
exp.prepare(scf.pendingFields())
for f in scf.getFeatures():
    if exp.evaluate(f)==1:
        closed.append(f.id())
scf.setSelectedFeatures(closed)
```

First, the previous code creates a list, closed, to store the IDs where the expression evaluates to true. Next the expression is declared. The expression checks for two conditions on the **Type** and **Status**. The expression is prepared and passed the fields in the layer. The next line iterates through the features. If the expression is true (1), the id is put in the list. Lastly, the selected features are set to the IDs in the closed list.

The results of the previous code are shown in the screenshot as follows:

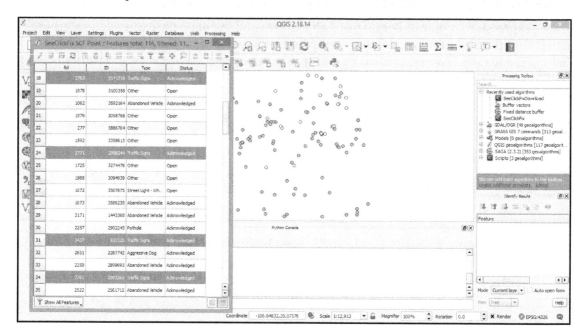

Features selected based on an expression

In the next section, you will learn how to use the toolboxes that come with QGIS to execute algorithms and perform geospatial tasks.

Using toolboxes in Python

QGIS has a processing library. If you go to the **Processing** menu in QGIS and select **Toolbox**, you will see a widget displayed with groups of toolboxes. The widget will look as shown:

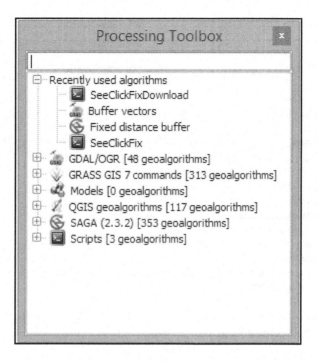

The processing widget

You have access to the toolboxes in Python by importing `processing`. You can see the available algorithms by executing the code as follows:

```
import processing
processing.alglist()
```

The previous code imports `processing` and calls the `alglist()` method. The results are all of the available algorithms from the installed toolboxes. You should see something similar to the following output:

```
Advanced Python field calculator---------------------
->qgis:advancedpythonfieldcalculator
 Bar plot----------------------------------------------->qgis:barplot
 Basic statistics for numeric fields------------------
->qgis:basicstatisticsfornumericfields
 Basic statistics for text fields---------------------
->qgis:basicstatisticsfortextfields
 Boundary----------------------------------------------->qgis:boundary
 Bounding boxes----------------------------------------->qgis:boundingboxes
 Build virtual vector---------------------------------
->qgis:buildvirtualvector
```

```
Check validity-------------------------------------->qgis:checkvalidity
Clip------------------------------------------------>qgis:clip
```

To search the algorithms by keyword, you can pass a string to `alglist()` as in the following code:

```
Processing.alglist("buffer")
```

The previous code passes a string to narrow the results. The output will be several algorithms containing the word `buffer`. See the output as follows:

```
Fixed distance buffer------------------------------
->qgis:fixeddistancebuffer
 Variable distance buffer---------------------------
->saga:shapesbufferattributedistance
 Buffer vectors-------------------------------------
->gdalogr:buffervectors
 v.buffer.column - Creates a buffer around features of given type.--
->grass:v.buffer.column
```

In this section, we will use the `Buffer vectors` algorithm. To see how the algorithm works, you can run the code as follows:

```
processing.alghelp("gdalogr:buffervectors")
```

The previous code calls `alghelp()` and passes the name of the algorithm found in the second column of the `alglist()`. The result will tell you the parameters and their type required for executing the algorithm. The output is shown as follows:

```
ALGORITHM: Buffer vectors
 INPUT_LAYER <ParameterVector>
 GEOMETRY <ParameterString>
 DISTANCE <ParameterNumber>
 DISSOLVEALL <ParameterBoolean>
 FIELD <parameters from INPUT_LAYER>
 MULTI <ParameterBoolean>
 OPTIONS <ParameterString>
 OUTPUT_LAYER <OutputVector>
```

If you run the algorithm from the GUI and then open `\.qgis2\processing\processing.log`, you will see the parameters used to execute the algorithm. Copy them and use them in your Python code.

The previous output shows the parameters needed to run the algorithm. By using `runalg()` you can execute the algorithm. The buffer vector is executed in the code as follows:

```
processing.runalg("gdalogr:buffervectors",r'C:/Users/Paul/Desktop/Projected
.shp',"geometry",100,False,None,False,"",r'C:/Users/Paul/Desktop
/ProjectedBuffer.shp')
layer = iface.addVectorLayer(r'C:\Users\Paul\Desktop\
ProjectedBuffer.shp', "Buffer", "ogr")
```

The previous code calls `runalg()` and passes the name of the algorithm we want to run, then the parameters required by the algorithm. In this case:

```
INPUT_LAYER = Projected.shp
 GEOMETRY = geometry
 DISTANCE = 100
 DISSOLVEALL = False
 FIELD = None
 MULTI = False
 OPTIONS = ""
 OUTPUT_LAYER = ProjectedBuffer.shp
```

The output layer is then added to the map. The result is shown in the following screenshot:

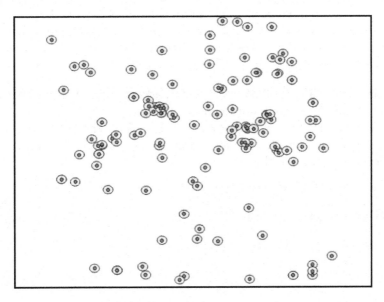

Results of the buffer algorithm

Now that you know how to use the Python console and call an algorithm let's write our own algorithm. The next section will show you how to make a toolbox that you can call using `runalg()` or by using the GUI.

Writing custom toolboxes

Writing toolboxes will allow you to automate several tasks and make that code available to users as a GUI, or to other developers as an algorithm that can be executed using processing. In this section, you will learn how to create a toolbox and call it from processing.

In this chapter, you have learned how to load data from a file and from a PostGIS database. In this example, you will learn how to bring data in to QGIS from the `SeeClickFix` **Application Program Interface (API)**.

 `SeeClickFix` is a 311 reporting system that is used by many cities in the United States. It contains geospatial data and has a very well documented, and user-friendly API.

To create a new script, open the processing toolbox in QGIS. This will open an editor window. You will write your code in this window and save it using the save icon. The file name will become a toolbox under **Tools | User scripts | File name**. Save the file and name it `SeeClickFix`.

Now that you have an empty toolbox, we can start adding code. Before the code, you need to create the parameters you will want to pass to this algorithm. Each parameter will also become a GUI widget with the parameter name as the label. The `SeeClickFix` API allows you to specify a city or neighborhood and also filter strings. The following code will add these as parameters to our algorithm:

```
##City_or_Neighborhood= string City
##Filter=string Nothing
##Output=output vector
```

The previous code uses double comment symbols (##), then the parameter name followed by the parameter type and a default value. Default values are required for numbers and strings. The first parameter in the code is the city or neighborhood, it is a `string` and defaults to Albuquerque. Next, is the filter keyword, which is also a `string` and defaults to `Nothing`. Lastly, the code has an output, which is a type of `output vector`. The output will be what is added to the map or saved to disk.

At this point, you can run the toolbox in the GUI and you will see the window shown in the following screenshot:

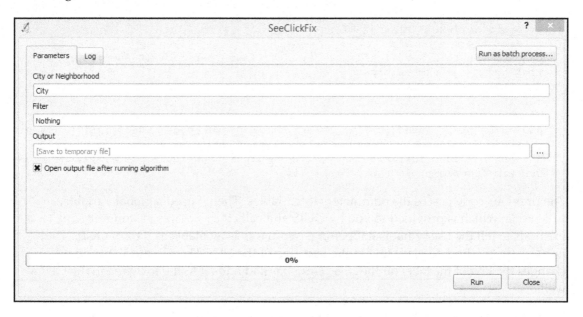

The GUI for the toolbox. Notice each parameter is a label

Next, you can import the libraries you need to perform the task. The following code will import what you need for the `SeeClickFix` toolbox:

```
import requests
import json
from qgis.core import *
from qgis.PyQt.QtGui import *
from qgis.PyQt.QtWidgets import *
from qgis.PyQt.QtCore import *
```

The previous code imports the `qgis` libraries and also `requests` and `json`. The `requests` library will be used to make the API call and `json` will parse the response from the request to `json`.

Now it is time to write some code. First, you will need to grab the parameters and set the variables needed to make the API call, and it would not hurt to give the user some information on what is happening. The following code will show you how:

```
scfcity=City_or_Neighborhood
searchterm=Filter
progress.setInfo("Wait while I get data from the API")
progress.setText("Calling API")
if searchterm=="None":
pagesURL="http://seeclickfix.com/api/v2/issues?per_page=100&amp;amp;place_u
rl="+scf city+"&amp;amp;page="
url="http://seeclickfix.com/api/v2/issues?per_page=100&amp;amp;place_url="+
scfcity
else:
pagesURL="http://seeclickfix.com/api/v2/issuesper_page=100&amp;amp;place_ur
l="+scfc ity+"&amp;amp;search="+searchterm+"&amp;amp;page="
url="http://seeclickfix.com/api/v2/issues?per_page=100&amp;amp;search="+sea
rchterm+"&amp;amp;place_url="+scfcity
```

The previous code passes the parameters to variables. Then, I used a global variable, `progress`, which is provided to you by QGIS and calls the `setInfo()` and `setText()` methods to tell the user what is happening. `progress` is available as part of QGIS. The `setInfo()` method displays text in the text area of the GUI. The `setText()` method changes the text of the label on the `progress` bar and adds it to the text area in the GUI as well.

Next, the code checks if the filter parameter is still `None`, and if it is, it assigns the **Uniform Resource Locator** (**URL**) to the API as a string with no filter parameter and uses the city or neighborhood parameter. If there is a filter, a different URL is assigned to make the API call.

Now you are ready for some GIS specific setup. The following code will start you off:

```
crs=QgsCoordinateReferenceSystem("epsg:4326")
scf=QgsVectorLayer('Point?crs=epsg:4326','SeeClickFix','memory')

fields = QgsFields()
fields.append(QgsField("ID", QVariant.Int))
fields.append(QgsField("Type", QVariant.String))
fields.append(QgsField("Status", QVariant.String))

writer = processing.VectorWriter(Output, None, fields.toList(),
```

```
QGis.WKBPoint, crs)
```

The previous code sets a coordinate reference system in WGS 84. Then, it creates a memory layer, and assigns fields. Lastly, it creates a `writer` vector and passes the output parameter, encoding (`None`), the fields, the geometry type, and a coordinate reference system. Now you can make the API call as shown in the code:

```
r = requests.get(url).text
rJSON=json.loads(r)
pages=rJSON['metadata']['pagination']['pages']
records=rJSON['metadata']['pagination']['entries']
progress.setInfo("Grabbing "+str(records) +" Records")
count=1

for x in range(1,pages+1):
    progress.setText("Reading page "+str(x))
    pageData=requests.get(pagesURL+str(x)).text
    pageDataJSON=json.loads(pageData)
```

The previous code uses `requests` to make an API call. It assigns a variable for the number of `pages` and the number of `records` returned. Using the `setInfo()` method, the code tells the user how many `records` are being processed. It then loops through each page and loads the items from the `page`. It tells the user what `page` it is currently reading.

Now, the code will parse each `record` on the `page` as a feature and send it to the vector `writer`. You do not need to add the output to the map. Processing will handle this for you if you run it from the GUI. When you run it from Python, you get the file path to the layer and can load it yourself. The following code will show you how:

```
for issue in pageDataJSON['issues']:
try:
    p=QgsFeature()
    point=QgsPoint(issue['lng'],issue['lat'])
    p.setGeometry(QgsGeometry.fromPoint(point))
    p.setAttributes([issue["id"],issue["request_type"]
    ["title"],issue["status"]])
    writer.addFeature(p)
    progress.setPercentage((count/float(records))*100)
    count+=1
except:
    pass
del writer
```

The previous code creates a feature and passes the geometry from the API to a `point`. It then passes the attributes and sends the completed feature to the vector `writer`. The `progress` bar on the GUI is updated using `progress.setPercentage()`. The method takes a `float`. In this example, the percentage is the number of `records` processed divided by the total number of `records`. Lastly, you delete the `writer`.

Your toolbox is complete, save it. Now a user can run it from the GUI or you can call it from Python. The following code will show you how to call it from Python and add the results to the map:

```
processing.alghelp("script:seeclickfix")

ALGORITHM: SeeClickFix
City_or_Neighborhood <ParameterString>
Filter <ParameterString>
Output <OutputVector>

out=processing.runalg("script:seeclickfix","Albuquerque","Juan Tabo",None)
```

The previous code calls the `alghelp()` method to show our new algorithm and the parameters. Next, it runs the algorithm using `runalg()` and assigns the results to the `out` variable. Printing the `out` variable shows a dictionary with a key of `Output` and a path to a temporary vector as follows:

```
out

{'Output':
u'C:\\Users\\Paul\\AppData\\Local\\Temp\\processingca7241c6176e42458ea32e8c
7264de1e\\014bc4d4516240028ce9270b49c5fcaf\\Output.shp'}
```

You can assign the vector to a layer and add it to the map, or you can iterate through the features and do something else with it, as follows:

```
out = iface.addVectorLayer(str(a["Output"]), "SeeClickFix","ogr")
for feature in out.getFeatures():
    Do something...
```

The results of adding the layer to the map will look like the following screenshot. All of the `SeeClickFix` incidents reported along the street, Juan Tabo:

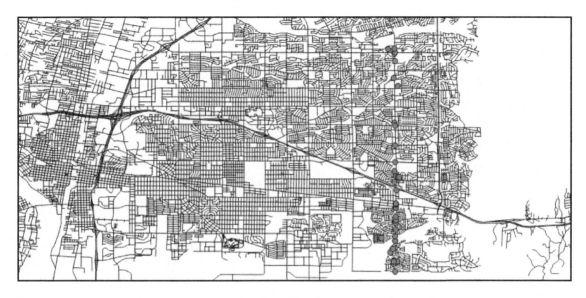

Results of the toolbox

Summary

In this chapter, you have learned how to use Python in QGIS. You started by learning the basics of loading a layer and displaying it on the map, and then progressed to adding, editing, and deleting features. You learned how to select features, highlight the selection, and how to use expressions. Then, we took advantage of pre-built geoprocessing tools and you learned how to call toolbox algorithms using processing. Lastly, you learned how to write your own toolbox.

In the next chapter, you will learn how to use Python with Esri tools. You will learn how to use Jupyter Notebooks in a browser to interact with cloud-based datasets and how to use the Esri API for Python to perform basic geospatial analysis and to create ArcGIS Online web maps.

9
ArcGIS API for Python and ArcGIS Online

This chapter will introduce the ArcGIS **Application Program Interface** (**API**) for Python and ArcGIS Online. The ArcGIS API for Python is a Python library for working with maps and geospatial data. This API can be installed locally using `conda` and interacts with Esri's cloud GIS, whether that's ArcGIS Online (SaaS) or Portal for ArcGIS, a server product that offers on-premises cloud GIS deployment for organizations. The API offers a modern solution to scripting for web mapping with Python and works well with Jupyter Notebooks.

The following topics will be covered in this chapter:

- Introducing the ArcGIS API for Python
- Installing the API
- Using the API with different Esri user accounts
- Introducing some modules of the API
- Interacting with the API's map widget
- Searching and displaying vector data
- Displaying and geoprocessing of raster data
- Setting up a personalized account for using ArcGIS Online
- Publishing and managing content in ArcGIS Online

Introducing the ArcGIS API for Python and ArcGIS Online

Esri, the geospatial software company known for its ArcGIS platform, adopted and integrated Python into their ArcGIS desktop software, as well as its successor ArcGIS Pro. The first Python site package developed by Esri was the `ArcPy` site package, which is a collection of Python modules that offers all existing, as well as extended, ArcMap and ArcGIS Pro functionality. Python can now be used as a scripting and programming language to automate repetitive tasks that involve a lot of interaction with the **Graphical User Interface (GUI)**. With `ArcPy`, these tasks could be carried out through a Python script, add-on, or toolbox.

Python was introduced successfully with ArcGIS desktop, while GIS itself was moving into the cloud—not only geospatial data but also the software itself. Esri offered organizations the possibility to do this through a variety of cloud environment offerings, using either public, private, or hybrid cloud services. In this chapter, we'll be using ArcGIS Online, the **Software as a Service (SaaS)** offering that allows users to create, store, and manage maps, applications, and data. Over the last few years, ArcGIS Online has become a key component and an integral part of Esri's ArcGIS system. Its users can share maps within an organization or the world, through ready-to-use tools that are available for the web, smartphones, and tablets.

A Pythonic web API

For users to be able to interact with their GIS data, services, and more, Esri developed a completely new Pythonic web API called the **ArcGIS API** for Python, which consists of a set of subroutine definitions, protocols, and tools for building software and applications. It is built on top of the ArcGIS **REpresentational State Transfer (REST)** API, along with the ArcGIS API for JavaScript. This same API is also used (in the background) within the Python API for displaying 2D and 3D web maps.

GIS users can download the freely available ArcGIS API for Python and use it to manage their cloud GIS environment, whether that's ArcGIS Online, ArcGIS Portal, or ArcGIS Enterprise (the product family formerly known as ArcGIS Server). The API requires Python 3.5 or higher. It's possible to use the API together with the `ArcPy` site package, but this is optional, the API also works without `ArcPy` (or any desktop-based GIS product), or even an ArcGIS Online or Portal environment.

The API has been written for a larger audience in mind than the current Python user, who would use it for data processing or map design—apart from the scripting capabilities, the API allows for GIS visualization and analysis, spatial data/content management, as well as organization administration. The API is a work-in-progress, since its first release in December of 2006, the API has seen a number of updates and the current version is 1.4 at the time of writing. Each new release introduces new features. Using the API is similar to working with any other Python library—you import the API with an `import` statement and can start using it right away, applying standard Python syntax and commands. As you're using it in a web environment to access a web GIS, it's best to use the browser-based Jupyter Notebook app.

Installing the API

The API can be installed in different ways. The easiest way is to use `conda`. If this is your first install of the API, you might want to create a separate virtual environment through Anaconda3 for the API because of its many dependencies. It is important that you install the latest available version of the API, as it will also ensure you have the latest available `conda` version installed and the API's dependencies. To install the API using `conda`, run the following command in a terminal:

```
conda install -c esri arcgis
```

The `-c` in the command refers to a channel (which is an online repository). When running this command in a terminal, you will be asked to install a list of dependencies. A partial list is displayed in the following screenshot. Notice that `NumPy` and `pandas` are also installed, two libraries from the `SciPy` stack that are used for data science. The API itself is the first package of the list, called `arcgis`:

```
The following NEW packages will be INSTALLED:

    arcgis:            1.3.0-py36hbb13de3_1   esri
    bleach:            2.1.1-py36h834942a_0
    colorama:          0.3.9-py36h029ae33_0
    decorator:         4.1.2-py36he63a57b_0
    entrypoints:       0.2.3-py36hfd66bb0_2
    html5lib:          1.0.1-py36h047fa9f_0
    icc_rt:            2017.0.4-h97af966_0
    intel-openmp:      2018.0.0-hd92c6cd_8
    ipykernel:         4.7.0-py36h2f9c1c0_0
    ipython:           6.2.1-py36h9cf0123_1
    ipython_genutils:  0.2.0-py36h3c5d0ee_0
    ipywidgets:        6.0.0-py36_0
```

Testing the API

After the installation, the ArcGIS package can be found in a separate folder named `arcgis` followed by the version number inside of the `C:\UserName\Anaconda3\pkgs` folder. If you have the API already installed on your computer, you might need to update it to the most recent version to ensure everything is working correctly, such as the map widget:

```
conda upgrade -c esri arcgis
```

The most recent version of the API at the time of writing is 1.4 and requires Python 3.5 or higher. You can test your installation by opening the Jupyter Notebook app, as follows, from a terminal or run the application directly from Anaconda3:

```
jupyter notebook
```

Then, run the following code and check to see if a map window opens up and you receive no error messages:

```
In: from arcgis.gis import GIS
    my_gis = GIS()
    my_gis.map()
```

If you have ArcGIS Pro installed, then you can install the API by using the `conda` environment inside Pro, using the Python package manager. Look for the **Python** tab and click on the **Add Packages** button. Search for `arcgis`, click **Install**, and accept the terms and conditions.

Troubleshooting

If for some reason, you are not able to install and use the API locally, you can also try the sandbox version of the API that runs in the cloud `https://notebooks.esri.com/`. By clicking this URL, a browser window will open with the Jupyter Notebook, where you can create your own Notebooks, run code examples, and use all of the functionality of the API.

For an online API reference showing all modules, classes with descriptions, and examples see `http://esri.github.io/arcgis-python-api/apidoc/html/index.html`.

For API updates, release notes, and more, refer to `https://developers.arcgis.com/python/guide/release-notes/`.

The main page for all info about the API can be found here. It's an excellent source with lots of documentation, a user guide and API reference: `https://developers.arcgis.com/python/`.

Authenticating your Esri user accounts

Now that we've installed the API on our machine, it's time to discuss how we can use it in combination with different Esri user accounts. As we've said before, the API has been created to manage and interact with a web GIS that can be located in a cloud environment. To be able to use the API and interact with this web or cloud GIS, we need some kind of additional Esri user account to make a connection with this web GIS. You can compare this to connecting to an FTP server or remote web server from your computer and performing a login procedure using a username and password (or token). This procedure ensures a secure connection between server and client and access to the right content.

Different Esri user accounts

The following Esri user accounts give access to ArcGIS Online using the ArcGIS API for Python:

1. An anonymous user account that gives you access to ArcGIS Online without passing in any user information. This is a quick solution for testing some basic functionality but doesn't offer any advanced functionality that comes with a personalized account. We'll cover this option as we proceed further in two of the three hands-on exercises in this chapter.

2. An ArcGIS Online organizational account (or Portal for ArcGIS account). This requires a (paid) subscription to ArcGIS Online or Portal for ArcGIS. This option gives you the most functionality possible but is not covered here.

3. An ArcGIS Enterprise trial account. This option is free and provides you with service credits that are required for creating maps and publishing content. This trial account only lasts for 21 days and after that has to be transferred to a paid account in order to be continued. Setting up a trial account is covered as we proceed further.

4. A free Esri developer account. This account is part of the ArcGIS Developer program that gives you 50 service credits for developing and testing personal apps, as well as using ArcGIS Online, among others. This option is covered as we proceed further.

5. Finally, there's the option to create a public ArcGIS account and log in to ArcGIS Online using a web browser. Using these login details, you can now connect to ArcGIS Online with the API, but with limited functionality. This option was added in the 1.3 version of the API and is not covered here.

Summarizing the previously mentioned points, we have covered a number of different user accounts to access ArcGIS Online with the API. A personalized account gives you added functionality over an anonymous one. We'll use both types for the exercises later in this chapter. Let's now look at how the API is organized into different modules and what functionality they offer.

Different modules of the ArcGIS API for Python

Just like other Python libraries, the API has Python modules, classes, functions, and types that can be used for managing and working with elements of the ArcGIS platform information model. Because the API is meant for different user groups that require their own unique tools, the API has been organized into 13 different modules. It's not necessary to cover them all here, but the most important ones for this chapter are mentioned as follows:

1. The GIS module: This is the most important module and is the entry point to a GIS that is hosted in ArcGIS Online or ArcGIS Portal. The GIS module lets you manage users, groups, and content in a GIS. The term GIS refers in this context to a collaborative environment for creating, visualizing, and sharing maps, scenes, apps, layers, analytics, and data.

2. The features module: This module represents the vector data part of the API. Vector data is represented through this module as feature data, feature layers, or collections of feature layers. Individual data elements are represented by feature objects, while classes such as `FeatureSet`, `FeatureLayer`, and `FeatureCollection` represent different groupings of feature data.

3. The raster module: This module contains classes and raster analysis functions for working with raster data and imagery layers. Whereas the features module represents the vector data component of the API, the raster module is the raster data component. This module uses the `Imagerylayer` class for displaying data from imagery services and offers raster functions for on-the-fly image processing. Imagery layers can be visualized using the map widget.

4. The geoprocessing module: This module is required for importing toolboxes with geoprocessing capabilities that are not part of the API but are available through ArcGIS Online. These geoprocessing toolboxes are imported as native Python modules so that you can call the functions available in the imported module to invoke these tools. The API itself also includes a rich collection of geoprocessing tools, that are available through other modules defined by spatial data type.

A geoprocessing tool is a function that performs an operation on GIS data, starting with an input dataset. Then, an operation is performed on that dataset, and finally the result of the operation is returned as an output dataset.

5. The widgets module: It provides components for visualizing GIS data and analysis and includes the MapView Jupyter Notebook widget. We'll use this widget next for visualizing maps and layers. This is not the only visualization module—the separate mapping module offers different mapping layers and 2D/3D mapping and visualization components.

As you can see, the API offers a broad range of modules for different tasks and users, ranging from publishing mapping data, performing geospatial analysis, and data manipulation. All modules use Python as the scripting language to manage GIS data and functionality. Let's now start using the API and explore some of the basic functionality before moving on to more advanced tasks.

Exercise 1 – importing the API and using the map widget

It's now time to start using the API. Follow the instructions as mentioned, open a new Notebook in the Jupyter Notebook application where you can access the API. Type and run the following code. We'll start by importing the API so that we can use its modules, functions, and classes:

```
In:    import arcgis
In:    from arcgis.gis import GIS
```

The second line of the code can be broken down as follows—`arcgis.gis` refers to a submodule (`gis`) in the `arcgis` module. What's being imported (`GIS`), is a `GIS` object that includes a map widget for displaying geographic locations, visualizing GIS content, as well as the analysis results. Next, we'll create a `GIS` object by assigning it to a variable with the same name, but spelled in lowercase:

```
In:    gis = GIS()
```

This is an example of an anonymous login as we don't pass in any login details between the parentheses of GIS(). Now we'll use the map widget by creating a map object and assigning it to a variable that can then be queried to bring up the widget in the Notebook:

```
In:    map1 = gis.map('San Francisco')
       map1
```

Note that you have to repeat and run the variable name on a separate, new line to have a map displayed. A map window will be opened in your Jupyter Notebook application showing a 2D color map of the city of San Francisco:

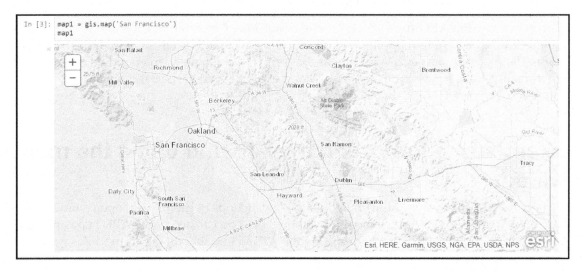

You can adjust the zoom level of the map through the zoom property and passing in an integer:

```
In:    map1.zoom = 5
```

A map display without a zoom-level value gives you a default zoom value of 2. A larger value will give you a smaller area showing more details, using a larger scale. This map is one of the several basemaps that ArcGIS Online offers as a backdrop for mapping data. We can query which type of basemap we're displaying currently:

```
In:    map1.basemap

Out:   'topo'
```

You might want to know how to access all of the object properties. This can be done by typing the object name, followed by a dot and pressing *Tab*. Then, a window with a drop-down list containing all available properties will be displayed:

```
map1.add_class
map1.add_layer
map1.add_traits
map1.basemap
map1.basemaps
map1.center
map1.class_config_rst_doc
map1.class_config_section
map1.class_get_help
map1.class_get_trait_help
In [ ]: map1.|
```

We can see the `basemap` property being listed in the previously mentioned screenshot. For more information on a given property, select the property of your choice followed by a question mark. Then, an information window will open at the bottom of your screen displaying more information:

```
In:    map1.basemaps?
```

The `basemaps` property can also be queried directly and returns a list object including new lines for each value:

```
In:    map1.basemaps

Out: ['dark-gray',
     'dark-gray-vector',
     'gray', ...
```

We can use the information from this window by changing our basemap, by passing in one of the available options in the basemap property (note the singular) as follows:

```
In: map1.basemap = 'satellite'
    map1
```

We can see that our basemap now shows a satellite image of San Francisco:

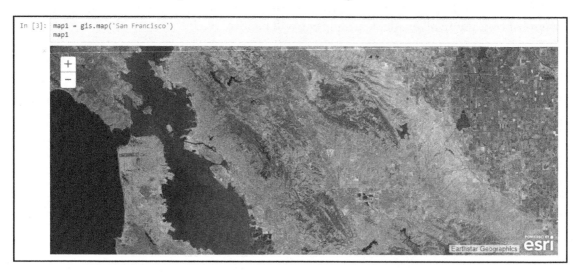

Next, we'll query the **coordinate reference system (CRS)** of the map that is displayed in our map widget. This information can be queried with the extent property, which also shows the four coordinates of our `extent`:

```
In: map1.extent

Out: {'spatialReference': {'latestWkid': 3857, 'wkid': 102100},
 'type': 'extent',
 'xmax': -13505086.994526163,
 'xmin': -13658266.799209714,
 'ymax': 4578600.169423444,
 'ymin': 4517450.546795281}
```

Let's have a look at the output. Our basemap is an example of a web map, which comes in **JavaScript Object Notation (JSON)** format for sharing 2D maps. Web maps are an example of an Esri specification that allows different applications, APIs, and SDKs to create, edit, and display maps. These web maps can be used for different Esri applications, such as ArcGIS Online in this particular example. The web map specification is in JSON, which is indeed the case with our output by looking at how it is structured using brackets and using key-value pairs.

Back to the spatial reference, this information is stored in the `spatialReference` object, located at the top-level of the web map JSON hierarchy. In our example, we can see the spatial reference being set as `latestWKid: 3857` and `wkid: 102100`. Consulting Esri's online web map specification available at `http://developers.arcgis.com`, we can see that both refer to a Web Mercator projection, the de facto standard for web mapping applications and used by most major online map providers.

This concludes our first hands-on exercise of the API in which we learned how to import the API, create a map object, display information on properties of an object, and use the map widget. In our next exercise, we'll start working with content from ArcGIS Online and add it to our map widget. We'll use a personalized account, which enables us to create our own web maps and host them online. Before we can do this, you'll need to create a personalized ArcGIS Online account, which we'll cover next.

Creating a personalized ArcGIS Online account

For the following exercise, you'll need a named user account for ArcGIS Online. This will enable you to create your own map content, save web maps in your own content folder in ArcGIS Online, share content with others, and more. We'll cover two free options to do this. The easiest and quickest way is to create a free ArcGIS developer account, which comes with the service credits required to use some of the capabilities of ArcGIS Online. It's also possible to create a free organizational trial account for ArcGIS Online, which has more options. Both options are covered here.

To create an ArcGIS Developer account, open a browser window and navigate to `https://developers.arcgis.com/sign-up`. Fill in the fields on the left (**First Name**, **Last Name**, and **Email**):

Next, you'll receive a confirmation email that is sent to the email address you entered online. The email contains a URL that you need to click on to active your account. After that, you can set up your account and choose a username and password. This username and password can be used to log in to ArcGIS Online using the ArcGIS API for Python. You will also be assigned an account URL path, something like `http://firstname-lastname.maps.arcgis.com`. This URL path is also required for logging into ArcGIS Online using the ArcGIS API for Python.

Next, we'll explain how to create a public ArcGIS account. Navigate to `www.arcgis.com` and click the orange **Free trial ->** button:

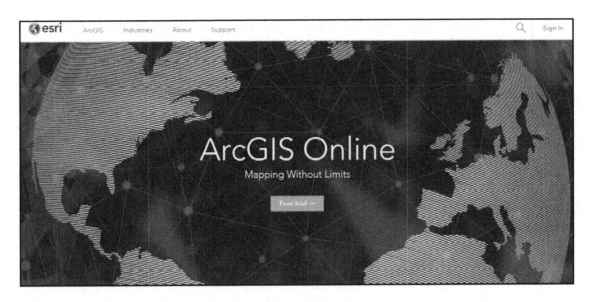

Next, you will be directed to a new page with a form that needs to be filled in with your personal details. After that, you can create an ArcGIS Online account. The username and password can be used as login details for ArcGIS Online.

Exercise 2 – searching, displaying, and describing geospatial content

In the following exercise, we'll search for online content, add it to our map, and describe the data. We'll finish by saving your map widget directly into a web map that is stored in your personal content folder in ArcGIS Online. This is a new feature that comes with the 1.3 version of the API, which makes it really easy to create web maps. The content we'll be using is a feature layer file containing bike trails in Solano County in California. This content is available through ArcGIS Online. We can use the API to search the content, reference it, and add it to our map widget in our Jupyter Notebook app.

First, we'll log into ArcGIS Online using a personal account. Read the code and follow the instructions as follows:

```
In:    import arcgis
In:    from arcgis.gis import GIS
       gis = GIS()
```

In the previous code, you are required to type your own personal details between the brackets following the capitalized GIS in the third line, starting with a personal URL, username, and password. If you've created a free ArcGIS developer account, this will look something like gis = GIS ("https://firstname-lastname.maps.arcgis.com", "username", "password"). If you've signed up for a trial period for ArcGIS Online, the first URL will be https://www.arcgis.com, followed by your username and password.

Next, we'll open up a map of Solano County, our area of interest:

```
In:   map = gis.map("Solano County, USA")
      map.zoom = 10
      map
```

To search for specific content outside of our own organization, use the following code that includes a query with specific search terms. Here, we've used trails in and near San Francisco:

```
In: search_result = gis.content.search(query="san francisco trail",
    item_type="Feature Layer", outside_org=True)
    search_result
```

In the previous code, we're using the content property of the GIS object to search for content. Using a personalized account, we specify we want to search for data outside of our own organization. Our query is looking for trails near San Francisco of the type "Feature Layer". Next, the results are returned by repeating the variable name. The output in this case looks like the following list but could be different for the reader. For brevity, only the first three search results are shown:

```
Out: [<Item title:"National Park Service - Park Unit Boundaries"
     type:Feature
     Layer Collection owner:imrgis_nps>,

     <Item title:"National Park Service - Park Unit Centroids"
     type:Feature Layer
     Collection owner:imrgis_nps>,

     <Item title:"JUBA_HistoricTrail_ln" type:Feature Layer Collection
      owner:bweldon@nps.gov_nps>,...
```

The items are returned as a list, with each item consisting of its title, type, and owner name. We can also show this items list in a different way if we use the Jupyter Notebook application:

```
In:   from IPython.display import display
      for item in search_result:
```

```
display(item)
```

Now, our search results are returned with a thumbnail picture, a title, and description. The title is also a hyperlink that will take you to an ArcGIS Online web page where you can display the content in a viewer and consult the metadata. We are interested in the following item showing bike trails in Solano County in a feature collection. This is a collection of feature layers and a table, meaning we have to find a way to access the right feature layer and add it to our map widget:

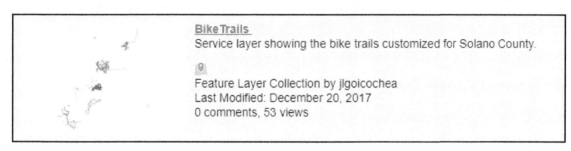

We now want to display the bike trail data from this feature collection on the map. To do this, we need to reference the data source in our code. We can do this as follows:

```
In:    bike_trails_item = search_result[8]
       bike_trails_item.layers
```

The code works as follows, the first line creates a variable that references the item from our search results list that contains the **Bike Trails** service layer. Next, we'll use the layers property on this item to see how many layers the item contains, in this case two layers, indexed 0 and 1.

Next, we want the names of both layers. Using a `for` loop, we can `print` the layer names:

```
In:    for lyr in bike_trails_item.layers:
           print(lyr.properties.name)

Out:   BikeTrails
       Parks
```

We can see that the bike trails are stored in the first layer. Next, we'll reference this layer within the service layer by assigning it the `name bike_trails_layer` variable. We'll also print the feature layer URL by repeating our newly created variable:

```
In: bike_trails_layer = bike_trails_item.layers[0]
In: bike_trails_layer
```

Using a `pandas` dataframe, we can visualize the attribute table that comes with the layer:

```
In:   bike_df = bike_trails_layer.query().df
In:   bike_df.head()
```

Limiting the output to the first five rows using the `head()` function, we get the following output:

Out[13]:

	City	FIPS	GlobalID	LASTEDITOR	LASTUPDATE	LastDateEd	NAME_PCASE	OBJECTID	ParkName	SHAPESTLen	STRNAME	Shape_Le_2
0	Vacaville	095	26e2b128-2807-4d21-baac-a8301f28b769	D. Brownell	None	1.487030e+12	Solano	1		1095.065524	Orange Tree Cir	2813.794665
1	Vacaville	095	f1550bcc-e86c-447a-9a2c-edfce5232e92	D. Brownell	None	1.487030e+12	Solano	2		956.589403	Fruitville Rd	2463.651154
2	Vacaville	095	a5048391-4fc2-435d-a089-68afa3303244	D. Brownell	None	1.487030e+12	Solano	3		1890.319478	Elmira Rd	4869.496672
3	Vacaville	095	b0ff14c1-5e84-4ca9-b4d3-4d4038e14e41	D. Brownell	None	1.487030e+12	Solano	4		570.585094	Marshall Rd	1470.048489
4	Vacaville	095	0a64de95-93ce-4d72-a3a3-7179d6f493a2	D. Brownell	None	1.487030e+12	Solano	5		542.662844	Foothill Dr	1396.921075

We can now add the layer to the map and look at the results:

```
In:   map.add_layer(bike_trails_layer)
      map
```

The bike trails will be displayed on top of our basemap in the map widget. If you don't see the trails, you may need to zoom in and out a few times, as well as pan the map to the right until you see the following result, showing the different bike trails as line segments on top of the basemap:

```
In [144]: map.add_layer(bike_trails_layer)
          map
```

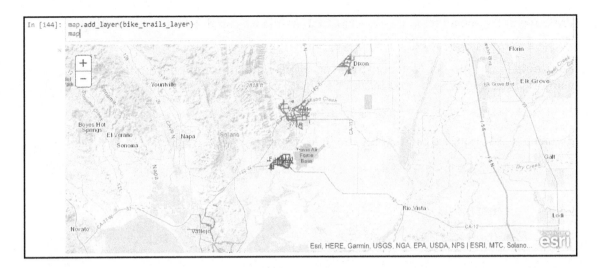

We'll now create our own web map from this map widget. This is a recent feature of the API, which is very powerful for creating and hosting your own web maps in ArcGIS Online. This is not the only way to create web maps, but serves as an example of how you can use the API to do this. By importing the WebMap class, we can create an instance of this class through a variable called wm, which will store our web map. Using the save function, we can simply save this map widget as a web map in our own organization's content folder:

```
In:    from arcgis.mapping import WebMap
       wm = WebMap()
       web_map_properties = {'title':'Bike Trails ',
       'snippet':'This map service shows bike trails in Solano County',
       'tags':'ArcGIS Python API'}
       web_map_item = wm.save(item_properties=web_map_properties)
       web_map_item
```

Python returns our item that we can immediately visit online by clicking the URL underlined in blue, after providing our login credentials to access our organizational page of ArcGIS Online:

```
Out[11]:
```

Bike Trails
This map service shows bike trails in Solano County

Web Map by
Last Modified: December 27, 2017
0 comments, 0 views

We can edit the metadata in the overview tab, while we can delete it in the **Settings** tab (scroll down to see this option marked in red).

Returning to our Jupyter Notebook, we can display the information from the service URL using Python, returning output in JSON format, showing only the first three results here:

```
In:    bike_trails_layer.properties
```

By using a `for` loop, we can display the field names:

```
In:    for field in bike_trails_layer.properties['fields']:
           print(field['name'])

Out:  OBJECTID
      SHAPESTLen
      STRNAME
      . . .
```

You can also access individual properties of the feature layer, for example the `extent`:

```
In:    bike_trails_layer.properties.extent

Out:   {
      "xmin": 6485543.788552672,
      "ymin": 1777984.1018305123,
      "xmax": 6634421.269668501,
      "ymax": 1958537.218413841,
      "spatialReference": {
      "wkid": 102642,
      "latestWkid": 2226
       }
      }
```

This concludes the second exercise, in which we learned how to search for content, add it to our map widget, and describe the data we're working with. We'll now have a look at the raster module to see how we can visualize and process raster imagery.

Exercise 3 – working with raster data and the API's geoprocessing functions

For this exercise, we'll have a look at the raster module. We'll work with raster data in the form of Landsat 8 satellite images and look at ways to describe the data and use geoprocessing functionality from ArcGIS Online. As always, we'll start with importing the arcgis package and gis module, this time using an anonymous login:

```
In: import arcgis
    from arcgis.gis import GIS
    from IPython.display import display
    gis = GIS()
```

Next, we'll search for content—we'll specify that we're looking for imagery layers, the data type for imagery used for the raster module. We limit the results to a maximum of 2:

```
In: items = gis.content.search("Landsat 8 Views", item_type="Imagery
    Layer",
    max_items=2)
```

Next, we'll display the items as follows:

```
In: for item in items:
        display(item)
```

The output shows the following two items:

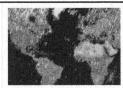

Landsat 8 Views
Landsat 8 OLI, 30m Multispectral 8 band scenes with visual renderings and indices. Updated daily.

Imagery Layer by esri
Last Modified: October 06, 2017
0 comments, 135,763 views

MDA NaturalVue Satellite Imagery
This image service presents NaturalVue 15m satellite imagery of the world created by MDA Information Systems Inc.

Imagery Layer by esri
Last Modified: August 25, 2017
0 comments, 42,934 views

We're interested in the first item of the results. We can reference it as follows:

```
In: l8_view = items[0]
```

Let's now investigate this item a little more by clicking the blue **Landsat 8 Views** URL. It takes you to a web page with a description of the dataset. Have a look at the band numbers and their description. The API offers raster functions available on this landsat layer, which we'll get to in a minute. First, we'll access the imagery layer through the layers property of the item:

```
In: l8_view.layers
```

Next, we can reference and visualize the layer as follows:

```
In: l8_lyr = l8_view.layers[0]
    l8_lyr
```

The output shows the layer, covering the whole earth:

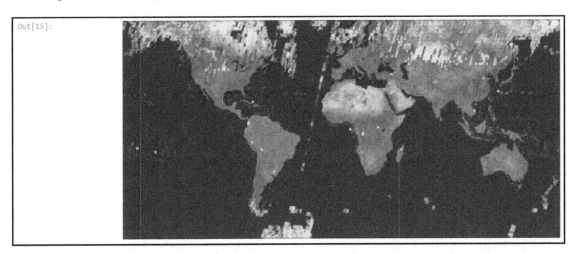

Having the image layer available as a Python object we can print all of available properties, returned, as before, in JSON:

```
In: l8_lyr.properties
```

A more visually attractive imagery layer item description can be printed using the following code:

```
In: from IPython.display import HTML
In: HTML(l8_lyr.properties.description)
```

Using a `pandas` dataframe, we can explore the different wavelength bands in more detail:

```
In:    import pandas as pd
In:    pd.DataFrame(l8_lyr.key_properties()['BandProperties'])
```

The output is now presented in a `pandas` dataframe object:

```
Out[13]:
              BandName    WavelengthMax   WavelengthMin
    0         CoastalAerosol        450             430
    1                 Blue          510             450
    2                Green          590             530
    3                  Red          670             640
    4          NearInfrared         880             850
    5    ShortWaveInfrared_1       1650            1570
    6    ShortWaveInfrared_2       2290            2110
    7               Cirrus         1380            1360
```

Now we'll get to the raster functions part. The API provides a set of raster functions to be used on the imagery layer that are rendered server-side and returned to the user. To minimize the output, the user needs to specify a location or area, whose screen extent will be used as input for a raster function. Raster functions can also be chained together and work on large datasets too. The following `for` loop displays all of the available raster functions available for this particular dataset:

```
In: for fn in l8_lyr.properties.rasterFunctionInfos:
        print(fn['name'])
```

The output shows all of the available raster functions on a separate line:

```
Agriculture with DRA
Bathymetric with DRA
Color Infrared with DRA
Natural Color with DRA
Short-wave Infrared with DRA
Geology with DRA
Agriculture
Bathymetric
Color Infrared
Geology
Natural Color
Short-wave Infrared
NDVI Colorized
Normalized Difference Moisture Index Colorized
NDVI Raw
NBR Raw
None
```

This information is also present in the full properties list we printed out earlier. Next, we'll try out some of these raster functions on a map showing the area of Madrid, Spain. We'll start by creating an instance of the map:

```
In: map = gis.map('Madrid, Spain')
```

Then, we'll add our satellite image to the map widget, which we can use for various raster functions:

```
In: map.add_layer(l8_lyr)
    map
```

The output will look like this:

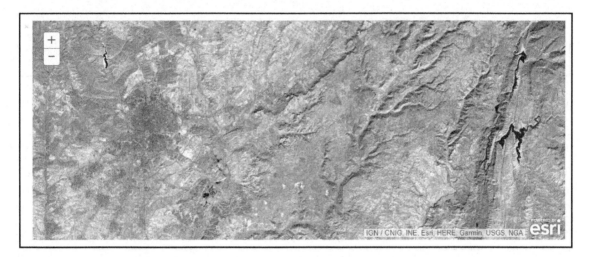

We'll now need to import the `apply` function from the raster module in order to apply the raster functions:

```
In: from arcgis.raster.functions import apply
```

First, we'll create a natural color image with dynamic range adjustment, using bands 4, 3, and 2:

```
In: natural_color = apply(l8_lyr, 'Natural Color with DRA')
```

Update the map as follows and see how it is different than before:

```
In: map.add_layer(natural_color)
```

The output will look like this:

We'll repeat the procedure, but this time we'll visualize the agricultural map:

```
In: agric = apply(l8_lyr, 'Agriculture')
In: map.add_layer(agric)
```

This raster function uses the bands 6, 5 and 2, referring to shortwave IR-1, near-IR and blue, respectively. We can see that our study area shows all of the three following categories—vigorous vegetation is bright green, stressed vegetation dull green, and bare areas as brown. We can verify the results in our map widget:

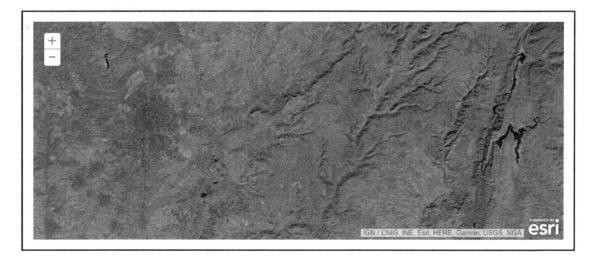

As you can see, the raster module enables quick geoprocessing of raster imagery in the cloud, and returns and displays the results on your screen quickly. This is just one of the many raster functions of the module, and there is much more to discover. This concludes this exercise where we looked at how we search for raster imagery, display it, and use geoprocessing capabilities of ArcGIS Online using the ArcGIS API for Python's raster module.

Summary

This chapter introduced the brand new ArcGIS API for Python, which is built on Python 3.5. You learned how to make use of the API, Jupyter Notebooks, and data processing with data stored in the cloud-based ArcGIS Online system. We covered how the API is organized into different modules, how to install the API, how to use the map widget, how to log in to ArcGIS Online using different user accounts, and working with vector and raster data. Using some of the API modules, we learned how to use the API for Python to perform basic geospatial analysis and to create ArcGIS Online web maps.

The next chapter will introduce Python tools for interacting with cloud-based data for search and fast data processing. In particular, it focuses on the use of Elasticsearch and MapD GPU databases, both of which are based on the AWS cloud infrastructure. The reader will learn to create cloud services for geospatial search, geolocated data processing, geolocated data, and learn how to use Python libraries to interact with these services.

Geoprocessing with a GPU Database **10**

With the emergence of multi-core GPUs, new database technologies have been developed to take advantage of this improved technology. MapD, a startup based in San Francisco, is one example of these companies. Their GPU-based database technology was made open source in 2017 and is available for use on cloud services, such as **Amazon Web Services** (**AWS**) and Microsoft Azure. By combining the parallelization potential of GPUs with a relational database, the MapD database improves the speed of database queries and visualizations based on the data.

MapD has created a Python 3 module, `pymapd`, that allows users to connect to the database and automate queries. This Python binding allows geospatial professionals to integrate the speed of a GPU database into an existing geospatial architecture, adding speed improvements to analysis and queries. Both of MapD's core offerings (the open source community version and the commercial enterprise version) are supported by `pymapd`.

In addition to the Python module, MapD has added geospatial capabilities to their database technology. Storage of points, lines, and polygons is now supported, as is a spatial analysis engine that offers distance and contains functionality. Also, MapD has developed a visualization component, **Immerse**, that allows for analytical dashboards to be built quickly, with the database as a backend.

In this chapter, we will cover the following topics:

- Create a GPU database in the cloud
- Explore data visualizations using Immerse and the SQL EDITOR
- Use `pymapd` to load spatial and tabular data into the database
- Use `pymapd` to query the database
- Integrate the cloud database into a GIS architecture

Cloud geodatabase solutions

Cloud storage of geospatial data has become a common part of many GIS architectures. Whether it is used as a backup to an on-premises solution, replaces an on-premises solution, or is combined with a local solution to provide internet support for an intranet-based system, the cloud is a big part of the future of GIS.

With ArcGIS Online, CARTO, MapBox, and now MapD, the options for a cloud data store that support geospatial data are more numerous than ever. Each offers a visualization component and a different type of data storage and each will integrate with your data and software in different ways.

ArcGIS Online, while also offering stand-alone options (that is, direct data upload), integrates with ArcGIS Enterprise (formerly ArcGIS Server) to consume enterprise **REpresentational State Transfer** (**REST**) web services that are stored on a local geodatabase. ArcGIS Online is built on top of **Amazon Web Services** (**AWS**) and all of the server architecture is hidden from users. Enterprise integration requires a high-level of licensing (cost), which includes a number of cloud tokens (that is credits), and storage and analysis within the cloud account itself can use lots of those tokens.

CARTO offers cloud PostGIS storage, allowing for geospatial data files to be uploaded. With the release of the Python package CARTOframes (covered in `Chapter 14`, *Cloud Geodatabase Analysis and Visualization*), the cloud datasets can be uploaded and updated using scripting. Using Python, a CARTO account can become a part of an enterprise solution that maintains up-to-date datasets while allowing them to be quickly deployed as custom web maps using the builder application. CARTO offers two tiers of paid accounts which have different levels of storage.

MapBox is focused on map tools for creating custom basemaps for mobile apps, but it also offers cloud data storage of datasets and map creation tools such as MapBox GL, the JavaScript library for maps built on the **Web Graphics Library** (**WebGL**). With the new MapBox GL—Jupyter module, the data can be accessed using Python.

MapD, while offering similar solutions to those mentioned, is different in a number of respects. It has an open source version of the database (MapD Core Community Edition) which can be used locally or on the cloud, and has an enterprise version for large customers. While MapD Core has a relational database schema and uses SQL for queries like a traditional RDBMS, it uses GPUs to accelerate queries. **MapD Core** can be cloud-deployed on AWS, Google Cloud Platform, and Microsoft Azure. MapD can be installed on servers without GPUs as well, though this reduces its effective speed gains over other geodatabases.

All of the geodatabases support Jupyter Notebook environments for data queries, but MapD has them integrated into the **SQL EDITOR** within the Immerse visualization platform. MapD uses Apache Arrow to upload data when using `pymapd` and also supports `INSERT` statements while allowing for data to be loaded using the Immerse data importer (including SHPs, GeoJSONs, and CSVs).

Big data processing

For data science analysis and geospatial analysis, encountering big data is more common than ever. MapD is incredibly fast when retrieving rows and return data to the client, making it really useful for powering real-time databases or for performing queries on huge datasets.

MapD offers amazing speed-ups on processing big datasets compared to CPU-bound databases. Because of the high number of cores that each GPU card contains, paralleled processes can run faster. This means that datasets numbering in the billions can be queried and analyzed in milliseconds.

MapD architecture

The architecture of MapD is a combination of **MapD Core** (the GPU-based database), **MapD Immerse** (the data visualization component), and other associated technologies and APIs that support data science operations and geospatial applications:

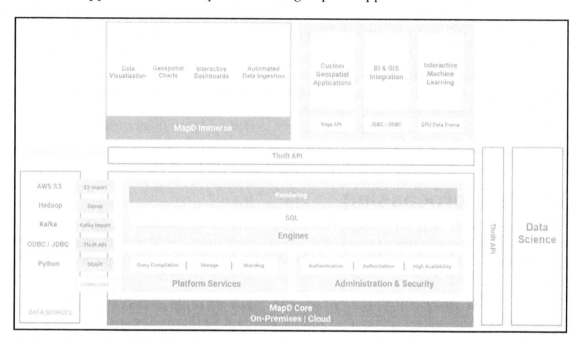

With the fast query speed and APIs, as well as `pymapd`, the components can be used together or separately to create geodatabases and visualizations. Drivers for multiple data importers exist to help data migration and the **Thrift API** can supply data for export or for communication with software packages and Immerse.

Cloud versus local versus combined

With many different types of organizations depending on geodatabases, the options for architecture are also quite varied. While some organizations have moved all of their data to the cloud, storing data and analysis tools on different servers, most maintain an on-premise geodatabase as the enterprise system.

A third architecture style, which balances between cloud-based and local geodatabases, is also very popular. This allows for database backups to be supported by always available cloud services and for data services to reach outside of organizational firewalls while limiting the datasets and services that are exposed to the internet.

The balance between these solutions depends on the need for processing speed and storage costs. MapD, which can be installed and maintained locally or can be hosted in the cloud, fits all kinds of organizational requirements. The speed of queries and data processing allows cloud data resources to be used in the same manner as locally-stored datasets. With `pymapd`, datasets can easily be mirrored in the cloud while maintained locally and can be integrated into geospatial analyses by comparing locally stored data to cloud-based data.

The technological structure your organization chooses will depend on your needs and the size of the datasets both produced and ingested from other sources. MapD can become a part of this structure or can be the entire GIS, supporting Spatial SQL queries at blazing speeds whether located on-premise, in the cloud or both.

Creating a MapD instance in the cloud

To explore the possibilities of using a mixed local and cloud-based GIS with **MapD Core** and **MapD Immerse**, let's create an instance (a virtual server) in the cloud. This cloud database will be accessed locally, using `pymapd` to perform queries and data management tasks.

Using AWS, we can create a server with GPU support. While I am using AWS here, MapD can be loaded into other cloud services, such as Google Cloud and Microsoft Azure, as well as installed locally. These other cloud services have a community edition available as well.

Finding the AMI

I'll use the MapD Community Edition, the open source version of the platform, on a **p2.xlarge** AWS instance. Pre-built **Amazon Machine Images (AMIs)** of the community edition are available. While the core database technology is free, the p2 instance will still have costs associated with it and is not available with the AWS free tier. I chose the **p2.xlarge** over the recommended **p2.8xlarge**, reducing the costs per hour from $7 to $1. For low-cost or free evaluation of the software, download and install it on a virtual machine or a dedicated Linux server:

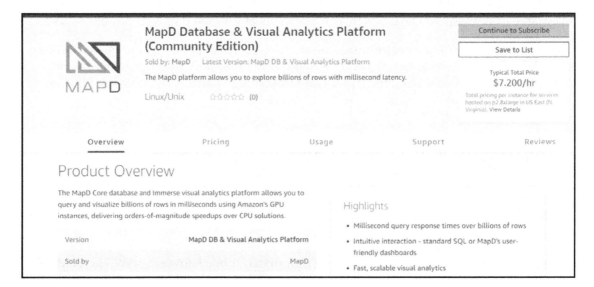

 For local installation, download the community edition (both compiled and the source code) from this website: https://www.mapd.com/community/.

Opening an AWS account

Creating the database instance will require an AWS account. Go to aws.amazon.com and sign up for an account. This account will require a credit or debit card that is tied to the account.

Explore the official documentation for installing a MapD AWS AMI here:
`https://www.mapd.com/docs/latest/getting-started/get-started-aws-ami/`.

Creating a key pair

Generating a key pair will allow you to use secure shell or SSH connections to remote in or remotely access AWS instances. To generate the pair from the **EC2 Dashboard**, select **Key Pairs** from the **NETWORK &amp; SECURITY** group in the left panel after scrolling down:

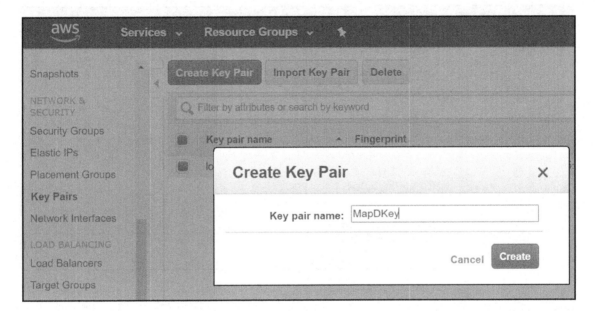

Give the key pair a name and push **Create** to save the private key (with a `.pem` extension) in a secure location on your computer or a USB stick. This key will be required each time you connect to the instance using SSH. The corresponding public key (with a `.pub` extension) is saved in your AWS account and used to match with the private key when connecting to the instance.

Launching an instance

Once the account is set up, go to EC2 from the **AWS Management Console**. In the **EC2 Dashboard**, select **Launch Instance** to open the AWS instance selection tool:

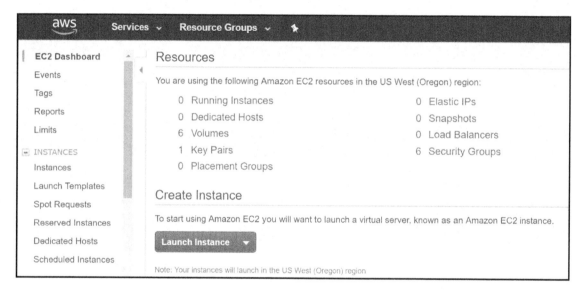

Picking a version

After clicking on **AWS Marketplace** on the left panel, search for the MapD database within the marketplace. Entering `MapD` into the search box brings up both versions. I chose the MapD core database community edition, as the MapD software is included for free:

Select the version of interest by pushing the **Select** button and go to the **Instance Types** menu.

Searching for an instance

Within the available **Instance Types**, only a few are supported. These p2 instances offer different levels of CPUs, memory, and GPUs. I chose the **p2.xlarge** instance for cost reasons, though the **p2.8xlarge** is recommended for production-level computing:

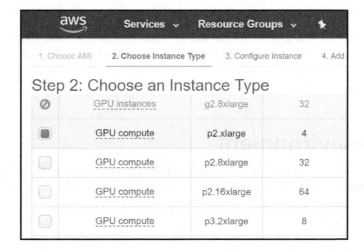

After selecting the instance type, there are a few menus describing the details of the instance and allowing for backup storage within the AWS ecosystem. Set these parameters as required by your organization.

Setting up a security group

The security group settings are important as they control who can access the instance, and where they can access it from. The **Source** tab allows you to set the machines that can connect to the instance, using IP addresses to determine who is allowed to connect:

For security, adjust the **Source** for SSH to my IP. This can be updated later to allow for connections from anywhere, that is the internet at large. Once that is complete, assign the existing key pair to the instance to ensure that it can be used for direct connections to the command line **MapD Core**.

Immerse environment

With the instance set up, accessing the installed Immerse environment can be done using a browser. In the Immerse environment, data can be imported, dashboards can be created, and SQL queries can be executed:

Logging in to Immerse

Within the **EC2 Dashboard**, ensure that the MapD instance is started. Copy the IP address of the instance (the **Public IP** address, not the **Private IP**) and the **Instance ID**, which is located underneath the instances list in the **EC2 Dashboard**. Ensure that the MapD instance is highlighted to ensure that the **Instance ID** is correct:

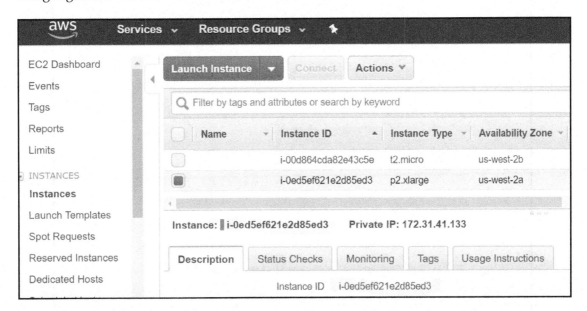

Open a browser and enter the **Public IP** address in the URL bar, along with port number 8443. Here is an example of the URL:

`https://ec2-54-200-213-68.us-west-2.compute.amazonaws.com:8443/.`

Make sure that you are using **Hyper Text Transfer Protocol Secure (HTTPS)** to connect and that the port number is included. If the browser warns you that the connection is insecure, click through using the **Advanced** link at the bottom of the page. Once the connection is made, the login page will open with the user and database pre-populated. Add the **Instance ID** as the password and push **Connect**:

Read the MapD conditions, click **I Agree**, and enter the Immerse environment.

> Read more about using MapD on AWS here: `https://www.mapd.com/`
> `docs/latest/getting-started/get-started-aws-ami/`.

Default dashboards

Once the Immerse environment is started, explore the included default **DASHBOARDS** to get a sense of what is possible:

NYC taxi dataset

The **NYC Taxi Rides** dashboard uses a database table with 13 million rows of data points to demonstrate the speed of the database. Every time the map is zoomed, the database is re-queried and the points regenerated in milliseconds. It's quite fun to explore the data and to alter the dashboard to include other chart and map types:

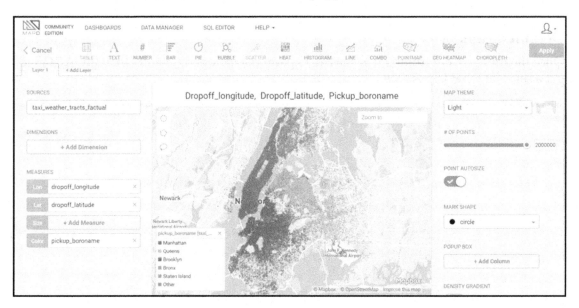

Importing a CSV

Importing a dataset in CSV format is easy using the data importer built into **MapD Immerse**. Go to the **DATA MANAGER** and select **Import Data**. On the next page, click on the **Add Files** button and load the included City of Juneau addresses CSV dataset using drag and drop.

The data will be loaded and, once loaded, a MapD database table is generated from the uploaded data. Review the data and add a new name or accept the default name (generated from the spreadsheet name). Once **Save Table** is clicked, the database table will be generated:

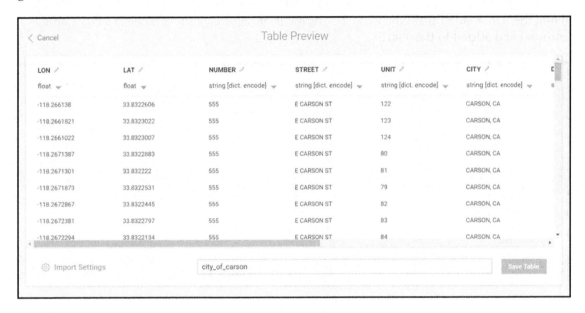

Creating a chart

With a dataset now added to the database, test out **MapD Immerse** by selecting the **DASHBOARDS** tab. Here, dynamic charts, tables, histograms, heat maps and more can be created and added to a new dashboard. In this example, a simple donut chart is created using the data loaded from the CSV. The number of records associated with a city name is counted and added to the chart:

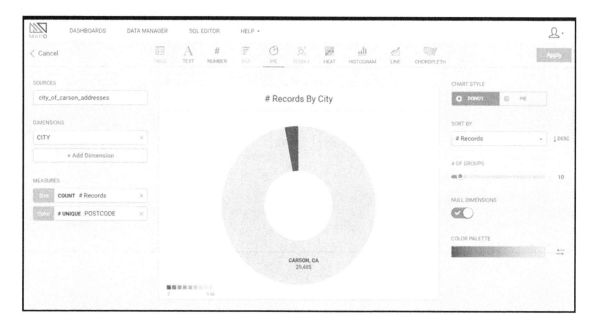

Selections with the SQL EDITOR

Using the built-in **SQL EDITOR**, SQL statements can be executed. The results will appear in the **SQL EDITOR** in a Jupyter Notebook-like interactive table:

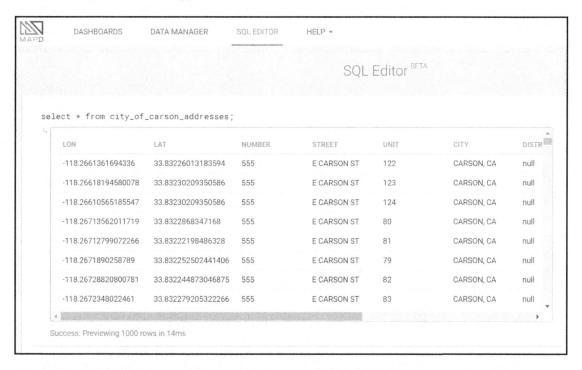

The SQL statements are executed really fast and will include spatial SQL commands that can perform analysis with an SQL select statement.

Use geospatial data

MapD Core supports geometry and geography data types and can also generate interactive maps using coordinate columns to display data with *x/y* or longitude and latitude pairs. Point maps, heat maps, and choropleth maps can easily be generated and styled using the Immerse dashboard environment:

This data visualization was created by loading the Calaveras County address CSV from **OpenAddresses** into my **MapD Immerse** instance using the **DATA MANAGER** and then using the **LON** and **LAT** columns to create a heat map.

Connecting to the database using a terminal

Connect to the database using the integrated Java-based terminal, or another terminal solution. As my local machine uses Windows, and does not have a terminal integrated into the OS, I have downloaded and installed PuTTY. This free SSH software allows me to connect to Linux command line servers from a Windows machine, using the key pair generated earlier for authentication.

If you are using another terminal solution for Windows or using another operating system, connect to the instance using the correct SSH procedure for the terminal. The steps will be similar, except for the required private key format conversion.

Download the PuTTY terminal
here: https://www.chiark.greenend.org.uk/~sgtatham/putty/.

PuTTYgen

To authorize any connection to the AWS instance, the private key generated for the AWS account must be converted into a PuTTY key format using the associated program PuTTYgen. Open PuTTYgen from the **Start** menu, and click on the **Conversions** menu. From the drop-down tab, select **Import Key**.

A file dialogue will open, allowing you to select the private key downloaded from AWS. This private key will have a .pem extension:

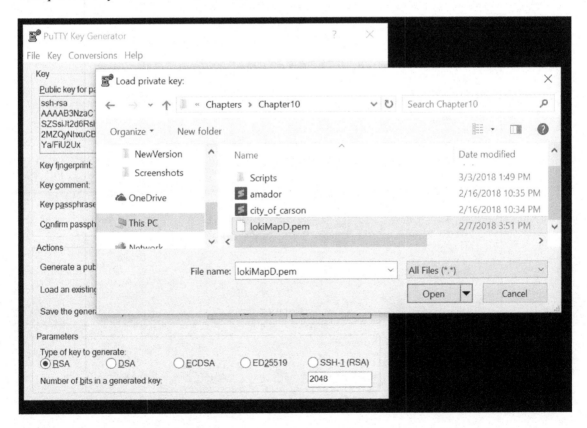

Click **Open**, and the key will be imported. To generate the private key in the PuTTY format, supply an optional key phrase (a word or few words that further identify the user and which must be remembered), and click the **Save Private Key** button in the **Actions** section. Select a folder and save the key, which will now have a .ppk file extension.

Connection configuration

Connecting to the instance using PuTTY requires some configuration. To create the connection, paste the public IP address of the instance into the **Host Name** field, check to ensure that the port is set to **22**, and that the connection type is **SSH**. Save the settings in the **Saved Sessions** section by clicking the **Save** button:

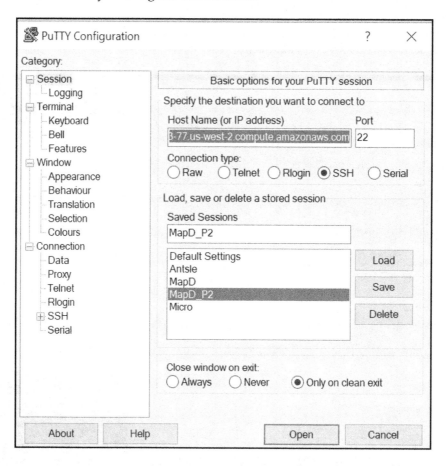

Using the private key

Once the setting is loaded, click on the **SSH** drop-down on the left. In the new menu, click **Auth** to switch to a new menu, and then browse to the private key that we converted into PuTTY format:

Once the key has been located, push **Open** to establish the connection. To start MapD on the server, go to the `/raidStorage/prod/mapd/bin` folder and run the following code, replacing `{Instance-ID}` with your instance ID:

```
./mapdql mapd -u mapd -p {Instance-ID}
```

If you are having trouble establishing the connection, check to make sure that the security group for the AWS instance is set to allow connections from the current computer being used. If the security group setting is my IP and the IP of the computer is different, the connection cannot be made.

Installing pymapd

Installing `pymapd` is simple, and supported by both `conda` and `pip`, the package installer included with Python. I am using `pip` for this chapter, but using `conda` will not cause any issues and may be recommended for integration with other `conda`-supported software.

The conda install command

Use `conda install -c conda-forge` to connect to `conda forge`, the repository where the `pymapd` module is stored. Refer to Chapter 1, *Package Installation and Management* for more information on `conda`:

```
conda install -c conda-forge pymapd
```

The pip install command

The `pymapd` module is also available using `pip`, the Python installer package. It pulls from `PyPi.org`, the Python foundation's repository:

```
pip install pymapd
```

Once the install command is run, the `pymapd` wheel is downloaded and installed along with the required supporting modules:

```
C:\Users\admin>pip install pymapd
Collecting pymapd
  Downloading pymapd-0.3.2.tar.gz (73kB)
    100% |████████████████████████████████| 81kB 706kB/s
Requirement already satisfied: six in c:\users\admin\appdata\local\programs\python\python36\lib\site-packages (from pymapd)
Requirement already satisfied: thrift==0.10.0 in c:\users\admin\appdata\local\programs\python\python36\lib\site-packages (from pymapd)
Requirement already satisfied: sqlalchemy in c:\users\admin\appdata\local\programs\python\python36\lib\site-packages (from pymapd)
Building wheels for collected packages: pymapd
  Running setup.py bdist_wheel for pymapd ... done
  Stored in directory: C:\Users\admin\AppData\Local\pip\Cache\wheels\07\1c\fa\d3b3a0059a53d74da5f891fa0b39f93ee43fa4131f1695289b
Successfully built pymapd
Installing collected packages: pymapd
Successfully installed pymapd-0.3.2
```

Test that the module was installed by opening a Python terminal (or IDLE) and typing `import pymapd`. If no errors occur, `pymapd` has successfully been installed.

> Another option is to download pymapd from GitHub: `https://github.com/mapd/pymapd`.

Creating a connection

The `pymapd` module includes a class called `connect` that requires connection information such as username, password, host server IP/domain, and database name (default value for both user and database name is `mapd`). For an AWS instance, the default password for **MapD Core** and **MapD Immerse** is the instance ID, available in the instance information section in the **EC2 Dashboard**, as shown earlier.

User and password

If you are connecting to the AWS AMI MapD instance, use the public IP address as the `host` and the instance ID as the `password`. Here is the `connection` pattern:

```
from pymapd import connect
connection = connect(user="mapd", password= "{password}",
    host="{my.host.com}", dbname="mapd")
cursor = connection.cursor()
```

Here is an example of what a filled out `connect` instantiation could look like:

```
connection = connect(user="mapd", password= "i-0ed5ey62se2w8eed3",
    host="ec2-54-212-133-87.us-west-2.compute.amazonaws.com", dbname="mapd")
```

Data cursor

To execute the SQL commands (spatial or otherwise), we will create a data `cursor`. The `cursor` is part of the `connection` class and will be used to execute statements using the `execute` command. It is also used to access query results, which are converted into a list and iterated using a `for` loop:

```
from pymapd import connect
connection = connect(user="mapd", password= "{password}",
    host="{my.host.com}", dbname="mapd")
cursor = connection.cursor()
sql_statement = """SELECT name FROM county;"""
cursor.execute(sql_statement)
results = list(cursor)
for result in results:
    print(result[0])
```

The result is a list of tuples, which contain (in this case) only the name of the `county`, accessed using a zero index to get it out of the tuple.

Creating a table

With the connection established, we can now execute SQL statements in the Python script that will generate tables in the **MapD Core** instance. The following statement will create a simple table called `county`, with a `MULTIPOLYGON` geometry type, an `integer id` field, and three `VARCHAR`-type fields (or strings, as they would be called in Python):

```
from pymapd import connect
connection = connect(user="mapd", password= "{password}",
    host="{my.host.com}", dbname="mapd")
cursor = connection.cursor()
create = """CREATE TABLE county ( id integer NOT NULL,
  name VARCHAR(50), statefips VARCHAR(3),
  stpostal VARCHAR(3), geom MULTIPOLYGON );
"""
cursor.execute(create)
connection.commit()
```

The next code block will create a table called `address`, with a `POINT` geometry type, an `integer id` field, and a `VARCHAR`-type field called `address`:

```
from pymapd import connect
connection = connect(user="mapd", password= "{password}",
    host="{my.host.com}", dbname="mapd")
cursor = connection.cursor()
create = """CREATE TABLE address ( id integer NOT NULL PRIMARY KEY,
  address VARCHAR(50), geom Point );
"""
cursor.execute(create)
connection.commit()
```

Insert statements

One way to add data to the database is to use SQL `INSERT` statements. These will generate rows of data within the database tables created in the last section. Using the `pyshp` module, we can read a shapefile and add the data it contains to an `INSERT` statement template. This statement is then executed by the `cursor`:

```
from pymapd import connect
import shapefile
connection = connect(user="mapd", password= "{password}",
    host="{my.host.com}", dbname="mapd")
import shapefile
import pygeoif
cursor = connection.cursor()
```

```
insert = """INSERT INTO county
    VALUES ({cid},'{name}','12','FL','{geom}');
"""
countyfile = r'FloridaCounties.shp'
county_shapefile = shapefile.Reader(countyfile)
county_shapes = county_shapefile.shapes()
county_records = county_shapefile.records()
for count, record in enumerate(county_records):
    name = record[3]
    county_geo = county_shapes[count]
    gshape = pygeoif.Polygon(pygeoif.geometry.as_shape(county_geo))
    geom = gshape.wkt
    insert_statement = insert.format(name=name, geom=geom, cid=count+1)
    cursor.execute(insert_statement)
```

This process can be time-consuming, so there are a few other ways to add data to the database.

Using Apache Arrow to load data

Using the `pyarrow` module and `pandas`, data can be written to the **MapD Core** database:

```
import pyarrow as pa
import pandas as pd
from pymapd import connect
import shapefile
connection = connect(user="mapd", password= "{password}",
    host="{my.host.com}", dbname="mapd")
cursor = connection.cursor()
create = """CREATE TABLE juneau_addresses (
  LON FLOAT, LAT FLOAT,
  NUMBER VARCHAR(30),STREET VARCHAR(200) );
"""
cursor.execute(create)
df = pd.read_csv('city_of_juneau.csv')
table = pa.Table.from_pandas(df)
print(table)
connection.load_table_arrow("juneau_addresses", table)
```

Contains queries

This code will test the speed of a data query against the county database table, using ST_Contains, a spatial SQL point in polygon analysis tool. The geometry column of the county table (called geom) is the first input into ST_Contains, and the **well-known text (WKT)** point is added second. Once the SQL statement is executed, the point will be compared against all of the rows in the table to find if one of the county geometries contains the point described by the WKT point:

```python
import pymapd
from pymapd import connect
connection = connect(user="mapd", password= "{password}",
        host="{my.host.com}", dbname="mapd")
import time
point = "POINT(-80.896146 27.438610)"
cursor = connection.cursor()
print(time.time())
sql_statement = """SELECT name FROM county where
ST_Contains(geom, '{0}');""".format(point)
cursor.execute(sql_statement)
print(time.time())
result = list(cursor)
print(result)
print(time.time())
```

The result of this script is as follows:

```
C:\Packt\PythonScripting\Chapters\Chapter10\Scripts>python Chapter10_4.py
1520266202.7939787
1520266202.8661702
('Okeechobee',)
('Okeechobee',)
1520266202.8661702
```

The geospatial query runs really fast, as you can see from the printed time signatures (in seconds). It takes only a few milliseconds to find that Okeechobee polygon contains the point location.

Other available spatial SQL commands

The number of spatial SQL commands available within a MapD Core database is growing all the time. These include:

- ST_Transform (for coordinate system transformations)
- ST_Distance (for distance analyses)
- ST_Point (to generate point objects)
- ST_XMin, ST_XMax, ST_YMin, ST_YMax (for bounding box access)

More functionality is being added every day and will reach spatial SQL feature parity with PostGIS and other spatial databases later this year. With these SQL commands, and the unique front-end dashboard publication tool MapD Immerse, MapD is a powerful new option for geodatabase deployment.

Summary

Using a cloud-based GPU database like **MapD Core**, and the Immerse visualization studio will pay dividends when designing and implementing a GIS. It offers speed and cloud reliability to both tabular and spatial queries and allows the data to be shared in interactive dashboards (which rely on JavaScript technologies such as D3.js and MapBox GL JavaScript) that are simple to create and publish.

With the MapD Python module, pymapd, cloud data can become an integrated part of a query engine. Data can be pushed to the cloud or pulled down to use locally. Analyses can be performed rapidly, using the power of GPU parallelization. It's worth installing MapD on a virtual server in the cloud, or even locally, to test out the potential of the software.

In the next chapter, we will explore the use of Flask, SQLAlchemy, and GeoAlchemy2 to create an interactive web map with a PostGIS geodatabase backend.

11
Flask and GeoAlchemy2

Python has always had strong internet capabilities. The standard library includes models for HTTP processing, STMP messages, and URL requests. Thousands of third-party modules have been written to extend or improve the built-in web functionality. Over time, a few modules coalesced into Python web frameworks—code libraries written to manage the creation and maintenance of complex and dynamic websites.

To better understand how to use a Python web framework and how to add geospatial capabilities, we'll implement the Flask **Model View Controller** (**MVC**) framework. A pure Python web framework, Flask can be combined with SQLAlchemy, GeoAlchemy2, and the Jinja2 HTML template system to create geospatially-enabled web pages.

In this chapter, you will learn about:

- The Flask web framework
- SQLAlchemy database management
- GeoAlchemy2
- Connecting to PostGIS using object-relational mapping (ORM)
- The Jinja2 web page template system

Flask and its component modules

Flask, as opposed to Django and GeoDjango (covered in `Chapter 12`, *GeoDjango*), does not include batteries. Instead, it allows a number of supporting modules to be installed as needed. This gives more freedom to you as the programmer, but it also makes it necessary to install the required components separately.

I've chosen some modules for this chapter that will allow us to create a Flask application with a geospatial component. The following sections will detail how to set up, install, and utilize these modules to generate a website, using a demonstration site with a PostGIS database backend (as covered in Chapter 7, *Geoprocessing with Geodatabases*) and the ability to perform spatial queries through a web-based interface.

Setup

A number of important Python modules must be in place to ensure that the Flask application and its connection to the PostgreSQL and PostGIS database components, will run as required. These modules will be downloaded and installed using pip, which connects to the **Python Package Index (PyPI)**, an online repository of registered modules located at https://pypi.python.org/pypi.

These modules include:

- Flask, a pure Python MVC web framework (http://flask.pocoo.org/).
- Flask-SQLAlchemy, a database ORM module that can connect to a multitude of database backends (http://flask-sqlalchemy.pocoo.org/2.3/). This module installs SQLAlchemy.
- GeoAlchemy2, a Python module that builds on the SQLAlchemy module and the Postgres/PostGIS backend (covered in Chapter 7, *Geoprocessing with Geodatabases*), is used to allow for geospatial data columns and ORM spatial queries (https://geoalchemy-2.readthedocs.io/en/latest/).
- Flask-WTForms, a web form module built on the WTForms (https://wtforms.readthedocs.io/en/latest/) that allows for Flask to carry the logic of each web page and to process the inputs (https://flask-wtf.readthedocs.io/en/stable/).
- SQLAlchemy-Utils, used to manage database creation and deletion (https://github.com/kvesteri/sqlalchemy-utils/).
- psycopg2, used to create connections to the PostgreSQL database and is used by the SQLAlchemy module (http://initd.org/psycopg/).
- pyshapefile (or pyshp), used to read the shapefiles used in this example and add it to the database tables (https://pypi.python.org/pypi/pyshp).
- Finally, pygeoif (https://pypi.python.org/pypi/pygeoif) is used to allow for the conversion of data from a shapefile binary encoding to a **well-known text (WKT)** encoding, for insertion of geometry data into the database.

Other important supporting modules are automatically installed along with Flask and the preceding modules, including the Jinja2 templating system (`http://jinja.pocoo.org/`) and the Werkzeug **Web Server Gateway Interface (WSGI)** module (`http://werkzeug.pocoo.org/`).

Installing modules using pip

If you have multiple versions of Python installed on your machine and you're not using a virtual environment with the `virtualenv` module, ensure that the `pip` version being called with the command line is the Python 3 version using the `pip -V` option:

```
C:\Python36\Scripts>pip -V
pip 9.0.1 from c:\python36\lib\site-packages (python 3.6)
```

Once it is clear that the correct `pip` is being called from the command line, the modules can be installed. Let's walk through the required `pip` commands and some examples of the expected output that each command will generate.

Installing Flask using pip

First, install the Flask module itself. Use the `pip` command `pip install flask`:

```
C:\Python36\Scripts>pip install flask
```

The `pip` will find Flask and its required dependencies on PyPI and will then run the included `setup.py` instructions (or the equivalent) to install the modules:

```
C:\Users\admin\AppData\Local\Programs\Python\Python36\Scripts>pip install flask
Collecting flask
  Using cached Flask-0.12.2-py2.py3-none-any.whl
Collecting itsdangerous>=0.21 (from flask)
  Using cached itsdangerous-0.24.tar.gz
Collecting Werkzeug>=0.7 (from flask)
  Using cached Werkzeug-0.12.2-py2.py3-none-any.whl
Collecting Jinja2>=2.4 (from flask)
  Using cached Jinja2-2.9.6-py2.py3-none-any.whl
Collecting click>=2.0 (from flask)
  Using cached click-6.7-py2.py3-none-any.whl
Collecting MarkupSafe>=0.23 (from Jinja2>=2.4->flask)
  Using cached MarkupSafe-1.0.tar.gz
Installing collected packages: itsdangerous, Werkzeug, MarkupSafe, Jinja2, click, flask
  Running setup.py install for itsdangerous ... done
  Running setup.py install for MarkupSafe ... done
Successfully installed Jinja2-2.9.6 MarkupSafe-1.0 Werkzeug-0.12.2 click-6.7 flask-0.12.2 itsdangerous-0.24
```

Installing Flask-SQLAlchemy via pip

Use the command `pip install flask-sqlalchemy` to install the `flask-sqlalchemy` wheel and its required dependencies:

```
C:\Python36\Scripts>pip install flask-sqlalchemy
```

The install command will find the `flask-sqlalchemy` wheel file (a pre-built file type used by `pip` to install modules) on PyPI and run the installation process:

```
C:\Users\admin\AppData\Local\Programs\Python\Python36\Scripts>pip install flask-sqlalchemy
Collecting flask-sqlalchemy
  Downloading Flask_SQLAlchemy-2.3.2-py2.py3-none-any.whl
Requirement already satisfied: SQLAlchemy>=0.8.0 in c:\users\admin\appdata\local\programs\python\python36\lib\site-packa
ges (from flask-sqlalchemy)
Requirement already satisfied: Flask>=0.10 in c:\users\admin\appdata\local\programs\python\python36\lib\site-packages (f
rom flask-sqlalchemy)
Requirement already satisfied: Jinja2>=2.4 in c:\users\admin\appdata\local\programs\python\python36\lib\site-packages (f
rom Flask>=0.10->flask-sqlalchemy)
Requirement already satisfied: itsdangerous>=0.21 in c:\users\admin\appdata\local\programs\python\python36\lib\site-pack
ages (from Flask>=0.10->flask-sqlalchemy)
Requirement already satisfied: Werkzeug>=0.7 in c:\users\admin\appdata\local\programs\python\python36\lib\site-packages
(from Flask>=0.10->flask-sqlalchemy)
Requirement already satisfied: click>=2.0 in c:\users\admin\appdata\local\programs\python\python36\lib\site-packages (fr
om Flask>=0.10->flask-sqlalchemy)
Requirement already satisfied: MarkupSafe>=0.23 in c:\users\admin\appdata\local\programs\python\python36\lib\site-packag
es (from Jinja2>=2.4->Flask>=0.10->flask-sqlalchemy)
Installing collected packages: flask-sqlalchemy
Successfully installed flask-sqlalchemy-2.3.2
```

Installing GeoAlchemy2 using pip

Use the command `pip install GeoAlchemy2` to call the module from PyPI, download the wheel file, and install it into the `Lib/site-packages` folder of the Python installation:

```
C:\Python36\Scripts>pip install GeoAlchemy2
```

Installing Flask-WTForms and WTForms using pip

With the WTForms module and the Flask-WTF interface, we can create the web forms that will make the webpage interactive. Install it using the `pip install flask-wtf` command:

```
C:\Python36\Scripts>pip install flask-wtf
```

Installing psycopg2 using pip

The `pscycopg2` is a Python module used to connect to PostgreSQL databases. If it is not installed yet (see `Chapter 7`, *Geoprocessing with Geodatabases*), install it using the `pip install psycopg2` command:

```
C:\Python36\Scripts>pip install psycopg2
```

Installing SQLAlchemy-Utils using pip

These utilities allow for quick database creation:

```
C:\Python36\Scripts>pip install sqlalchemy-utils
```

Installing pyshapefile (or pyshp) using pip

The `pyshapefile` module can read and write shapefiles:

```
C:\Python36\Scripts>pip install pyshp
```

Installing pygeoif using pip

The `pygeoif` module allows for geospatial data format conversion:

```
C:\Python36\Scripts>pip install pygeoif
```

Writing a Flask application

To explore the basics of Flask and GeoAlchemy2, we'll build a Flask web application and test and deploy it locally using the included web server. This web application allows the user to find the county, state, and congressional district associated with different arena's located throughout the country. This application will involve downloading shapefiles from a **United States Geological Survey (USGS)** data catalog and will have views (Python functions that process web requests) performing geospatial queries using the GeoAlchemy2 ORM and table relationship searches using the SQLAlchemy ORM.

This application requires the use of two scripts that create the database and database tables. These scripts are detailed as we proceed further and are in the `Chapter11` folder of the book's code package. The final product will be a web application that uses a `Leaflet` JavaScript map to display the results of ORM-based spatial queries and a relationship query.

Downloading the data from a data source

To start this project, let's download data from the USGS data catalog. This project will use four US-based shapefiles—an NBA arena shapefile, a states shapefile, a congressional districts shapefile, and a counties shapefile.

The USGS has a lot of USA shapefiles for download available here: `https://www.sciencebase.gov/catalog/item/503553b3e4b0d5ec45b0db20`.

County, district, state, and arena shapefiles

The `US_County_Boundaries` data is a polygon shapefile available from the USGS data catalog at this address: `https://www.sciencebase.gov/catalog/item/4f4e4a2ee4b07f02db615738`.

Click on the download zip link, as shown in the image. Unzip the file into a project folder (for example, `C:\GeospatialPy3\Chapter11`) so it can be accessed throughout the chapter:

Attached Files ⚓▾

Click on title to download individual files attached to this item or ⬇ download all files listed below as a compressed file.

Shapefile: ⬇ Arenas_NBA.zip

⬇ Arenas_NBA.shp	912 Bytes
⬇ Arenas_NBA.dbf	20.88 KB

The `Arenas_NBA` shapefile is available here: `https://www.sciencebase.gov/catalog/item/4f4e4a0ae4b07f02db5fb54d`.

The `Congressional_Districts` shapefile is available here: `https://www.sciencebase.gov/catalog/item/4f4e4a06e4b07f02db5f8b58`.

The `US_States` shapefile is available here: `https://www.sciencebase.gov/catalog/item/4f4e4783e4b07f02db4837ce`.

These shapefiles are not current (for example, the Nets arena is still listed as being in New Jersey and not in Brooklyn), but it's the application techniques that we're exploring here (and how they deal with geometry data types) and not the data itself, so ignore the temporal quality of the data.

Creating the database and data tables

To create our database and the tables that will hold the application data, we will use the SQLAlchemy and GeoAlchemy2 classes and methods. The following code is in the script called Chapter11_0.py. This code will allow us to connect to a PostgreSQL data server to create a database and data tables that will form the backend of the web application. Import these libraries:

```
from sqlalchemy import create_engine
from sqlalchemy_utils import database_exists, create_database,
                            drop_database
from sqlalchemy import Column, Integer, String, ForeignKey, Float
from sqlalchemy.orm import relationship
from geoalchemy2 import Geometry
from sqlalchemy.ext.declarative import declarative_base
```

Connecting the database server to both generate and query the data tables is achieved using the create_engine function and the connection string format, demonstrated as follows:

```
conn_string = '{DBtype}://{user}:{pword}@{instancehost}:{port}/{database}'
engine = create_engine(conn_string, echo=True)
```

Connection strings are used throughout all Python database modules. They usually include a specification of the **relational database management system (RDBMS)** type, the username, the password, the instance host (that is the IP address or localhost for a database server installed on the local machine), an optional port number, and a database name. For example, a connection string might look like this:

```
connstring = 'postgresql://postgres:bond007@localhost:5432/chapter11'
engine = create_engine(connstring, echo=True)
```

In this example, postgresql is the RDBMS type, postgres is the user, bond007 is the password, localhost is the instance host, 5432 is the port (and the default port for PostgreSQL installations; if the port wasn't changed on installation, it can be left out of the connection string), and chapter11 is the name of the database. The echo=True statement is used to generate logs of the database interactions to the standard output window. To turn these messages off, change the echo value to False.

A more thorough explanation of this pattern can be found here: `http://docs.sqlalchemy.org/en/latest/core/engines.html`.

For our database, we can use the following format. Replace `{user}` and `{pword}` (including the brackets) with your PostgreSQL server username and password:

```
conn_string ='postgresql://{user}:{pword}@localhost:5432/chapter11'
engine = create_engine(conn_string, echo=True)
```

If the connection string is valid, the `create_engine` function will return an object to the `engine` variable, which will be used to perform database interactions throughout the script.

The code in the comment (`#drop_database(engine.url)`) is commented out but can be uncommented if the database needs to be dropped and then recreated using the script. It calls the SQLAlchemy create_engine's `url` property, which is a reference to the connection string:

```
# Uncomment the line below if you need to recreate the database.
#drop_database(engine.url)
```

The database and the data tables it will contain is created within an `if not` conditional that relies on the `database_exists` function. If the conditional returns `True` (indicating that the database does not exist), the `engine` variable is passed to the `create_database` function:

```
# Check to ensure that the database doesn't exist
# If it doesn't, create it and generate the PostGIS extention and tables
if not database_exists(engine.url):
    create_database(engine.url)
```

Adding the PostGIS extension tables to the new database

Just underneath the `create_database` function, we will need to connect to the database using the `engine.connect` function to pass an SQL statement directly to the database. This SQL statement, (`"CREATE EXTENSION postgis"`) enables spatial columns and queries within the new database:

```
# Create a direct connection to the database using the engine.
# This will allow the new database to use the PostGIS extension.
conn = engine.connect()
```

```
conn.execute("commit")
try:
     conn.execute("CREATE EXTENSION postgis")
 except Exception as e:
     print(e)
     print("extension postgis already exists")
conn.close()
```

A try/except block is used here in case the database has already been spatially enabled. Check the output from the print statements to ensure that no other exception occurs.

Defining the database tables

Within the world of Python MVC web frameworks, the database tables are the **models**. Used by the website to store data, they are generated with and modeled by Python classes. These classes subclass or inherit pre-written functionality from a superclass that contains a majority of the database management code, leaving us to simply define the columns of the table using basic data types such as strings and integers, as well as advanced classes such as geometries.

These class-defined tables can be generated in multiple RDBMS without the need to revamp how the model code is written. While GeoAlchemy2 only works on top of PostgreSQL/PostGIS, SQLAlchemy models can be used to generate tables in a variety of databases, including SQL Server, Oracle, Postgres, MySQL and more.

The declarative base

For SQLAlchemy database classes, a base class called the declarative_base allows for inheritance of database methods and properties (this is where the superclass magic of SQLAlchemy exists, handling database SQL statements in multiple SQL versions, which simplifies the code required to write to any RDBMS):

```
# Define the model Base
Base = declarative_base()
```

Database table model classes

Once the base has been called or instantiated, it can be passed to the model classes. These classes, like all Python classes, could include functions, properties, and methods which are useful for processing data internally to the class. In this chapter, the models do not include any internal functions, but instead only define columns.

Explore SQLAlchemy models and their internal functions here: `http://docs.sqlalchemy.org/en/latest/orm/tutorial.html`.

Table properties

The name of the data table generated in the RDBMS database will correspond to the `__tablename__` property of a model class. The primary key for each table is used for relationships and queries and must be defined using the keyword `primary_key`. The `Column` class and the `String`, `Float` and `Integer` type classes are called from SQLAlchemy and are used to define table columns to be generated within the underlying RDBMS (thus allowing the programmer to avoid crafting `CREATE TABLE` statements for each variety of SQL used by the major RDBMS).

For example, the `Arena` class will be used to manage a table that has four columns—a `String` name field, two `Float` fields (`longitude` and `latitude`), and a `POINT` geometry type with an SRID or EPSG spatial reference system ID of `4326`, corresponding to the WGS 1984 coordinate system (`http://spatialreference.org/ref/epsg/wgs-84/`):

```
# Define the Arena class, which will model the Arena database table
class Arena(Base):
    __tablename__ = 'arena'
    id = Column(Integer, primary_key=True)
    name = Column(String)
    longitude = Column(Float)
    latitude = Column(Float)
    geom = Column(Geometry(geometry_type='POINT', srid=4326))
```

Like the `Arena` class, the following classes use a `String` name column. For the geometry type, they also use SRID `4326`, but they use the `MULTIPOLYGON` geometry type to store the complex multipolygon geometries used to model these geographies. For tables with relationships, as in the case of the `County`, `District`, and `State` classes, there are also special classes used to manage table relationships and queries between tables.

These special classes include the `ForeignKey` class and the `relationship` function. The `ForeignKey` class is passed an `id` parameter and passed to a `Column` class, associating the child row's with the parent. The `relationship` function allows two-way queries. The `backref` keyword generates a function that instantiates an instance of the joined table's model:

```
# Define the County class
class County(Base):
```

```
    __tablename__ = 'county'
    id = Column(Integer, primary_key=True)
    name = Column(String)
    state_id = Column(Integer, ForeignKey('state.id'))
    state_ref = relationship("State",backref='county')
    geom =   Column(Geometry(geometry_type='MULTIPOLYGON',srid=4326))
# Define the District class
class District(Base):
    __tablename__ = 'district'
    id = Column(Integer, primary_key=True)
    district = Column(String)
    name = Column(String)
    state_id = Column(Integer, ForeignKey('state.id'))
    state_ref = relationship("State",backref='district')
    geom = Column(Geometry(geometry_type='MULTIPOLYGON',srid=4326))
```

The County class and the District class will have a relationship with the State class, allowing session queries that call the State class. This relationship makes it easy to find which US state a county or congressional district is located in. The state_id column builds the relationship, and the state_ref field references the parent State class. For the State class, the counties and districts have their own backref references, allowing the parent State class to access the associated counties/districts:

```
# Define the State class
class State(Base):
    __tablename__ = 'state'
    id = Column(Integer, primary_key=True)
    name = Column(String)
    statefips = Column(String)
    stpostal = Column(String)
    counties = relationship('County', backref='state')
    districts = relationship('District', backref='state')
    geom =
    Column(Geometry(geometry_type='MULTIPOLYGON',srid=4326))
```

Creating the tables

To actually generate the tables, there are two methods that can be used. Table model classes have an internal __table__ method that has a create function, which can be used to create each table separately. There is also a drop function that can be called to drop a table.

In the script, we use `try`/`except` blocks to generate the tables. If an exception is incurred (that is, if the table already exists), the table is dropped and then created. Here is the `State` table creation statement as an example:

```
# Generate the State table from the State class.
# If it already exists, drop it and regenerate it
try:
    State.__table__.create(engine)
except:
    State.__table__.drop(engine)
    State.__table__.create(engine)
```

Alternatively, all database tables can be generated from the defined classes using the `Base` method `metadata` and its `create_all` function:

```
Base.metadata.create_all(engine)
```

Inserting data into the new data tables

Once the database has been created and the database tables have been defined and created within the database, the data can be added. A second script, `Chapter11_1.py`, will be used to find and read the data contained within the downloaded shapefiles and `for` loops will be used to read through the data and write it to the respective database table. An SQLAlchemy session manager will be used to query and commit data to the tables.

Importing the required modules

For the data to be processed and imported, a few new modules will be used. The `pyshapefile` module (or `pyshp`, imported as shapefile) is used to connect to the shapefiles and to read both the geometries and attribute data that they contain. The `pygeoif` module is a pure Python module that implements a protocol known as the `geo_interface`.

This protocol allows Python object-level introspection of geospatial data, for example, it converts geospatial data formats into Python objects. It will be used to convert between shapefile geometries stored in binary into WKT geometries that can be inserted into the database using the GeoAlchemy2 ORM:

```
# The pyshapefile module is used to read shapefiles and
# the pygeoif module is used to convert between geometry types
import shapefile
import pygeoif
```

More discussion of the `geo_interface` protocol is available here: `https://gist.github.com/sgillies/2217756`.

To connect to the database and the tables, import the SQLAlchemy ORM and other SQLAlchemy functions:

```
from sqlalchemy import create_engine
from sqlalchemy.ext.declarative import declarative_base
from sqlalchemy import Column, Integer, String, ForeignKey, Float
from sqlalchemy.orm import sessionmaker
from sqlalchemy.orm import relationship
```

To add data to the geometry columns of the database tables, the GeoAlchemy2 `Geometry` data type will be used:

```
# The Geometry columns from GeoAlchemy2 extend the SQLAlchemy ORM
from geoalchemy2 import Geometry
```

To enable the script to find the downloaded shapefiles, use the `Tkinter` module and its `filedialog` method, as it is built into Python and is OS-agnostic:

```
# The built-in Tkinter GUI module allows for file dialogs
from tkinter import filedialog
from tkinter import Tk
```

Connections to the database will again be created using the `create_engine` function from SQLAlchemy. This section also generates a `session` using the session manager, binding it to the `engine` variable that connects to the database:

```
# Connect to the database called chapter11 using SQLAlchemy functions
conn_string = 'postgresql://postgres:password@localhost/chapter11'
engine = create_engine(conn_string)
Session = sessionmaker(bind=engine)
session = Session()
```

The `session` will allow for queries and commits (that is, writing to the database) to them being managed. We will need to query against database tables inside the `for` loop, to create the database relationships between the counties, districts, and states.

The database table models are again defined within the script, subclassing from the `declarative_base` class. These class definitions will match those within the last script.

Locating and reading the shapefiles

To create file dialogs that allow the user to search for and locate shapefiles, Tkinter's `Tk` class is instantiated and assigned to the variable `root`. The `Tk` class creates a small console window that is not necessary, so it is withdrawn using the `root.withdraw` method:

```
# Initiate the Tkinter module and withdraw the console it generates
root = Tk()
root.withdraw()
```

The file dialogs are generated using the `filedialog.askopenfilename` method. The method accepts a number of arguments, including the `title` of the file dialog window, the initial directory, and the file extensions that should be visible while using the file dialog. Here is the `Select Arena Shapefile` dialog code as an example:

```
# Navigate to the Arena shapefile using the Tkinter file dialog
root.arenafile = filedialog.askopenfilename(initialdir = "/",
                        title = "Select Arena Shapefile",
                        filetypes = (("shapefiles","*.shp"),
                        ("all files", "*.*")))
```

Within the script, this is repeated for each of the downloaded shapefiles. After using the file dialogs, each of the shapefiles located will pass a string type file path to the `root` variable and the file path will be held in a property.

Accessing shapefile data

To access the data within the shapefiles, the `pyshp Reader` class is invoked by passing the respective file path property to the `Reader` class. The instantiated class will have both `records` and a `shapes` method, to allow access to the shapefile's attribute data and geometry data respectively:

```
# Read the Arena shapefile using the Reader class of the pyshp module
import shapefile
arena_shapefile = shapefile.Reader(root.arenafile)
arena_shapes = arena_shapefile.shapes()
arena_records = arena_shapefile.records()
```

Once the data has been read and assigned to iteratable variables, they can be iterated using `for` loops. Because the data accessed using the `pyshp Reader records` method corresponds to the data accessed using the `shapes` method, a loop counter generated using the `enumerate` function is used to match indexes between the current record and the corresponding geometry data in the list of geometries generated by the `shapes` method.

For the `Arena` shapefile geometry, the `Reader shapes` method returns the data as a list with coordinate pairs. As the `Arena` class geometry column is a `POINT` data type, the data can be written to the database table using a `POINT(X Y)` WKT template. The SRID (`4326`) is included at the beginning of the string, as per GeoAlchemy2 Extended WKT (EWKT) requirements.

Read more on the GeoAlcheym2 ORM here: `http://geoalchemy-2.readthedocs.io/en/0.4/orm_tutorial.html`.

With each loop, a new `Arena` class is instantiated and assigned to the variable `arena`. The `name` field is extracted from the `Reader record` data item located at index 6 and assigned to the `arena` variable, while the geometry data is extracted from the `arena_shapes` data item at `count` (that is, the current loop number) and assigned to the `Arena` columns called `arena.longitude` and `arena.latitude`.

These coordinates are then passed to the string `format` method to format the EWKT template and assigned to the `arena.geom` property. Once the data for the `arena` row has been assigned, it's added to the session using `session.add`. Finally, the data is written to the database using the session's `commit` method:

```
# Iterate through the Arena data read from the shapefile
for count, record in enumerate(arena_records):
    arena = Arena()
    arena.name = record[6]
    print(arena.name)
    point = arena_shapes[count].points[0]
    arena.longitude = point[0]
    arena.latitude = point[1]
    arena.geom = 'SRID=4326;POINT({0} {1})'.format(point[0],
    point[1])
    session.add(arena)
session.commit()
```

For the `State` class (and the `County` and `District` classes), the name, **Federal Information Processing Standards (FIPS)** code, and postal code abbreviation are extracted from the attribute data using indexing. The `pygeoif` is used to convert the geometry first into a `pygeoif MultiPolygon` format and then into WKT, which is passed to a string template and written to the `geom` field as EWKT:

```
# Iterate through the State data read from the shapefile
for count, record in enumerate(state_records):
    state = State()
```

```
        state.name = record[1]
        state.statefips = record[0]
        state.stpostal = record[2]
        state_geo = state_shapes[count]
        gshape =
        pygeoif.MultiPolygon(pygeoif.geometry.as_shape(state_geo))
        state.geom = 'SRID=4326;{0}'.format(gshape.wkt)
        session.add(state)
        if count % 10 == 0:
            session.commit()
    session.commit()
```

Because of the large size of the geometry data for states, they are committed to the database every 10 loops. The final commit catches any remainder.

Using queries

For the District and County data tables, a final wrinkle is added, querying against the newly added state data to find the associated state by FIPS code. By querying the State class using session.query and filtering the state's data using the filter_by method (passing the FIPS code from the district records as the filter argument), and then specifying that the first result should be used, the correct state can be called. The variable state's id field is used to populate the district's state_id column to create the relationship:

```
# This uses the STFIPS data to query the State table and find the state
for count, record in enumerate(district_records):
    district = District()
    district.district = record[0]
    district.name = record[1]
    state = session.query(State).filter_by(statefips=record[4]).first()
    district.state_id = state.id
    dist_geo = district_shapes[count]
    gshape=pygeoif.MultiPolygon(pygeoif.geometry.as_shape(dist_geo))
    district.geom = 'SRID=4326;{0}'.format(gshape.wkt)
    session.add(district)
    if count % 50 == 0:
        session.commit()
session.commit()
```

The County table is similarly looped and also includes a State query. Check the script to see the completed code. Once all of the data has been written to the data tables, close the session and dispose of the connection engine:

```
session.close()
engine.dispose()
```

Components of the Flask application

Now that the backend database and tables have been created and loaded with data and the relationships between the tables have been modeled and generated, it's time to write the scripts that will create the Flask application. These scripts will contain views, models, and forms that process web requests, query the database, and return an HTTP response.

The web application is called the Arena application, as it lists all of the NBA arenas stored in the arena table in a drop-down list, and allows the user to display the location on a map along with a popup that contains information about the arena from spatial queries and table relationships.

The MVC method of web development allows for separation between the necessary components of a web application. These components include database models (the SQLAlchemy models described earlier), web forms for accepting application input, and a controller object that routes requests. The separation of components is reflected in the separate scripts. Making each component independent makes it easier to adjust without affecting other components of the application.

The database model will be contained in a script called models.py, along with the required module imports. The web forms (Python classes that create web page components such as drop-down lists and entry fields) will be contained in a script called forms.py. All of the views, which include the URL endpoints and the processing of the web requests to those URLs, will be contained within a script called views.py.

A controller is an object generated from the Flask class and assigned to the variable called app. Each URL endpoint of the web application is defined using app.route and has an associated Python function (the view) that contains the logic to process the web request and return an HTTP response. The controller is used to route web requests to the correct URL endpoint and can distinguish between GET and POST HTTP requests. It is created in the views.py script.

HTML templates are used to present the processed results of a web request. Using the Jinja2 templating system, the data contained within the web forms will be passed to HTML templates and sent back to the requesting web browser as a complete web page. The template for this application contains links to JavaScript libraries, including Leaflet, which allows the web page to present a map within the web page.

Folder structure and the controller object

To contain the separate components of the application, a specific folder structure is recommended. It will allow for the components to reference each other as needed, while still maintaining independence. Adjustments made to one portion of a component shouldn't require the overhaul of a separated component (at least as much as possible).

The Arena application is contained within a folder called `arenaapp`:

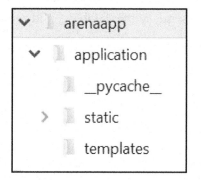

Inside the `arenaapp` folder is a script called `app.py` and a folder called `application`:

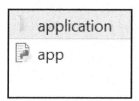

The `app.py` script imports the `app` controller object from the `application` and calls the `app.run` method to start the web application:

```
from application import app
app.run()
```

Making the folder `application` importable and allowing `app` access to code inside the component scripts is made possible by adding a Python __init__.py script. This special script indicates to the Python executable that the folder is a module:

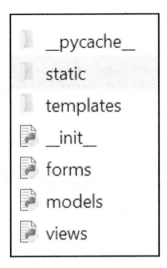

Inside __init__.py, the app object is defined and configured. The app object contains a configuration dictionary that allows the web application to connect to the backend ('SQLALCHEMY_DATABASE_URI') and to perform session management and encryption. While we have included the configuration settings within this script, note that larger applications will separate out the configuration settings into a separate config.py script:

```
import flask
app = flask.Flask(__name__)
conn_string = 'postgresql://postgres:password@localhost:5432/chapter11'
app.config['SQLALCHEMY_DATABASE_URI'] = conn_string
app.config['SECRET_KEY'] = "SECRET_KEY"
app.config['DEBUG'] = True
import application.views
```

To make it easier to debug the application, the DEBUG configuration has been set to True. Set it to False in production. Replace 'SECRET KEY' with your own secret key.

 Read more about configuring a Flask web application here: http://flask.pocoo.org/docs/latest/config/.

Models

For the Arena application, a script called `models.py` contains the models that will be used for the application. As described earlier, these models are Python classes that contain database column definitions and can have internal functions for processing data. Our simplified models contain only data column definitions using SQLAlchemy and GeoAlchemy2 classes.

To connect to the database, the `app` object is imported. This makes the application configuration variables, including `app.config['SQLALCHEMY_DATABASE_URI']` which stores the database connection string, available to the SQLAlchemy `create_engine` function:

```
from application import app
# The database connections and session management are managed with
SQLAlchemy functions
from sqlalchemy import create_engine
from sqlalchemy.ext.declarative import declarative_base
from sqlalchemy import Column, Integer, String, ForeignKey, Float
from sqlalchemy.orm import sessionmaker
from sqlalchemy.orm import relationship
from geoalchemy2 import Geometry
engine = create_engine(app.config['SQLALCHEMY_DATABASE_URI'])
Session = sessionmaker(bind=engine)
session = Session()
Base = declarative_base()
```

For the sake of brevity, I've skipped detailing the model class definitions here as they were explained previously. Look for them inside the `arenaapp/application` folder's `models.py` script.

Forms

Web forms are used in web applications to accept data from a user and send it to the server for validation and processing. To generate the required forms (for example drop-downs, entry fields, and even password fields that hide their contents from the user), the Flask-WTF module and the WTForms module are used. These modules contain classes that make it possible to create the form components and to ensure that the data entered into them is valid for that field.

For our simple application, only one form is created. The `ArenaForm` form inherits from the `FlaskFor` class and contains a `description` attribute and field called `selections`. This field is a `SelectField`, which will create a drop-down list on the web page. It requires a description string and uses the keyword `choices` to generate the list of the choices available in the drop-down list. As the members of the drop-down list will be generated dynamically within the view (explained as follows), an empty list is passed to the `choices` keyword here:

```
from flask_wtf import FlaskForm
from wtforms import SelectField
class ArenaForm(FlaskForm):
    description  = "Use the dropdown to select an arena."
    selections = SelectField('Select an Arena',choices=[])
```

Other field classes, such as `TextField`, `BooleanField`, `StringField`, `FloatField`, `PasswordField`, and many others, are available from WTForms for implementation of complex web applications. Also, because they are Python objects, forms can be updated to include other data attributes on the fly, as we will see as we proceed further.

Views

Flask views are Python functions that, when paired with the `app` controller object and its `app.route` URL definitions, allows us to write Python code to accept a web request, process it, and return a response. They are the heart of the web application, making it possible to connect web pages and their forms to the database and its tables.

To create views, we will import all of the application components along with a number of Flask functions. The forms and models are imported from their respective scripts, as is the `app` object:

```
from application import app
from flask import render_template,jsonify, redirect, url_for, request
from .forms import *
from .models import *
```

For the Arena application, we have two views defined that create two application URL endpoints. The first view, `home`, is in place only to redirect requests to the IP address root. Using the Flask functions `redirect` and `url_for`, any web requests sent to the `root` address will be redirected to the `arenas` view:

```
@app.route('/', methods=["GET"])
def home():
  return redirect(url_for('arenas'))
```

The second view, `arenas`, is more complex. It accepts both GET and POST request methods. Depending on the `request` method, the data processed and returned will be different, though they both rely on the template `index.html` which is stored in the `application/templates` folder (where all Flask HTML templates are stored). Here is the complete view:

```
@app.route('/arenas', methods=["GET","POST"])
def arenas():
    form = ArenaForm(request.form)
    arenas = session.query(Arena).all()
    form.selections.choices = [(arena.id,
                                 arena.name) for arena in arenas]
    form.popup = "Select an Arena"
    form.latitude = 38.89517
    form.longitude = -77.03682
    if request.method == "POST":
        arena_id = form.selections.data
        arena = session.query(Arena).get(arena_id)
        form.longitude = round(arena.longitude,4)
        form.latitude = round(arena.latitude,4)
        county=session.query(County).filter(
                    County.geom.ST_Contains(arena.geom)).first()
        if county != None:
            district=session.query(District).filter(
                    District.geom.ST_Intersects(arena.geom)).first()
            state = county.state_ref
            form.popup = """The {0} is located at {4}, {5}, which is in
            {1} County, {3}, and in {3} Congressional District
            {2}.""".format(arena.name,county.name, district.district,
            state.name,
            form.longitude, form.latitude)

        else:
                form.popup = """The county, district, and state could
                not be located using point in polygon analysis"""

        return render_template('index.html',form=form)
    return render_template('index.html',form=form)
```

Dissecting the view

The views's URL is `http://{localhost}/arenas`. Using a special Python object called a **decorator** (such as `@app.route`) allows us to connect the URL that we want to use with the function that will accept and handle the request processing. The function and the URL do not need to have the same name, though it is common for them to do so:

```
@app.route('/arenas', methods=["GET","POST"])
def arenas():
```

Using forms

Underneath the decorator and the function declaration, the `ArenaForm` from `forms.py` is called and the function `request.form` is passed as a parameter. This adds functionality to the `ArenaForm` and allows it to access the request's own parameters as needed.

Once the `ArenaForm` object is passed to the variable `form`, it can be populated with data. This data will come from an SQLAlchemy session `query` on the `Arena` model. This query requests all rows of data from the `Arena` table and passes it to the variable `arenas` using `all` method (as opposed to the `filter_by` method which would limit the rows returned).

Because the ArenaForm's `selections` field is currently blank, we'll use a list comprehension to loop through the `arena` objects contained within the list called `arenas`, adding their `id` and `name` fields to tuples inside the list. This populates the drop-down list and makes it so each selection in the list has a value (the `id`) and a label (the `name`):

```
form = ArenaForm(request.form)
arenas = session.query(Arena).all()
form.selections.choices = [(arena.id,
                              arena.name) for arena in arenas]
form.popup = "Select an Arena"
form.latitude = 38.89517
form.longitude = -77.03682
```

After populating the selections choices, three new attributes are added to the form—popup, `latitude`, and `longitude`. Initially, these are just placeholders and are not derived from the `arena` data. However, once the web application is running and users are selecting `arenas` from the drop-down list, these placeholder values will be replaced with data derived from the `arenas` tables and from queries against the other tables.

Evaluating the request method

The next line is an `if` conditional that uses the `request.method` property to see if the HTTP request method is `POST`:

```
if request.method == "POST":
```

Because the initial request to the URL `arenas` is a `GET` request, the code initially evaluates the `if` conditional as `False`, skipping the indented code section to the bottom of the view to return the template `index.html` and the now populated `form`:

```
return render_template('index.html',form=form)
```

This function returns uses the `render_template` function to return the template called `index.html` and passes the populated `ArenaForm` variable called `form` into the template, making it possible for the Jinja2 templating system to generate the completed web page and send it to the requesting web browser. All of the template's double-bracketed variables are filled in with the corresponding data from `form` (for example, the selections are added to the drop-down list).

POST requests

If a user selects an `arena` from the list and pushes the **Find Data** button, the HTML form issues a `POST` request to the view. With the `if` conditional resolving to `True`, the view handles the request by generating an `arena` location coordinate pair and a custom `popup`, instead of using a default coordinate pair and `popup` value:

```
if request.method == "POST":
    arena_id = form.selections.data
    arena = session.query(Arena).get(arena_id)
    form.longitude = round(arena.longitude,4)
    form.latitude = round(arena.latitude,4)
```

The property `form.selections.data` is used to retrieve the `id` of the `arena` chosen from the list and is passed to a variable called `arena_id`. This `id` is then used to query the database through the SQLAlchemy ORM's `get` method. The `form.longitude` and `form.latitude` fields can be populated from data fields of the `arena` object returned by the query.

Spatial queries

To find the county and the congressional district, two PostGIS spatial analysis techniques are used—ST_Contains and ST_Intersects. The first query determines if the arena is contained within a county; if not, the result is null (or None in Python):

```
county=session.query(County).filter(
                County.geom.ST_Contains(arena.geom)).first()
if county != None:
    district=session.query(District).filter(
                District.geom.ST_Intersects(arena.geom)).first()
```

While ST_Contains could be used for both queries, I wanted to demonstrate that the GeoAlchemy2 ORM allows for access to all PostGIS functions when using Geometry columns. These searches combine the SQLAlchemy filter method with the GeoAlchemy2 ORM to make it possible to return query results based on a spatial analysis.

Relationship query

If the county query was successful, the district query is performed, and then a relationship attribute (state_ref) is used to find the state within which the county is placed:

```
state = county.state_ref
```

The two-way relationship established in the County, District, and State model definitions make this possible. This state object is a member of the State model class and can be used to retrieve the name of the state.

To create the custom popup, string template formatting is used to populate the popup with the specifics describing the arena requested. The result is assigned to the variable form.popup.

Finally, the populated form is then passed once again to the index.html template, but this time it contains data about the selected arena:

```
return render_template('index.html',form=form)
```

Here is a screenshot of the application query results for The Oracle Arena:

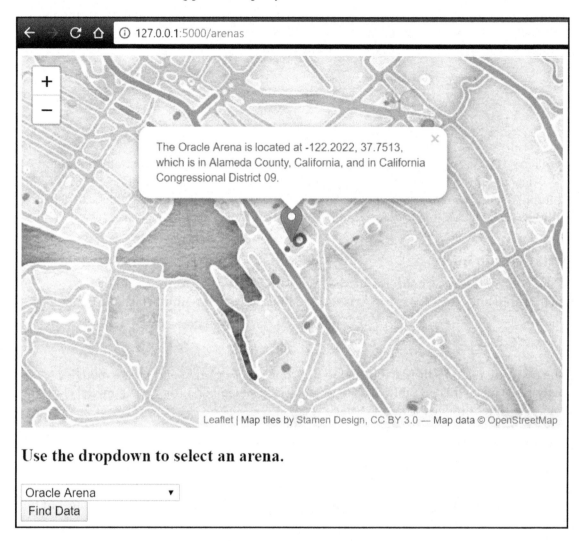

The web map template

Within the index.html template, the form data is accessed inside double-bracketed variables. These variables can be located inside the JavaScript or within the HTML. In this example, the form.latitude and form.longitude variables are located inside the map JavaScript that defines the initial center point of the map:

```
var themap = L.map('map').setView([{{form.latitude}},
{{form.longitude}}], 13);
```

To create the marker at the location of the arena requested, with a custom popup, the location coordinates and the popup fields are added:

```
L.marker([{{form.latitude}},{{form.longitude}}]).addTo(themap)
  .bindPopup("{{form.popup}}").openPopup();
```

To make the POST requests possible, an HTML form with a POST method houses the form.description and form.selection (the drop-down list) attributes. The HTML form's button generates the POST request when it is pushed:

```
<form method="post" class="form">
  <h3>{{form.description}}</h3>
  {{form.selections(class_='form-control',placeholder="")}}
  <br>
  <input type="submit" value="Find Data">
</form>
```

Running the web application locally

To run the application locally, we can call the app.py script, located in the arenaapp folder, using the Python executable. Open up a command line and pass a script argument:

```
C:\Python36>python C:\GeospatialPy3\Chapter11\Scripts\arenaapp\app.py
```

To run this application on a web server is beyond the scope of the chapter, but it involves configuring a web server with a WSGI handler to allow for web requests to be processed by the Python executable and app.py. For Apache web servers, the mod_wsgi module is popular. For Windows servers using **Internet Information Services (IIS)**, the wfastcgi module is very useful and is available from the Microsoft Web Platform Installer.

Explore more about Apache and the `mod_wsgi` module here: `http://flask.pocoo.org/docs/latest/deploying/mod_wsgi/`.

For IIS, these installation instructions are very useful: `http://netdot.co/2015/03/09/flask-on-iis/`.

Summary

In this chapter, we learned how to use the Flask MVC web framework and some of the available component modules that add extra functionality. These modules include the SQLAlchemy ORM, the GeoAlchemy2 ORM for geospatial queries, WTForms for processing of web data, and the Jinja2 templating system for creating web page templates. We created database tables, added data tables and tables relationships, and created a web application that utilized geospatial and relationship queries to generate dynamic web pages.

A fun challenge, building on the code reviewed here, would be to explore adding editing capabilities to the Arena application, allowing the user to move the `arenas` into their correct location if the data is out of date. Explore the GeoAlchemy2 ORM documentation for more advanced capabilities.

In the next chapter, we will review a similar MVC web framework, Django, and its GeoDjango spatial component. With more batteries included philosophy, Django solves the same problems inherent to web applications in different ways, but with less freedom of module choice, when compared to Flask.

12
GeoDjango

The Django Python web framework was made available in 2005 and has been steadily supported and improved throughout the years. One major improvement was additional support for spatial data types and queries. This effort produced GeoDjango, allowing Django to support geospatial database models and web views that utilize geospatial queries.

GeoDjango is now a standard Django component, which can be activated using a specific configuration. In December 2017, Django 2 was released as the new long-term support version. It currently supports Python 3.4, 3.5, and 3.6.

In this chapter, we will learn about the following:

- Installation and configuration of Django and GeoDjango
- Django admin panel functionality, including map editing
- How to load shapefiles into database tables using LayerMapping
- GeoDjango queries
- Django URL patterns
- Django views

Installing and configuring Django and GeoDjango

Django, compared to Flask, is a batteries-included framework. It includes modules that allow for database backend support, without requiring a separate database code package (unlike Flask, which relies on SQLAlchemy). Django also includes an admin panel that allows for easy data editing and management through a web interface. This means fewer modules are installed and more code is included to handle database interactions and web processing.

There are some major differences between Flask and Django. Django separates URLs from views and models in a more structured manner than Flask. Django also uses Python classes for databases tables, but it has built-in database support. For geospatial databases, no extra module is required. Django also supports geometry columns in a wider range of databases, though PostgreSQL and PostGIS are used the most often.

Like many Python 3 modules, Django development is geared towards Linux development environments. While it supports Windows installation, it requires a few modifications of the environment variables within Windows, requiring administrative control of the machine. Administrative-level permissions are required for configurations, allowing Django to access **Geospatial Data Abstraction Library (GDAL)** and **OGR Simple Features** libraries.

Steps from Django to GeoDjango

Within this section, we'll install Django add GeoDjango configurations, and add the required libraries (including the GDAL and OGR) that bring spatial functionality to Django. Installing the Django 2 module for Python 3, and configuring the GeoDjango components, depends on a number of steps. These include:

1. Using `pip` to install Django 2
2. Installing and enabling a spatial database (if not already installed)
3. Installing GDAL/ OGR/PROJ4/GEOS
4. Configuring the Windows environment variables
5. Generating a project
6. Opening `settings.py`
7. Adding `django.contrib.gis` to `INSTALLED_APPS`
8. Configuring database settings to point to the spatial database

Installing Django

Django 2 is hosted in **Python Package Index (PyPI)**, so use `pip` to install it. It can also be downloaded and installed manually. Using `pip` to install Django will also install the required dependency, `pytz`. Django will be downloaded from PyPI as a wheel and installed.

Because Django 2 is a major update which has been recently released, we have to ensure that `pip` installs the correct version. With this command, we will install Django 2.0:

```
C:\Python36\Scripts>pip install Django==2.0
```

The module will be installed, along with the supporting modules:

```
Collecting Django==2.0
  Downloading Django-2.0-py3-none-any.whl (7.1MB)
    100% |                                    | 7.1MB 173kB/s
Collecting pytz (from Django==2.0)
  Using cached pytz-2017.3-py2.py3-none-any.whl
Installing collected packages: pytz, Django
Successfully installed Django-2.0 pytz-2017.3
```

Django 2.0 is used in this chapter. Use the latest version of Django 2 available to start a project. Check out Django 2.0 documentation (as well as other Django versions) here: https://www.djangoproject.com/.

> If you are using virtual environments, you can specify a specific version of Django for each environment. If not, and you have multiple versions of Python installed, be sure to use the correct `pip` version to install Django within the `Python 3` folder structure.

Installing PostGIS and psycopg2

This chapter will use PostGIS. Refer to `Chapter 7`, *Geoprocessing with Geodatabases*, if you do not have PostGIS installed on your machine as it explains how to install the spatial extension add-on to PostgreSQL. Also, ensure that the `psycopg2` module is installed by using the following code:

```
C:\Python36\Scripts>pip install psycopg2
```

Creating the database

Generating the database table is made possible by the `Chapter12_0.py` script, which creates a PostgreSQL database called `chapter12` and adds spatial functionality to the new database. Adjust the credentials, host, and port (as needed) in the connection configuration below.

Connect to the database server using `psycopg2` and its `connect` function, which creates a `connection` class. The class has a `cursor` function that creates a `cursor` object, which is able to execute SQL statements. This section creates the database for the chapter:

```
import psycopg2
connection = psycopg2.connect(host='localhost',
user='{user}',password='{password}', port="5432")
connection.autocommit = True
cursor = connection.cursor()
cursor.execute('CREATE DATABASE chapter12')
```

To make the database geospatial, ensure that the PostGIS spatial add-on has been installed. Connect to the new database and pass the following SQL statement, which adds the spatial functionality tables to the database:

```
import psycopg2
connection = psycopg2.connect(dbname='chapter12', host='localhost',
user='{user}', password='{password}', port="5432")
cursor = connection.cursor()
connection.autocommit = True
cursor.execute('CREATE EXTENSION postgis')
connection.close()
```

The PostGIS database for this chapter is now created and spatially enabled.

GDAL/OGR

Django's built-in geospatial support requires the use of code libraries available from the **Open Source Geospatial Foundation (OSGeo)**. The GDAL library, which includes OGR, handles vector and raster datasets. It must be installed (see Chapter 5, *Vector Data Analysis*, and Chapter 6, *Raster Data Processing*, for more details on using it for analysis).

If it is not already installed, use the OSGeo4W installer available at: `https://trac.osgeo.org/osgeo4w/`. Select the correct installer for your machine. The installer will also install QGIS and GRASS and other open source geospatial programs. Download and run the installer and place the output files on your local drive. This file path (for example: `C:\OSGeo4w`) will be important when modifying the Windows environment variables.

 Find installation instructions for configuring GeoDjango for Linux and macOS from the Django project documentation here: `https://docs.djangoproject.com/en/2.0/ref/contrib/gis/install/`.

Modifying Windows environment variables

Editing the system path and other environment variables within Windows requires administrative permissions. Here are the steps to edit them for our purposes:

1. Log into an account with administrative permissions.
2. Open Windows Explorer and right-click on the PC icon in the left pane.
3. Select **Properties** from the context menu.
4. Click on **Advanced system settings**.
5. In the next menu, click on **Environment Variables**.
6. Select **Path** from the system variables and click **Edit** (or double-click on the path value).
7. Add the file path of the `bin` folder in the `OSGeo4W` folder (for example, `C:\OSGeo4W\bin`) to the path:

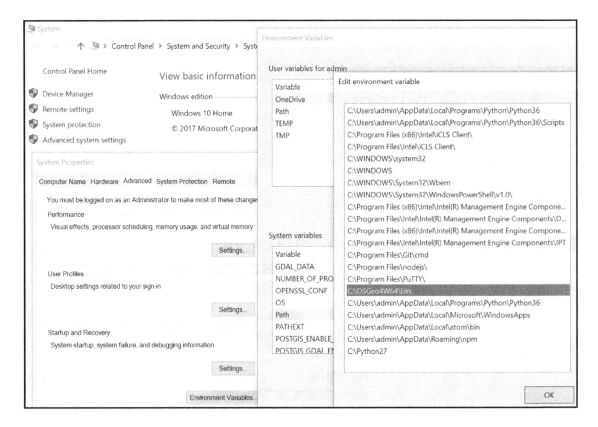

The `Python 3.6` folder has also been added to the path in this example, as well as `Python 2.7`, which is ordered behind `Python 3.6` because of its position in the path environment variable value. This means that when Python is passed to a command line, the `Python 3.6` executable will be run.

Two other variables that may be required are the **GDAL_DATA** variable and the **PROJ_LIB** variable. If PostGIS has been installed, it will have created a **GDAL_DATA** variable already, but if it is not present, click the **New** button underneath the system variables box. Add the name of the variable (**GDAL_DATA**) and the variable value (for example, `C:\OSGeo4W64\share\gdal`).

Add the **PROJ_LIB** variable the same way:

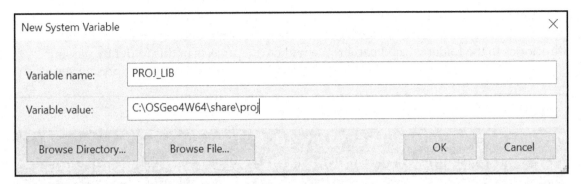

Click **OK** to save the new variables, and **OK** again to get out of the first settings dialog. Close the **System Properties** menu.

Creating a project and application

Now that Django is installed, let's create a project. Django has two levels that are managed by scripts accepting command-line arguments. These two levels are projects and applications. A project can have many applications, and sometimes an application has multiple projects as well. This organization allows you to reuse of code between related applications, governed by project-level code.

Django uses an administration file, `django-admin.py`, to control the creation of projects. It is installed in the `Scripts` folder of the `Python 3` folder. I usually copy the `django-admin.py` file into a new project folder, and pass the required command-line arguments while working in the project folder, but it can also be called from the command line if the `Scripts` folder is included in the path environment variable.

Create a folder for your project; something like `C:\Projects`. Copy `django-admin.py` into `C:\Projects`.

Command-line argument – startproject

A command-line argument is used with `django-admin.py` to create the project—`startproject`. To create a project, open the command prompt and change directories to the folder created earlier. We will create projects in this folder by passing `startproject` and the name of our new project (`chapter12`) to `django-admin.py`:

```
Command Prompt
Microsoft Windows [Version 10.0.15063]
(c) 2017 Microsoft Corporation. All rights reserved.

C:\Users\admin>cd C:\Projects

C:\Projects>django-admin.py startproject chapter12

C:\Projects>
```

What is created by startproject?

By passing the two arguments to `django-admin.py`, `startproject`, and `chapter12` (the name of the project), a folder is created with a number of scripts and subfolders. The outer (`root`) folder is called `chapter12`, and it contains an important script called `manage.py`, and a folder also called `chapter12`, which is the project folder:

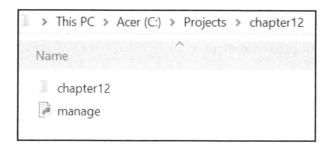

Inside the project folder are some important scripts, including `settings.py` and `urls.py`:

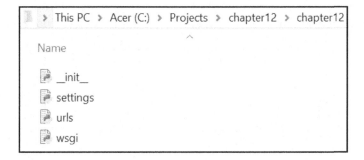

These files are default placeholders, waiting for us to configure our project and applications. We will edit `setting.py` and `urls.py` too, with the specifics of our project as we go along. The third file, `wsgi.py`, is used for production deployment of the web application.

Creating an application using manage.py

Now, the `root` folder, `Projects` folder, and associated scripts have been created. Within the `root` folder is the `manage.py` file, which is used for configuration and management of the applications and project. In this section, we'll create an application using `manage.py` and the command-line argument `startapp`.

With the command prompt, change directories into the `root` folder. Unlike `django-admin.py`, we have to run `manage.py` by passing it as an argument to the Python executable. In turn, to `manage.py` we pass the argument `startapp` and the name of the application, `arenas`. It should look like this:

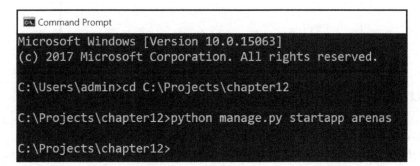

What is created by manage.py

Passing the `startapp arenas` command to `manage.py` created a folder called `arenas`. All applications are created within the `root` folder, next to the project folder:

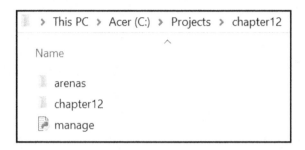

Inside the folder are auto-generated scripts that we will configure and add to later. There is also a folder called `migrations`, which is used by Django to store scripts describing edits to the database. The scripts `admin.py`, `models.py`, and `views.py` will be used in this chapter:

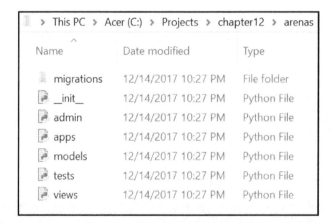

Configuring settings.py

With the project created and a new application, the next step towards using GeoDjango is to configure the `settings.py` script contained in the project folder. We'll add the specifics about the database connection (user, password, database name, and so on), and adjust the `INSTALLED_APPS` setting.

Adding a new database connection

Using IDLE or another IDE, open `settings.py` from the `chapter12` project folder. Scroll down to the variable called `DATABASES`. This variable, which is set to a local SQLite database, will be adjusted to the PostgreSQL database with the PostGIS extension.

This is the default:

```
DATABASES = {
    'default': {
        'ENGINE': 'django.db.backends.sqlite3',
        'NAME': os.path.join(BASE_DIR, 'db.sqlite3'),
    }
}
```

Change it to the following, substituting the `username` and `password` for your PostGIS installation (see `Chapter 3`, *Introduction to Geospatial Databases*):

```
DATABASES = {
    'default': {
        'ENGINE': 'django.contrib.gis.db.backends.postgis',
        'NAME': 'chapter12',
        'USER': '{username}',
        'PASSWORD': '{password}',
        'HOST': '127.0.0.1',
        'PORT':'5432'
    },
}
```

An empty string can also be used for the `HOST` option to indicate `localhost`. If the PostgreSQL installation is on a different machine, adjust the `HOST` option to the IP address of the database server. If it is on a different port, adjust the `PORT` option.

Save the script, but don't close it.

Adding new installed apps

Within `settings.py`, scroll to the variable `INSTALLED_APPS`. This lists the built-in, core applications used to support our application. To it, we'll add `django.contrib.gis`, the built-in Django GIS application, and our own new application, Arenas.

`INSTALLED_APPS` is a list and can be edited. Initially, `INSTALLED_APPS` looks like this:

```
INSTALLED_APPS = [
    'django.contrib.admin',
    'django.contrib.auth',
```

```
        'django.contrib.contenttypes',
        'django.contrib.sessions',
        'django.contrib.messages',
        'django.contrib.staticfiles',
    ]
```

Edit it to look like this:

```
INSTALLED_APPS = [
    'django.contrib.admin',
    'django.contrib.auth',
    'django.contrib.contenttypes',
    'django.contrib.sessions',
    'django.contrib.messages',
    'django.contrib.staticfiles',
    'django.contrib.gis',
    'arenas',
]
```

Save `settings.py` and close the script. Now we've added our custom arenas app and Django's GIS library to the installed app package manager, so GeoDjango is now configured. Next, we'll use `manage.py` and OGR to read shapefiles and automatically generate data models.

Creating the application

This application will perform geospatial analysis using the geometry fields of database tables. To make this possible, we have to create and populate the database tables using shapefiles and a built-in method called `LayerMapping`.

The completed application will need URL pattern matching to link URLs with the views that will process the requests and return the response. Templates will be used to pass processed data to the browser. Views will be written to be able to handle both `POST` and `GET` requests and to redirect to other views.

Now that GeoDjango is configured, the NBA Arenas application can be created using the Django project management script called `manage.py`.

manage.py

The script `manage.py` performs a number of jobs to help set up and manage the project. For testing purposes, it can create a local web server (using `runserver` as the argument); it manages database schema migrations, generating tables from data models (using `makemigration` and `migrate`); it even has a built-in Python 3 shell (using `shell`) for testing and more:

```
C:\Projects\chapter12>python manage.py shell
Python 3.6.3 (v3.6.3:2c5fed8, Oct  3 2017, 18:11:49) [MSC v.1900 64 bit (AMD64)] on win32
Type "help", "copyright", "credits" or "license" for more information.
(InteractiveConsole)
>>>
```

In this section, we'll use `manage.py` to create and populate database tables, using shapefiles as the data and schema source.

Generating data models

After configuring GeoDjango, a new available function in `manage.py` is available, `ogrinspect`, which automatically generates data table models with geometry columns that can be placed in `models.py`. By inspecting or reading the shapefile data using OGR, Django's built-in functionality creates a Python class data model and a field mapping dictionary that maps between the names of shapefile fields and database columns.

For this section, we will use the shapefiles downloaded in `Chapter 11`, *Flask and GeoAlchemy2*. They are also available in the code package. Copy the four shapefiles (and all of the associated files) into a folder called `data` within the arenas application folder:

« Acer (C:) › Packt › PythonScripting › Chapters › Chapter12 › Scripts › chapter12 › arenas › data			
Name	Date modified	Type	Size
Arenas_NBA.shp	10/25/2017 1:18 PM	SHP File	1 KB
Congressional_Districts.shp	10/30/2017 8:17 PM	SHP File	7,276 KB
US_County_Boundaries.shp	10/30/2017 8:18 PM	SHP File	91,028 KB
US_States.shp	10/30/2017 8:22 PM	SHP File	45,607 KB

Open a command prompt, and change the directory to the project folder. The `data` folder with the four shapefiles (`Arenas_NBA.shp`, `US_States.shp`, `US_County_Boundaries.shp`, and `Congressional_Districts.shp`) will be inspected to generate data models using `manage.py`. The results are copied to `models.py`. From these models, the database tables will be generated, and then the tables will be populated using the field mapping dictionaries:

```
C:\Projects\chapter12>python manage.py ogrinspect
arenas\data\Arenas_NBA.shp Arenas --srid=4326 --mapping
```

This command will produce a data model with a geometry column and a `4326` SRID. The field mapping dictionary, generated by the `--mapping` option, is a Python dictionary that maps between the keys (data model column names) and the values (shapefile field names). This is a part of the output:

```
C:\Projects\chapter12>python manage.py ogrinspect arenas\data\Arenas_NBA.shp Arenas --srid=4326 --mapping
# This is an auto-generated Django model module created by ogrinspect.
from django.contrib.gis.db import models


class Arenas(models.Model):
    sector = models.CharField(max_length=30)
    subsector = models.CharField(max_length=22)
    primary_ty = models.CharField(max_length=45)
    date_creat = models.CharField(max_length=15)
    date_modif = models.CharField(max_length=24)
    comp_affil = models.CharField(max_length=29)
    name1 = models.CharField(max_length=66)
```

Copy the output, including the `import` line, data model, and the field mapping dictionary into `arenas\models.py`. Copy the `import` line over the data model class definition over the auto-generated `import` line in `models.py`.

Copying from the command line is easy when the **Quick Edit** option is turned on in the command prompt defaults. Once it is on, select text by dragging the mouse. Push *Enter* when the text block has been selected.

Multipolygons

For the three other shapefiles with multipolygon geometry types, we'll pass the argument—`multi` to `manage.py` and `ogrinspect`. Using this option generates a `MultiPolygon` geometry column in the data model.

This command generates a data model from the US States shapefile:

```
C:\Projects\chapter12>python manage.py ogrinspect arenas\data\US_States.shp
US_States \
      --srid=4326 --mapping --multi
```

The output will look like this:

```
# This is an auto-generated Django model module created by ogrinspect.
from django.contrib.gis.db import models
class US_States(models.Model):
    stfips = models.CharField(max_length=2)
    state = models.CharField(max_length=66)
    stpostal = models.CharField(max_length=2)
    version = models.CharField(max_length=2)
    dotregion = models.IntegerField()
    shape_leng = models.FloatField()
    shape_area = models.FloatField()
    geom = models.MultiPolygonField(srid=4326)
# Auto-generated `LayerMapping` dictionary for US_States model
    us_states_mapping = {
    'stfips': 'STFIPS',
    'state': 'STATE',
    'stpostal': 'STPOSTAL',
    'version': 'VERSION',
    'dotregion': 'DotRegion',
    'shape_leng': 'Shape_Leng',
    'shape_area': 'Shape_Area',
    'geom': 'MULTIPOLYGON',
}
```

Copy the output to `models.py`, including both the data model and the field mapping dictionary. Repeat the process for the counties and districts shapefiles by adjusting the arguments to `manage.py` (that is, the shapefile name and the table name), and save `models.py` once the models have been added.

Database migrations

Django uses a concept of database migrations to record and execute changes to the database. These changes include table creation and schema alterations. Now that we have generated the data models, we need to migrate the database, which involves inspecting `models.py` for changes, calculating the SQL syntax to generate the database alterations, and then running the required migrations to make the database table columns match their `models.py` code definitions. These migrations can also be reverted.

makemigrations

To start the migration, pass `makemigrations` to `manage.py`. This argument will start the migration process by inspecting the contents of `models.py`. All of the Python class data models will be read, and the corresponding SQL is generated:

```
C:\Projects\chapter12>python manage.py makemigrations
Migrations for 'arenas':
  arenas\migrations\0001_initial.py
    - Create model Arenas
    - Create model Counties
    - Create model Districts
    - Create model US_States
```

A new script has been generated and added to the `migrations` folder. This initial database migration script creates a `Migration` class and includes a number of migration operations using the `CreateModel` method. Each of these migrations creates operations will generate a new (empty) table in the `chapter12` database. `Migration` classes also have methods for performing table alterations, when you need to add or remove fields.

sqlmigrate

Use the command `sqlmigrate` to see the SQL statements generated from the `makemigration` operation. Pass `sqlmigrate`, the application label (`arenas`), and the migration name (`0001`) to `manage.py` to generate the output:

```
C:\Projects\chapter12>python manage.py sqlmigrate arenas 0001
BEGIN;
--
-- Create model Arenas
--
CREATE TABLE "arenas_arenas" ("id" serial NOT NULL PRIMARY KEY, "sect
or" varchar(30) NOT NULL, "subsector" varchar(22) NOT NULL, "primary_
ty" varchar(45) NOT NULL, "date_creat" varchar(15) NOT NULL, "date_mo
```

All of the data models have been translated to SQL, with definitions for primary keys and field lengths added automatically.

migrate

With the migration script generated, we can finally perform the database migration. This operation will generate the tables within the database specified in `settings.py`.

Pass the argument `migrate` to `manage.py`:

```
C:\Projects\chapter12>python manage.py migrate
```

The result of the operation should look like this:

```
Operations to perform:
  Apply all migrations: admin, arenas, auth, contenttypes, sessions
Running migrations:
  Applying contenttypes.0001_initial... OK
  Applying auth.0001_initial... OK
  Applying admin.0001_initial... OK
  Applying admin.0002_logentry_remove_auto_add... OK
  Applying arenas.0001_initial... OK
  Applying contenttypes.0002_remove_content_type_name... OK
  Applying auth.0002_alter_permission_name_max_length... OK
  Applying auth.0003_alter_user_email_max_length... OK
  Applying auth.0004_alter_user_username_opts... OK
  Applying auth.0005_alter_user_last_login_null... OK
  Applying auth.0006_require_contenttypes_0002... OK
  Applying auth.0007_alter_validators_add_error_messages... OK
  Applying auth.0008_alter_user_username_max_length... OK
  Applying auth.0009_alter_user_last_name_max_length... OK
  Applying sessions.0001_initial... OK
```

The database tables have been created in the database. Open pgAdmin4 (or another database GUI tool) to check on the tables within the database, or open psql and use the command line interface.

> Explore the Django documentation to explore all of the available arguments for `django-admin.py` and `manage.py`:
> https://docs.djangoproject.com/en/2.0/ref/django-admin/.

LayerMapping

To populate the database tables created from the shapefiles, Django has a built-in concept called `LayerMapping`. By using the field mapping dictionary generated by `manage.py`, along with the `LayerMapping` class from `django.contrib.gis.utils`, the data contained in the shapefiles can be extracted and loaded into the database tables. To instantiate a `LayerMapping` instance, we will pass the data model, the associated field mapping, and the location of the shapefile to the class.

Create a new file called `load.py` and save it inside the Arenas application. Add this line to the file:

```
import os
from django.contrib.gis.utils import LayerMapping
from .models import US_States, Counties, Arenas, Districts
```

Open `models.py` and copy all of the field mapping dictionaries into `load.py`. Then, use the `os` module to assign the shapefile path to a variable. Here is the dictionary and path variable for `US_County_Boundary.shp`:

```
us_counties_mapping = {
'stfips' : 'STFIPS', 'ctfips' : 'CTFIPS', 'state' : 'STATE', 'county' :
'COUNTY',
'version' : 'VERSION', 'shape_leng' : 'Shape_Leng', 'shape_area' :
'Shape_Area', 'geom' : 'MULTIPOLYGON'
}
counties_shp = os.path.abspath(os.path.join(os.path.dirname(__file__),
'data','US_County_Boundaries.shp'),
)
```

Repeat this step for all of the shapefiles, as demonstrated in the `load.py` provided in the code package. These path variables and mapping dictionaries are required to perform the layer mapping.

Running the layer mapping

At the bottom of `load.py`, create a function called `run` that contains the following code. Note that the names of the mappings (for example, `us_states_mapping`) will have to match the names of the dictionaries:

```
def run(verbose=True):
    lm = LayerMapping(
        US_States, states_shp, us_states_mapping,
        transform=False, encoding='iso-8859-1',
    )
```

```
lm.save(strict=True, verbose=verbose)
lm = LayerMapping(
    Counties, counties_shp, us_counties_mapping,
    transform=False, encoding='iso-8859-1',
)
lm.save(strict=True, verbose=verbose)
lm = LayerMapping(
    Districts, districts_shp, districts_mapping,
    transform=False, encoding='iso-8859-1',
)
lm.save(strict=True, verbose=verbose)
lm = LayerMapping(
    Arenas, arenas_shp, arenas_mapping,
    transform=False, encoding='iso-8859-1',
)
lm.save(strict=True, verbose=verbose)
```

To run the script, we will use the `manage.py shell` argument to invoke a Python shell, and then import the `load.py` file and execute the `run` function inside this local shell:

```
>>> from arenas import load
>>> load.run()
```

Once the `run` function is called and executed, the rows of data in the shapefiles are imported into the database tables:

```
C:\Projects\chapter12>python manage.py shell
Python 3.6.3 (v3.6.3:2c5fed8, Oct  3 2017, 18:11:49) [MSC v.1900 64 bit (AMD64)] on win32
Type "help", "copyright", "credits" or "license" for more information.
(InteractiveConsole)
>>> from arenas import load
>>> load.run()
Saved: US_States object (1)
Saved: US_States object (2)
Saved: US_States object (3)
Saved: US_States object (4)
Saved: US_States object (5)
```

Once the function completes successfully, the database tables will be populated. We can now explore a very useful feature of Django—the built-in admin panel.

Administrative panel

The Django framework was developed in a busy newsroom environment, and from the beginning, it required a built-in administrative panel that would allow reporters and editors to access their stories. This concept has continued to be supported, as most websites require an interface for administrative tasks. It's a very useful and convenient interface that requires no technical knowledge about the site to use.

GeoDjango administrative panel

Websites built with the GeoDjango configuration are no different, and the administrative panel for GeoDjango websites even supports the display and editing of geometry data. The OpenLayers JavaScript library is included in the panel template to allow for the data visualizations. It also allows for the normal administrative tasks such as editing groups or users and their permissions.

admin.py

To access the data models stored in models.py through the administrative panel, the autogenerated script called admin.py inside the Arenas application must be updated. Open the file in an IDE and add the following lines, copying the original code:

```
from django.contrib.gis import admin
from .models import US_States, Counties, Arenas, Districts
admin.site.register(US_States, admin.GeoModelAdmin)
admin.site.register(Counties, admin.GeoModelAdmin)
admin.site.register(Arenas, admin.GeoModelAdmin)
admin.site.register(Districts, admin.GeoModelAdmin)
```

Save the script and close it.

createsuperuser

The first step is to create a superuser. This user will be able to access the administrative panel. To do this, we will pass the createsuperuser argument to manage.py and follow the instructions as they appear one by one:

```
C:\Projects\chapter12>python manage.py createsuperuser
Username: loki
Email address: email@server.com
Password:
Password (again):
Superuser created successfully.
```

The superuser is now available for logging into the administrative panel, using the password and username supplied.

runserver

Once the superuser has been created, pass the `runserver` argument to `manage.py` to start the local development web server:

```
C:\Projects\chapter12>python manage.py runserver
Performing system checks...

System check identified no issues (0 silenced).
December 19, 2017 - 13:01:24
Django version 2.0rc1, using settings 'chapter12.settings'
Starting development server at http://127.0.0.1:8000/
Quit the server with CTRL-BREAK.
```

This will make the `localhost` open at port `8000` by default (`http://127.0.0.1:8000`). The administrative panel is available at: `http://127.0.0.1:8000/admin`. Open a web browser and navigate to the administrative panel URL. Enter the superuser credentials:

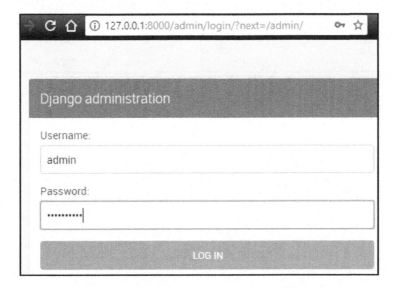

Once they are entered, the administrative panel will list the available models, as well as the authentication and authorization section. These models are initially shown with an **s** at the end of their name (pluralizing them by default). This behavior can (and should) be overridden, though we won't focus on that task here:

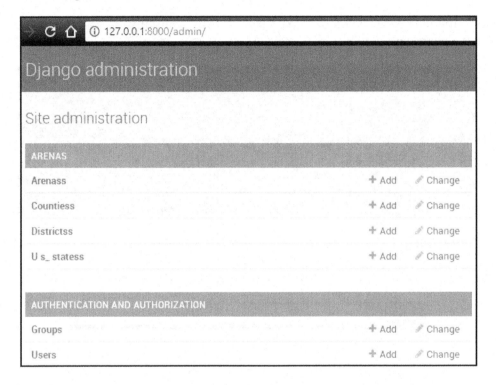

Click on the **U_s_statess** model under **ARENAS**, and then click on the first object in the list of states objects. It should look like this:

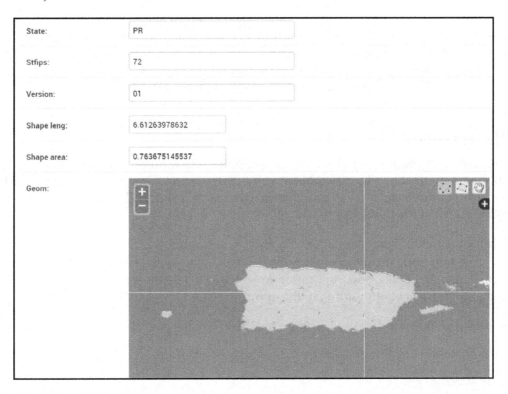

These fields can be edited through this administrative panel, and even the geometry of the state (or, in this case, Puerto Rico) can be edited using the OpenLayers editing plugin included. Click **Save** after any edits. The data row can also be deleted from this interface.

 Explore the complete administrative panel documentation here: https://docs.djangoproject.com/en/2.0/ref/contrib/admin/.

URLs

Finally, within the HTML form section, we designate where the description and a drop-down list will go and include a hidden token (CSRF), which is required for authentication.

With the models generated and data added to the associated tables, it's time to generate some views, which will process our web requests and return the data required to complete our request.

To correctly route our requests, we have to first create some URLs that will be paired with a view. This will require both project-level and application-level configuration. Unlike Flask, URLs are not attached to views using Python decorators. Instead, they are contained in separate scripts that will either map to an application or a view.

URL patterns

Django URL patterns are very clean and simple and make for nice websites where the URLs are short and memorable. To make this possible, there is matching of the requested URL with a view (or application-level URL that matches with a view). The URLs and their destination are matched inside a list called `urlpatterns`.

Within the project folder (`C:\Projects\chapter12\chapter12`), there is a script called `urls.py` just underneath `settings.py`. This script controls project-level URL routing. For this application, we'll also add application-level URLs inside the `arenas` folder and will point the project-level URL routing to the application URLs.

Open up the project-level `urls.py`, and copy the following code over any existing code:

```
from django.urls import include, path
from django.contrib.gis import admin
urlpatterns = [
  path('', include('arenas.urls')),
  path('arena/', include('arenas.urls')),
  path('admin/', admin.site.urls),
]
```

This code will redirect the requests to two different URLs in the application-level `urls.py` file, where they can be further sorted. Any requests sent to the admin URL are handled by the administrative code. The `path` function accepts two required parameters: the URL path (for example, `'arenas/'`, which goes to `http://127.0.0.1:8000/arenas`), and the view or application-level code that will accept the request. The `include` function is used to add the available URLs from the Arenas application into the project level URLs.

To create the application-level URLs, create a script called `urls.py` inside the Arenas application folder. Copy the following code:

```
from django.urls import path
from . import views
```

```
urlpatterns = [
    path('', views.index, name='index'),
    path('arena', views.arena, name='arena'),
]
```

This time, the function `path` directs requests to views (that will be) inside the `views.py` script. Both the base URL and the arena URL are redirected to a view. The optional parameter `name` is also included.

 Note that a major change in Django URL patterns was introduced in Django 2.0. Earlier Django versions do not use the `path` function but use a similar function called `url`. Ensure that you are using the newest version of Django to match the code here.

Views

Views are at the heart of the application, and in Django take the form of Python functions. They accept both `GET` and `POST` web requests, allowing for multiple actions, with various responses, to occur inside the same function. Within view functions, we design how the request is parsed, how database tables are queried, how the query results (**QuerySets** in Django) are processed, and which forms and templates are sent to the browser along with the processed data.

Now that the URL patterns are in place, we need to write some views that will accept and process the web requests sent to the URLs. These views will query the database table model classes in `models.py` to find the location data associated with each NBA arena included in the `Arenas` class.

Required folders and files

The first step is to create the necessary folders with files of forms and templates, as web responses from the views require a pre-generated template that can display the requested data (in this case, the location of the NBA `arena` requested).

forms.py

A web form is used in Django to capture user input and submit it to a view. To make it possible to select an NBA `arena` name from a drop-down list and have the web map zoom to that location, a new script, `forms.py`, must be created. Open an IDE and copy the following code into a new file:

```
from django import forms
from .models import Arenas
class ArenaForm(forms.Form):
    name = ""
    description = "Use the dropdown to select an arena."
    selections =
    forms.ChoiceField(choices=Arenas.objects.values_list('id','name1'),
                            widget=forms.Select(),required=True)
```

This section creates a form class by subclassing from `forms.Form`. It has a `name` field, a `description` field, and a `ChoiceField`. The `ChoiceField` will create a drop-down list, populated by the IDs and names of the `arenas`. Other fields will be added to the `ArenaForm` class within the view and are not defined here. This form and its fields will be inserted into the template created in the next section. Save this file as `forms.py` into the Arenas application folder.

templates folder

Copy the `templates` folder from the completed code package into the Arenas application folder. Inside the `templates` folder is a folder called `arenas`, with a template HTML file called `index.html`. This file contains a JavaScript portion that generates a web map. On that map, the location of an NBA `arena` is displayed.

Django templates use placeholders (demarcated with a `{{form.field }}` format) that allow for data to be passed at runtime into the template, providing the specifics of the request. These placeholders are located throughout `index.html`. Django has its own built-in template language, which we will use here, and also includes Jinja2, which Flask also uses (see `Chapter 11`, *Flask and GeoAlchemy2*).

The first portion of `index.html` is to highlight is where the `longitude` and `latitude` of the current NBA `arena` have been added to the Leaflet JavaScript, which centers the map window on that location at zoom level `13`:

```
var themap = L.map('map').setView([ {{form.latitude}},
{{form.longitude}}], 13);
```

The next portion to highlight is where the `longitude`, `latitude`, and custom `popup` about the current NBA `arena` are added to a marker:

```
L.marker([ {{form.latitude}},{{form.longitude}}]).addTo(themap)
.bindPopup("{{form.popup}}").openPopup();
```

Finally, within the HTML `form` section, we designate where the `description` and a drop-down list will go and include a hidden token (CSRF), which is required for authentication of the `POST` request. The button is generated by the input HTML:

```
<form method="post" class="form">
   <h3>{{form.name}}</h3>
   <h4>{{form.description}}</h4>
   {{form.selections}}
   <br>
   <input type="submit" value="Find Data">
   {% csrf_token %}
</form>
```

All of these placeholders will be populated when the view is processed and data is returned to the requesting browser.

Writing views

Everything is finally set to write our views. Open up `views.py` from the Arenas application folder within an IDE. Import the required libraries, models, forms, and modules:

```
from django.shortcuts import render, redirect
from django.http import HttpResponse, HttpResponseNotFound
from .models import US_States, Counties, Districts, Arenas
from .forms import ArenaForm
from django.views.decorators.http import require_http_methods
import random
```

Next, we will create two views—`index` and `arena`, and one non-view function called `queryarena`. These match with the URLs we added to `urls.py`. The return from the `index` function is very simple—it will redirect to the function `arena`. For the views, a decorator is used to determine the HTTP request methods allowed.

index view

The `index` view is a Python function that accepts the request data and redirects it to the `arena` view, with a decorator (`require_http_methods`) prior to restricting the HTTP requests allowed:

```
@require_http_methods(["GET", "POST"])
def index(request):
    return redirect(arena)
```

queryarena function

The `arena` function below selects a random `arena` for the initial GET request, getting data from the database model about the selected NBA `arena`. The queries themselves are handled by the `queryarena` function.

In this function, the name of the selected `arena` is accepted as a parameter. It is used to query (or `filter`) all of the `Arenas` model objects. This **object-relational mapping (ORM)** `filter` method requires a field as a parameter; in this case, the field is called `name1`. As an example of what the `filter` is doing, if the name of the `arena` is *Oracle Arena*, the `filter` translated to English would be *find all NBA arenas with the name Oracle Arena*. The results of the `filter` method are returned as a list, so the first result is retrieved from the list using zero-indexing. A result is an object representing the data row from the `Arenas` class that met the `filter` parameters:

```
def queryarena(name):
    arena = Arenas.objects.filter(name1=name)[0]
    state = US_States.objects.filter(geom__intersects=arena.geom)
    if state:
        state = state[0]
        county = Counties.objects.filter(geom__contains=arena.geom)[0]
        district = Districts.objects.filter(geom__contains=arena.geom)[0]
        popup = "This arena is called " + arena.name1 + " and it's
        located at "
        popup += str(round(arena.geom.x,5))+ "," +
        str(round(arena.geom.y,5) )
        popup += "It is located in " +state.state + " and in the county
        of " + county.county
        popup += " and in Congressional District " + district.district
        return arena.name1, arena.geom.y, arena.geom.x, popup
    else:
        return arena.name1, arena.geom.y, arena.geom.x, arena.name1 + "
        is not in the United States"
```

Once the `arena` object is instantiated, its geometry field is used in a `filter` operation. Instead of using a field to `filter`, however, this `filter` uses geospatial analysis. Passing `arena.geom` to the `geom__intersects` method (provided by GeoDjango) performs an intersect operation to find the state in which the `arena` resides. An if/else conditional checks to ensure that the `arena` is located in the United States (for instance, not Toronto's `arena`) to determine the correct value to return.

If the `arena` is located inside the United States, the `arena` geometry is again used to determine the `county` and congressional `district` that contain the `arena`. This time, the geospatial operation is `geom_contains`. The `filters` return a `county` object and a `district` object. They are used to generate the custom `popup` that will be added to the map marker on the leaflet map. This `popup` contains the `longitude` and `latitude` of the `arena`, the name of the `arena`, and the name of its `county`, `state`, and the number of the congressional `district` within its `state`.

arena view

The `arena` view accepts the `request` object and then instantiates an `ArenaForm` object to gather the data needed to respond to the `request`. A query of the `Arenas` model objects and its `values_list` method creates a Python list that contains tuples with the ID and name of every `arena`. The `request` method (either GET or POST) is used in a conditional to determine the appropriate response.

If a GET request is received (that is, the web page is first opened), a random `arena` object is generated and passed to the template, which shows the `arena` on the included map. To get a random `arena`, we use the list of `arena` names and IDs (values). Once the list is generated, a list comprehension is used to generate a new list containing `arena` names.

Using the `random` module and the # of names in the list (`length`) generates a random `index` that is used to select an `arena` name from the list. This `name` is then passed to the `queryarena` function, which populates the `form` with the `arena` name, location, and the `popup`.

These values are returned to the browser using the `render` function. This function is used to pass `forms` to templates along with the `request`, and knows where the `templates` folder is located inside the Arenas application:

```
@require_http_methods(["GET", "POST"])
def arena(request):
    values = Arenas.objects.values_list('id','name1')
    if request.method=="GET":
        form= ArenaForm(request.GET)
        names = [name for id, name in values]
        length = len(names)
        selectname = names[random.randint(0, length-1)]
        form.name, form.latitude, form.longitude, form.popup =
queryarena(selectname)
        return render(request, "arena/index.html", {"form":form})
    else:
        form= ArenaForm(request.POST)
```

```
if form.is_valid():
    selectid = int(request.POST['selections'])
    selectname = [name for ids, name in values if ids == selectid][0]
    form.name, form.latitude, form.longitude, form.popup =
    queryarena(selectname)
    return render(request, "arena/index.html", {"form":form})
```

If a POST request is received (that is, an arena was selected), an ArenaForm class is called by passing the POST data to the class, and the form is validated. The ID of the selected arena is used as a conditional in a list comprehension, allowing us to retrieve the name of the arena. The name is then passed to queryarena, and the details of its location are queried and added to the form before it is returned using render.

The views are complete and the script can be saved. The next step is to run the application.

Running the application

Open, the command prompt and change directories to the root folder (C:\Projects\chapter12). Start the local development server with the following command:

C:\Projects\chapter12>python manage.py runserver

The result should look like this:

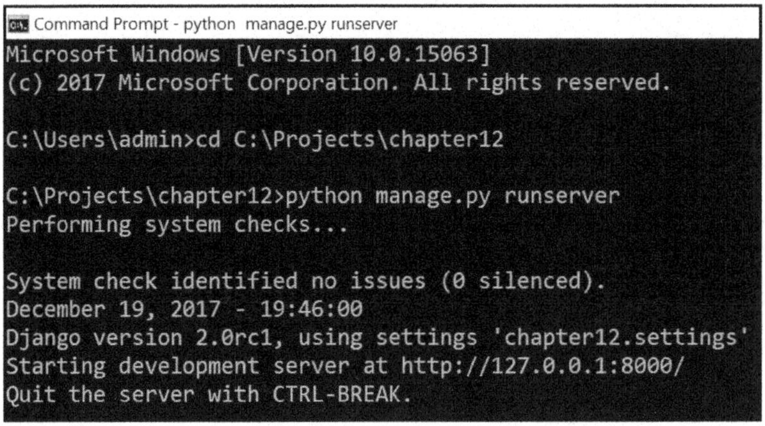

Open a browser and go to: `http://127.0.0.1:8000`. The initial `GET` request will be redirected to the `arenas` view and processed, returning a random `arena`. Selecting another `arena` from the list and pushing the **Find Data** button will perform a `POST` request and will locate the selected `arena`. Each time an `arena` is selected, the text of the `arena` name will change, along with the map location and popup displayed.

Here is an example of the results of a `POST` request:

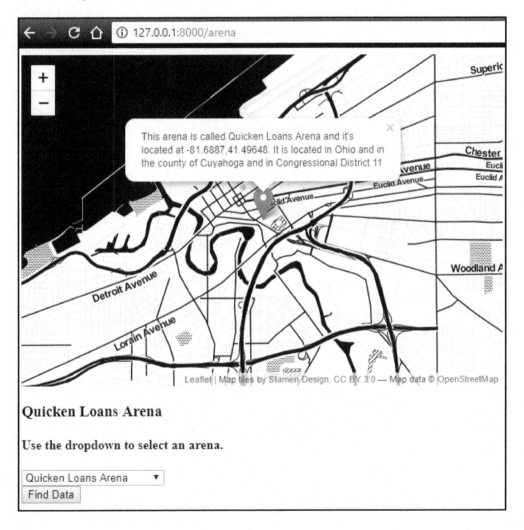

Test the application by selecting different NBA arenas, and for extra credit, change the popup message.

Summary

Django, with its batteries-included philosophy, creates complete applications with very few outside libraries required. This application performs data management and data analysis using only the Django built-in tools and the GDAL/OGR library. Enabling the GeoDjango functionality is a relatively seamless experience because it is an integral part of the Django project.

Creating web applications with Django allows for a lot of instant functionality, including the administrative panel. The LayerMapping makes it easy to import data from shapefiles. The ORM model makes it easy to perform geospatial filters or queries. The templating system makes it easy to add web maps as well as location intelligence to a website.

In the next chapter, we will use a Python web framework to create a geospatial REST API. This API will accept requests and return JSON encoded data representing geospatial features.

13
Geospatial REST API

Publishing data for consumption on the web is a major component of modern GIS. To transfer data from remote servers to remote clients, most geospatial publishing software stacks use **Representational State Transfer** (**REST**) web services. In response to web requests for specific data resources, REST services return **JavaScript Object Notation** (**JSON**)-encoded data to the requesting client machine. The web services are combined in an application programming interface, or API, which will contain the endpoints that represent each data resource available for querying.

By combining a Python web framework with **object-relational mapping** (**ORM**) and a PostGIS backend, we can create a custom REST API that will respond to web requests with JSON. For this exercise, we will use the Flask web framework and the SQLAlchemy module with GeoAlchemy2 providing spatial ORM capabilities.

In this chapter, we will learn about the following:

- REST API components
- JSON response formatting
- How to process GET, POST, PUT, and DELETE request methods
- Performing geospatial operations using the API
- How to deploy a Flask website using IIS

Writing a REST API in Python

To understand the components of a REST API with JSON response, we will utilize the Flask web framework, a PostgreSQL/PostGIS database, and SQLAlchemy and GeoAlchemy2 for ORM queries. Flask will be used to create the URL endpoints for the API. PostGIS will store the data in tables defined by SQLAlchemy models, which define the column types for all columns except the geometry columns, which are defined by GeoAlchemy2 column types.

REST

REST is a standard for web services, designed to accept requests and parameters and return a representation of that data, usually in a JSON format but sometimes in XML or HTML format. APIs that use REST architecture must meet these architectural constraints:

- Client-server interactions
- Statelessness
- Cacheablitity
- Uniform interface
- Layered system

The client (a web browser or a remote computer) will send a request to a server at a designated URL endpoint. The request can include parameters that limit the data objects returned, much like conditionals in an SQL statement. It is stateless, meaning that each request must contain the request parameters and cannot refer to the results of another request. The data returned must be explicitly marked as cacheable or non-cacheable, to allow clients to decide if the data can be stored, or must be requested when required. When data is requested, all available API endpoints relating to the data (including links for adding or deleting data, if available) are returned as links along with the data representation. The underlying architecture of the server is not revealed by the API and can be manipulated (machines added or removed) without any change in the API structure.

JSON

JSON is designed to be understood by humans and machines alike. JavaScript data objects are easily generated from Python dictionaries, as they use the same key value structure and curly bracket notation. Python contains a built-in library for generating JSON (the `json` module), and web frameworks such as Flask also include code for generating JSON responses.

Multiple JSON standards exist for geospatial data, including GeoJSON and Esri JSON. Within this chapter, the REST API will use the GeoJSON format to respond to requests.

 Read more about GeoJSON here: `http://geojson.org/`.

Python for REST API

Python is a fantastic language for writing a REST API. It has modules that allow for database queries and others that process the HTTP web requests into the URL and parameter components. Using these modules, the requested resource is retrieved from the database and returns the data as JSON using modules that convert between Python dictionaries and JSON objects.

While a Python-based API can be built using the standard library, using a web framework to build the API will speed up the development time and enable component modules to be added as needed.

Flask

Flask is a good choice for a Python web framework for a REST API. Partnered with SQLAlchemy and GeoAlchemy2 (see `Chapter 11`, *Flask and GeoAlchemy2*, for more information on both), it allows the REST URL endpoints to be paired with a view (a Python function) that will process the request in different ways depending on the request method (such as `GET` and `POST`, to name two examples) and return JSON data.

REST modules

As Flask is built to be extensible, there are many add-on modules that are designed to ease the creation of REST APIs. These include:

- Flask-RESTful (`https://flask-restful.readthedocs.io/en/latest/`)
- Eve (`http://python-eve.org/`), which is built on top of Flask and Cerberus
- Flask-REST-JSONAPI (`https://github.com/miLibris/flask-rest-jsonapi`)

This chapter will use vanilla Flask capabilities, along with SQLAlchemy and GeoAlchemy2 for database queries, to illustrate the basics of API creation.

Other frameworks

Django and GeoDjango (covered in `Chapter 12`, *GeoDjango*) are used extensively for REST API creation. With its batteries-included design motto, Django allows for easy API development. The Django REST framework adds easy API publication to the code base.

> **TIP**
>
> Explore the Django REST Framework here: `http://www.django-rest-framework.org/`.

Variables in Flask URLs

When using Flask for URL processing, it is useful to understand how to add variables into URLs, as each resource may be requested using an ID or string identifier (for example, a state name). Flask URLs use placeholders to pass data into function parameters and utilize it as variables within the view for each endpoint. Using a converter, numerical data can be assigned a type within the placeholder; the default is a string type.

Number converters

In this example, a placeholder with a converter for an integer ID is added at the end of the URL. By adding `int:` before the placeholder variable (`arena_id`), the ID can be used to query the `Arena` model/database table using the `get(id)` method of `session.query`, which expects an integer. If the datatype converter is not specified in the placeholder, the `arena_id` variable will contain a string character and won't be used by the `get(id)` method:

```
@app.route('/nba/api/v0.1/arena/<int:arena_id>', methods=['GET'])
def get_arena(arena_id):
  arena = session.query(Arena).get(arena_id)
```

With the parameter datatype specified, the requested `arena` object is returned by the ORM query and can be processed for a response.

Other data converters

Besides integers, which use the converter `int`, floating point data can be converted using `float`, and URL data can be converted using `path`. Strings, which use the converter `string`, are the default. In this case, a `float` value is captured and used to compare against `county` geometry areas. As the SRID for this data is in WKID, the area is in an odd format, but this query will work:

```
@app.route('/nba/api/v0.1/county/query/size/<float:size>', methods=['GET'])
def get_county_size(size):
  counties = session.query(County).filter(County.geom.ST_Area() >
size).all()
```

```
data = [{"type": "Feature",
 "properties":{"name":county.name,"id":county.id
,"state":county.state.name},
 "geometry":{"type":"MultiPolygon",
"coordinates":[shapely.geometry.geo.mapping(to_shape(county.geom))["coordin
ates"]]},
 } for county in counties]
 return jsonify({"type": "FeatureCollection","features":data})
```

In this example, the value captured from the URL variable is compared to the county geometry using the ST_Area function, which borrows from PostGIS spatial SQL.

 Read more about GeoAlchemy2 spatial functionality, and its use of spatial SQL, here: http://geoalchemy-2.readthedocs.io/en/latest/spatial_functions.html.

Request methods

When using a REST API, multiple HTTP request methods can be utilized. The GET method is used to request data, the POST method is used to add new data, the PUT method is used to update data, and the DELETE method is used to remove data from the database.

GET

For Flask URL endpoints, GET requests are specified using the method GET. Data can be passed as an argument and accessed using request.args:

```
from flask import requests, jsonify
@app.route('/nba/api/v0.1/arenas', methods=['GET'])
def get_arenas():
  if 'name' in request.args:
      arenas = session.query(Arena).filter(name=request.args['name'])
  else:
      arenas = session.query(Arena).all()
  data = [{"type": "Feature",  "properties":{"name":arena.name,
"id":arena.id},
  "geometry":{"type":"Point","coordinates":[round(arena.longitude,6),
round(arena.latitude,6)]},
  } for arena in arenas]
  return jsonify({"type": "FeatureCollection","features":data})
```

The response data, processed into a list of Python dictionaries using a list comprehension, is added to another Python dictionary, and then converted to JSON using `jsonify` from Flask.

POST

The `POST` requests carry data that can be processed to add to a database. To differentiate a `POST` request, the Flask requests object has the `method` property, which can be checked to see if the request method was `GET` or `POST`. If we create a `form` (called `AddForm`) to add new arenas to the `Arenas` table, we could process the data submitted as a `POST` request and add it the database using the session manager:

```
from flask import request
from .forms import AddForm
@app.route('/nba/api/v0.1/arena/add', methods=['GET', 'POST'])
def add_arenas():
  form = AddForm(request.form)
  form.name.data = "New Arena"
  form.longitude.data = -121.5
  form.latitude.data = 37.8
  if request.method == "POST":
    arena = Arena()
    arena.name = request.form['name']
    arena.longitude =float(request.form['longitude'])
    arena.latitude = float(request.form['latitude'])
    arena.geom = 'SRID=4326;POINT({0} {1})'.format(arena.longitude,
arena.latitude)
    session.add(arena)
    data = [{"type": "Feature", "properties":{"name":arena.name},
    "geometry":{"type":"Point",
    "coordinates":[round(arena.longitude,6), round(arena.latitude,6)]},}]
    return jsonify({'added':'success',"type":
"FeatureCollection","features":data})
  return render_template('addarena.html', form=form)
```

As this method will accept both `GET` and `POST` requests, it sends a different response based on each request method.

Other available request methods

While GET and POST are the main request methods, others are available for processing data. For the example API, we will only use GET, and POST, and DELETE.

PUT

Similar to a POST request, a PUT request will carry data to update or add to a database. It will attempt to update the data multiple times to ensure complete transmission of the update.

DELETE

The DELETE method will remove a resource from the specified endpoint, for example, deleting an arena from the Arenas table. It requires a record identifier to specify the resource to be removed:

```
@app.route('/nba/api/v0.1/arena/delete/<int:arena_id>', methods=['DELETE'])
def delete_arena(arena_id):
  arena = session.query(Arena).delete(arena_id)
```

The REST API application

To enable access to a database of NBA Arenas, US States, US Counties, and US Congressional Districts, we will build a REST API. The API will allow for queries about tables and about specific table resources, that is, rows of data. It will also allow for geospatial queries.

Application components

The components of this application include:

- The database, created in Chapter 11, *Flask and GeoAlchemy2*, which contains the tables for NBA Arenas, US States, US Counties, and US Congressional Districts
- The app.py file, which initiates the application when called by a Python executable
- The application folder, which contains the application code and folders

- The __init__.py file, which makes the application folder into a module, defines the Flask object and connects to the database
- The views.py file, which defines the API endpoints, the view functions, and the return responses
- The models.py file, which defines the database table models as Python classes that subclass from SQLAlchemy
- The forms.py file, which defines the HTML forms
- The static and templates folders, which contain templates and data

Application folder and file structure

The example REST API requires specific files and folders to be created. The outer folder, called arenaapp, will contain the app.py file and the folder called application. Create the folder called arenaapp. Inside of it, create a folder called application. Inside of application, create the folders static and templates:

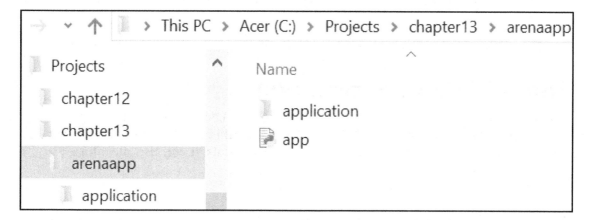

The other files, views.py, models.py, and forms.py, will be located inside of application. Two folders, static and templates, will store application data and HTML forms:

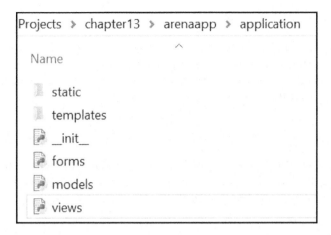

app.py

Using an IDE or text editor, create a file inside `arenaapp` called `app.py`. Open this file and add the following lines; this file will be run by the Python executable to initiate the REST API application:

```
from application import app
app.run()
```

The `__init__.py` file allows the `application` folder to be imported by `app.py`, allowing the Flask object `app` and its `app.run()` method to be called.

__init__.py

Within the `application` folder, create a file called `__init__.py`. Inside of the file, add the following code (while adjusting the username and password to your specific database credentials:

```
import flask
app = flask.Flask(__name__)
conn_string = 'postgresql://{user}:{password}@localhost:5432/chapter11'
app.config['SQLALCHEMY_DATABASE_URI'] = conn_string
app.config['SECRET_KEY'] = "SECRET_KEY"
import application.views
```

Within this file, the Flask object, `app`, is created and configured. To connect to the database, a connection string is used and stored in the `app.config` dictionary as the `'SQLALCHEMY_DATABASE_URI'`. Remember to add the username and password into the connection string.

The database

This will connect to the database created in `Chapter 11`, *Flask and GeoAlchemy2*. It is generated from shapefiles that have been imported and structured to match the models described as we proceed. To ensure that the application will work, be sure that the database has been created and that the shapefiles were imported.

models.py

Within `models.py`, the SQLAlchemy and GeoAlchemy2 modules are imported and the database session is initiated. The database models have their schemas defined as Python classes, allowing for queries and data updates.

Importing required modules

These modules enable the application to define the models and connect to the database:

```
# The database connections and session management are managed with
SQLAlchemy functions
from sqlalchemy import create_engine
from sqlalchemy.ext.declarative import declarative_base
from sqlalchemy import Column, Integer, String, ForeignKey, Float
from sqlalchemy.orm import sessionmaker, relationship
# The Geometry columns of the data tables are added to the ORM using the
Geometry data type
from geoalchemy2 import Geometry
```

Declaring the session

From the `app.config` dictionary, the database connection string is passed to the `create_engine` function. Once `engine` is bound to the `sessionmaker`, a `session` can be initiated:

```
from application import app
# Connect to the database called chapter11 using SQLAlchemy functions
engine = create_engine(app.config['SQLALCHEMY_DATABASE_URI'])
Session = sessionmaker(bind=engine)
session = Session()
Base = declarative_base()
```

A Python class called `Base` is created from the `declarative_base()` function. The `Base` class is then used to subclass all application classes.

Declaring the models

For the models, all of the field types (for example, `Integer`, `String`, and `Float`) are defined using SQLAlchemy ORM-column classes, except for the geometry columns, which use the GeoAlchemy2 `Geometry` class. The `Geometry` class requires a geometry type and SRID:

```
# Define the Arena class, which will model the Arena database table
class Arena(Base):
    __tablename__ = 'arena'
    id = Column(Integer, primary_key=True)
    name = Column(String)
    longitude = Column(Float)
    latitude = Column(Float)
    geom = Column(Geometry(geometry_type='POINT', srid=4326))
```

The `County` class has a primary key field and a `name` field, as well as fields that define the many-to-one relationship with the `State` class. Instead of a `POINT` geometry type, it uses `MULTIPOLYGON`:

```
# Define the County class, which will model the County database table
class County(Base):
    __tablename__ = 'county'
    id = Column(Integer, primary_key=True)
    name = Column(String)
    state_id = Column(Integer, ForeignKey('state.id'))
    state_ref = relationship("State",backref='county')
    geom = Column(Geometry(geometry_type='MULTIPOLYGON', srid=4326))
```

The `District` class represents US Congressional Districts. Stored with a `MULTIPOLYGON` geometry type and an SRID of `4326`, it has a many-to-one relationship with the `State` class. Each `district` stored is linked to the state in which it resides:

```
# Define the District class, which will model the District database table
class District(Base):
    __tablename__ = 'district'
    id = Column(Integer, primary_key=True)
    district = Column(String)
    name = Column(String)
    state_id = Column(Integer, ForeignKey('state.id'))
    state_ref = relationship("State",backref='district')
    geom = Column(Geometry(geometry_type='MULTIPOLYGON', srid=4326))
```

The State class has one-to-many relationships with the County and District classes respectively, defined using the relationship function. It also has a MULTIPOLYGON geometry column with an SRID of 4326:

```
# Define the State class, which will model the State database table
class State(Base):
    __tablename__ = 'state'
    id = Column(Integer, primary_key=True)
    name = Column(String)
    statefips = Column(String)
    stpostal = Column(String)
    counties = relationship('County', backref='state')
    districts = relationship('District', backref='state')
    geom = Column(Geometry(geometry_type='MULTIPOLYGON', srid=4326))
```

With the fields and relationships defined, the next step is to create the REST API endpoints and write the views that will query the database and return GeoJSON responses.

forms.py

To capture data from the user, such as a new arena, a form will be used. Create a file called forms.py inside the application folder, and add the following code:

```
from flask_wtf import FlaskForm
from wtforms import TextField, FloatField
class AddForm(FlaskForm):
  name = TextField('Arena Name')
  longitude = FloatField('Longitude')
  latitude = FloatField('Latitude')
```

This code will add the fields to a template, which will be discussed in the section on using POST methods. It will allow for code to be entered from an HTML template and passed to the server to add a new arena.

views.py

The API endpoints and processing are contained within views.py. The views are imported within __init__.py to make them available to the app object. Open an IDE and save a file called views.py inside the application folder.

Importing modules

To enable the processing of web requests, we need to import functionality from Flask, GeoAlchemy2, and Shapely, a Python module for creating and processing geospatial data. We will also `import` the models and forms:

```
from application import app
from flask import render_template,jsonify, redirect, url_for, request,
Markup
from .forms import *
from .models import *
import geoalchemy2,shapely
from geoalchemy2.shape import to_shape
```

Base URL

Each API pattern can be different, but should generally include a base URL that indicates the API version and should link to the other endpoints available within the API. This application will use a base URL pattern of `nba/api/v0.1`. In this case, the home URL (`'/'`) will `redirect` to the base URL of the API:

```
@app.route('/', methods=['GET'])
def get_api():
  return redirect('/nba/api/v0.1')

@app.route('/nba/api/v0.1', methods=['GET'])
def get_endpoints():
  data= [{'name':"Arena", "endpoint":"/arena"},
  {'name':"State", "endpoint":"/state"},
  {'name':"County", "endpoint":"/county"},
  {'name':"District", "endpoint":"/district"},]
  return jsonify({"endpoints":data})
```

The endpoints for each of the following sections are available from the base URL. Each resource URL can be constructed by adding the resource-specific endpoint to the base URL.

Arenas

To request data from the `Arenas` table, we will define API endpoints and use view functions to query the `Arenas` model. Each response will be a package as GeoJSON. This endpoint (`'/arena'`) will return a GeoJSON response, which will vary based on the presence of variables added to the URL. These variables include arena ID and name.

Getting all arenas

To generate a response containing a representation of all `arenas`, a query is made using the SQLAlchemy ORM. To convert the query results into GeoJSON, a list comprehension is used to generate a list of dictionaries that describe each `arena` returned from the ORM query. The resulting list (`data`) is then added to a dictionary, which is converted from a Python dictionary to a JSON object using the `jsonify` function:

```python
@app.route('/nba/api/v0.1/arena', methods=['GET'])
def get_arenas():
    arenas = session.query(Arena).all()
    data = [{"type": "Feature", "properties":{"name":arena.name,
"id":arena.id},
    "geometry":{"type":"Point", "coordinates":[round(arena.longitude,6),
round(arena.latitude,6)]},
    } for arena in arenas]
    return jsonify({"type": "FeatureCollection","features":data})
```

The `name` and `id` field is returned, as well as the `longitude` and `latitude`. To limit the amount of data transmitted, the `latitude` and `longitude` are rounded to 6 decimals. The low amount of precision required to describe the location of an `arena` makes this a reasonable limitation. While point data types are easier to return given that they consist of only two points, producing less data, polygon and polyline data are much larger and require more precision.

Compared to loops, list comprehensions decrease the processing time required for iterating over lists. Learn more about list comprehensions here:
https://docs.python.org/3/tutorial/datastructures.html#list-comprehensions.

Getting arenas by ID

By adding a numeric ID to the `arena` endpoint, the specific `arena` will be located and returned. The `session.query` method `get` is used to retrieve the requested `arena` object:

```python
@app.route('/nba/api/v0.1/arena/<int:arena_id>', methods=['GET'])
def get_arena(arena_id):
    arena = session.query(Arena).get(arena_id)
    data = [{"type": "Feature",  "properties":{"name":arena.name,
"id":arena.id},  "geometry":{"type":"Point",
"coordinates":[round(arena.longitude,6), round(arena.latitude,6)]},
    return jsonify({"type": "FeatureCollection","features":data})
```

The selected `arena` is added to a dictionary inside a list, which is then added to a dictionary and returned as JSON `data`.

Getting arenas by name

An `arena` can be requested by `name` at this endpoint. By utilizing a query condition, known as a `filter`, an `arena` matching the `name` provided will be retrieved. To add flexibility, a `like` operator is used (along with a `"%"` wildcard operator) to make it possible for the `arena name` entered to be complete. Instead, the string entered will be used to `filter` the query and return only `arena` objects whose names start with the string entered:

```
@app.route('/nba/api/v0.1/arena/<arena_name>', methods=['GET'])
def get_arena_name(arena_name):
  arenas =
session.query(Arena).filter(Arena.name.like(arena_name+"%")).all()
  data = [{"type": "Feature",
"properties":{"name":arena.name,"id":arena.id},
  "geometry":{"type":"Point",  "coordinates":[round(arena.longitude,6),
round(arena.latitude,6)]},
  } for arena in arenas]
  return jsonify({"type": "FeatureCollection","features":data})
```

A list comprehension is used to generate the `arena` dictionaries. Here is an example of a response to a string query to the `arena` endpoint:

A geospatial query

By adding one more URL component, the API is spatially enabled. Passing an `arena` ID and adding `"/intersect"` will use spatial queries to find data describing the requested NBA Arena. In this view function, the `County` and `District` tables are queried using an `intersect filter` (that is, the `county` containing the `arena` is identified using a point in polygon function). The underlying state is retrieved using a table relation between the `county` and the `state`. All of the geometry and the selected fields are returned:

```python
@app.route('/nba/api/v0.1/arena/<int:arena_id>/intersect', methods=['GET'])
def arena_intersect(arena_id):
    arena = session.query(Arena).get(arena_id)
    county =
session.query(County).filter(County.geom.ST_Intersects(arena.geom)).first()
    district=session.query(District).filter(District.geom.ST_Intersects(arena.g
eom))
    district = district.first()
    if county != None:
        data = [{"type": "Feature", "properties": {"name":arena.name,
"id":arena.id,} ,
        "geometry":{"type":"Point", "coordinates":[round(arena.longitude,6),
round(arena.latitude,6)]},
        },{"type": "Feature", "properties": {"name":county.name,
"id":county.id,} ,
        "geometry":{"type":"MultiPolygon",
        "coordinates":[shapely.geometry.geo.mapping(to_shape(county.geom))]},
        },{"type": "Feature", "properties": {"name":district.district,
"id":district.id,},
        "geometry":{"type":"MultiPolygon",
        "coordinates":[shapely.geometry.geo.mapping(to_shape(district.geom))]},
        },{"type": "Feature", "properties": {"name":county.state_ref.name,
"id":county.state_ref.id,}, "geometry":{"type":"MultiPolygon",
"coordinates":[shapely.geometry.geo.mapping(to_shape(county.state_ref.geom)
)]},
        }]
        return jsonify({"type": "FeatureCollection","features":data})
    else:
        return redirect('/nba/api/v0.1/arena/' + str(arena_id))
```

To ensure that the function is valid, the `if` conditional checks if the `arena` is inside a US county; if not, the `county`, `district`, and `state` objects are not used. Instead, the request is redirected to the non-geospatial query view function.

States

The US States data can be large, due to the many vertices that make up each `state`. Within the endpoint for the `states`, we will add some URL parameters that will enable us to decide the geometry of each requested `state` should be returned.

Getting all states

By checking for a URL argument in the `request.args` dictionary, and then checking if the argument evaluates as true, we can determine if all of the `state` geometries should be returned. The GeoJSON response is generated from the state's geometry by using the `to_shape` function and the `shapely.geometry.geo.mapping` (shortened to `smapping`) function:

```
@app.route('/nba/api/v0.1/state', methods=['GET'])
def get_states():
  smapping = shapely.geometry.geo.mapping
  states = session.query(State).all()
  data = [{"type": "Feature",
  "properties":{"state":state.name,"id":state.id},
  "geometry":{"type":"MultiPolygon",
  "coordinates":"[Truncated]"},
  } for state in states]
  if "geometry" in request.args.keys():
    if request.args["geometry"]=='1' or request.args["geometry"]=='True':
      data = [{"type": "Feature",
      "properties":{"state":state.name,"id":state.id},
      "geometry":{"type":"MultiPolygon",
      "coordinates":[smapping(to_shape(state.geom))["coordinates"]]},
      } for state in states]
  return jsonify({"type": "FeatureCollection","features":data})
```

If the `geometry` argument or parameter is not included, the geometry will be represented as truncated.

Getting a state by ID

To get a specific `state` using the primary key ID of the `state`, we can add a URL variable that will check for an integer ID. It is returned with the `geometry` as a `geojson`:

```
@app.route('/nba/api/v0.1/state/<int:state_id>', methods=['GET'])
def get_state(state_id):
  state = session.query(State).get(state_id)
  geojson = shapely.geometry.geo.mapping(to_shape(state.geom))
```

```
        data = [{"type": "Feature",  "properties":{"name":state.name},
        "geometry":{"type":"MultiPolygon",
    "coordinates":[geojson["coordinates"]]},
        }]
        return jsonify({"type": "FeatureCollection","features":data})
```

Getting a state by name

Using a `filter` will allow for a URL variable to be used as a `query filter`. The string variable will be checked against the state `name` field in the database table, and uses a `like` operator to do a fuzzy comparison (that is, it will get all `states` that start with `'M'` if the `state_name` variable is `'M'`:

```
@app.route('/nba/api/v0.1/state/<state_name>', methods=['GET'])
def get_state_name(state_name):
    states =
session.query(State).filter(State.name.like(state_name+"%")).all()
    geoms = {state.id:smapping(to_shape(state.geom)) for state in states}
    data = [{"type": "Feature", "properties":{"state":state.name},
    "geometry":{"type":"MultiPolygon",
"coordinates":[shapely.geometry.geo.mapping(to_shape(state.geom)["coordinat
es"]]},
    } for state in states]
    return jsonify({"type": "FeatureCollection","features":data})
```

This function has no URL parameters and will return the specified fields and `geometry` of the selected states.

Getting arenas by state

This function uses spatial analysis to find all `arenas` that are contained by the `state`. The `state` is identified by the ID, and the URL component within which it will select all `arenas` whose `geometry` is within the `state geometry`:

```
@app.route('/nba/api/v0.1/state/<int:state_id>/contains', methods=['GET'])
def get_state_arenas(state_id):
    state = session.query(State).get(state_id)
    shp = to_shape(state.geom)
    geojson = shapely.geometry.geo.mapping(shp)
    data = [{"type": "Feature", "properties":{"name":state.name},
    "geometry":{"type":"MultiPolygon", "coordinates":[geojson]},
    }]
    arenas = session.query(Arena).filter(state.geom.ST_Contains(arena.geom))
    data_arenas =[{"type": "Feature",
    "properties":{"name":arena.name}, "geometry":{"type":"Point",
```

```
            "coordinates":[round(arena.longitude,6), round(arena.latitude,6)]},
            } for arena in arenas]
            data.extend(data_arenas)
            return jsonify({"type": "FeatureCollection","features":data})
```

The data returned will include the state `data` and `data` for all `arenas`, as GeoJSON allows for multiple datatypes to be packaged as a feature collection.

Counties

Similar to the `State` database table, this will retrieve all of the `county` data. It accepts a `geometry` parameter to decide if it will return the `geometry` of each `county`:

```
@app.route('/nba/api/v0.1/county', methods=['GET'])
def get_counties():
    counties = session.query(County).all()
    geoms = {county.id:smapping(to_shape(county.geom)) for county in
counties}
    if 'geometry' in request.args.keys():
        data = [{"type": "Feature",
        "properties":{"name":county.name, "state":county.state.name},
        "geometry":{"type":"MultiPolygon",
"coordinates":[shapely.geometry.geo.mapping(to_shape(state.geom)["coordinat
es"]]},
            } for county in counties]
    else:
        data = [{"type": "Feature",
        "properties":{"name":county.name, "state":county.state.name},
        "geometry":{"type":"MultiPolygon",
    "coordinates":["Truncated"]},
            } for county in counties]
    return jsonify({"type": "FeatureCollection","features":data})
```

Getting a county by ID

After retrieving all counties using the `get_counties` function, the ID of a specific `county` can be passed to this function. Using `session.query.(County).get(county_id)` allows for the retrieval of the `county` of interest:

```
@app.route('/nba/api/v0.1/county/<int:county_id>', methods=['GET'])
def get_county(county_id):
    county = session.query(County).get(county_id)
    shp = to_shape(county.geom)
    geojson = shapely.geometry.geo.mapping(shp)
    data = [{"type": "Feature",
```

```
"properties":{"name":county.name, "state":county.state.name},
"geometry":{"type":"MultiPolygon",
"coordinates":[geojson]},
}]
return jsonify({"type": "FeatureCollection","features":data})
```

Getting a county by name

Again, we can use a URL variable to collect a string, and use the string supplied for a query filter. If `Wash` is used as the URL variable `county_name`, the query will find all `counties` with names that start with `Wash`:

```
@app.route('/nba/api/v0.1/county/<county_name>', methods=['GET'])
def get_county_name(county_name):
  counties =
session.query(County).filter(County.name.like(county_name+"%")).all()
  data = [{"type": "Feature",
  "properties":{"name":county.name, "state":county.state.name},
  "geometry":{"type":"MultiPolygon",
"coordinates":[shapely.geometry.geo.mapping(to_shape(county.geom))["coordin
ates"]]},
  } for county in counties]
  return jsonify({"type": "FeatureCollection","features":data})
```

The `filter` method can be used on spatial fields as well as non-spatial fields.

Districts

Districts can be similarly added to the API. In this case, we will add a geometry parameter to decide if the geometry should be returned. This allows for the requesting machine or browser to get all of the districts and their IDs, which can be used to get the individual district in the next section, or to get all of the data at once, as needed.

Getting all districts

This endpoint, (`'/district'`), will query against the `District` model using `session.query(District).all()`:

```
@app.route('/nba/api/v0.1/district', methods=['GET'])
def get_districts():
  districts = session.query(District).all()
  if 'geometry' in request.args.keys() and request.args['geometry'] in
('1','True'):
    data = [{"type": "Feature",
```

```
    "properties":{"representative":district.name,
"district":district.district,
 "state": district.state_ref.name, "id":district.id},
    "geometry":{"type":"MultiPolygon",
"coordinates":shapely.geometry.geo.mapping(to_shape(district.geom))["coordi
nates"]},
    } for district in districts]
  else:
    data = [{"type": "Feature",
    "properties":{"representative":district.name,
"district":district.district,
    "state": district.state_ref.name, "id":district.id},
    "geometry":{"type":"MultiPolygon",
    "coordinates":["Truncated"]},
    } for district in districts]
  return jsonify({"type": "FeatureCollection","features":data})
```

Getting a district by ID

Passing the integer `district` ID will return only the requested representation of the `district`. The `geometry` is converted to GeoJSON format using `shapely` and the `to_shape` method from `geoalchemy2.shape`:

```
@app.route('/nba/api/v0.1/district/<int:district_id>', methods=['GET'])
def get_district(district_id):
  district = session.query(District).get(district_id)
  shp = to_shape(district.geom)
  geojson = shapely.geometry.geo.mapping(shp)
  data = [{"type": "Feature",
  "properties":{"district":district.district,"id":district.id},
  "geometry":{"type":"MultiPolygon",
  "coordinates":[geojson['coordinates']]},
  }]
  return jsonify({"type": "FeatureCollection","features":data})
```

Getting a district by name

In this case, the `name` of the district is the congressional `district` number. There is a `name` field, but it contains the name of the elected representative from that `district`:

```
@app.route('/nba/api/v0.1/district/<dist>', methods=['GET'])
def get_district_name(dist):
  districts =
session.query(District).filter(District.district.like(dist+"%")).all()
  data = [{"type": "Feature",
  "properties":{"district":district.district,"id":district.id,
```

```
    "representative":district.name},    "geometry":{"type":"MultiPolygon",
"coordinates":shapely.geometry.geo.mapping(to_shape(district.geom))["coordi
nates"]},
    } for district in districts]
    return jsonify({"type": "FeatureCollection","features":data})
```

All of these methods can be adjusted to include more parameters. Try adding in conditionals that check for fields to return, or another conditional. All URL parameter arguments are added after a question mark ('?') in the query.

API POST endpoints

Adding an `arena` can be accomplished using both JSON data and using an HTML form. In this section, we'll create an HTML template, use the `AddForm` from `forms.py`, and use it to collect data from the `Leaflet.js` map included in `Chapter 12`, *GeoDjango*, code bundle. It also uses the library jQuery to allow the user to click on the map at any location, thus updating the `longitude` and `latitude` data from the map:

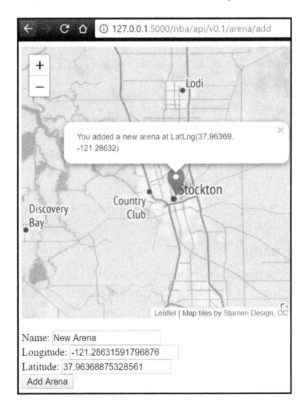

New arenas

To add new arenas to the database Arena table, a view function for processing and a Jinja2 HTML template will be created and used. The function will determine the request method and will send the appropriate response to the request. If it is a GET request, it will send an HTML template with the AddForm form. From the HTML template, filling in the data and pushing the button will submit a POST request, which will go to the same view function, and will use the submitted data to add a new row to the Arena table.

The view function

The view function that will process the request accepts both GET and POST request methods. The endpoint '/add' is used in this case, though it could have been anything that differentiated it from the arena endpoint:

```
@app.route('/nba/api/v0.1/arena/add', methods=['GET', 'POST'])
def add_arenas():
  form = AddForm(request.form)
  form.name.data = "New Arena"
  form.longitude.data = -121.5
  form.latitude.data = 37.8
  if request.method == "POST":
    arena = Arena()
    arena.name = request.form['name']
    arena.latitude = float(request.form['latitude'])
    arena.longitude = float(request.form['longitude'])
    arena.geom = 'SRID=4326;POINT({0} {1})'.format(arena.longitude,
arena.latitude)
    session.add(arena)
    data = [{"type": "Feature", "properties":{"name":arena.name},
    "geometry":{"type":"Point",
    "coordinates":[round(arena.longitude,6), round(arena.latitude,6)]},}]
    return jsonify({'added':'success',"type":
"FeatureCollection","features":data})
  return render_template('addarena.html', form=form)
```

Once the button is pushed, the data is submitted. The view function will determine what to do based on the request method—if it is a POST request, the data submitted in the form will be used to create a new arena object, and the session manager will save the object, adding it to the database.

The addarena.html head

Next, let's create the template called `addarena.html`, which will be added to the `templates` folder inside the `application` folder. At the top of the HTML file, in the head section, add the CSS, JavaScript, and jQuery libraries:

```
<!DOCTYPE html>
<html>
<head>
  <title>Arena Map</title>
  <meta charset="utf-8" />
  <meta name="viewport" content="width=device-width, initial-scale=1.0">
   <link rel="stylesheet"
href="https://unpkg.com/leaflet@1.2.0/dist/leaflet.css" />
    <script src="https://unpkg.com/leaflet@1.2.0/dist/leaflet.js"></script>
    <script
src="https://ajax.googleapis.com/ajax/libs/jquery/3.2.1/jquery.min.js"></sc
ript>
</head>
```

The addarena.html script

Create the map `<div>` section and add the JavaScript that will enable map interactivity. If the map is clicked on, the JavaScript function `showMapClick` (which accepts an event `e` as a parameter) will move the marker. Within the function, jQuery is used to set the value of the `latitude` and `longitude` form elements, getting the values from the event argument's `e.latlng` method:

```
<body>
<div id="map" style="width: 600px; height: 400px;"></div>
<script>
  var themap = L.map('map').setView([
{{form.latitude.data}},{{form.longitude.data}}], 13);
L.tileLayer('https://stamen-tiles-{s}.a.ssl.fastly.net/toner/{z}/{x}/{y}.e
xt}', {
  subdomains: 'abcd',
  minZoom: 1,
  maxZoom: 18,
  ext: 'png'
  }).addTo(themap);
  marker = L.marker([
{{form.latitude.data}},{{form.longitude.data}}]).addTo(themap)
    .bindPopup("Click to locate the new arena").openPopup();
  var popup = L.popup();
  function showMapClick(e) {
    $('#longitude').val(e.latlng.lng);
```

```
    $('#latitude').val(e.latlng.lat);
    marker
      .setLatLng(e.latlng)
      .bindPopup("You added a new arena at " + e.latlng.toString())
      .openPopup();
  }
  themap.on('click', showMapClick);
</script>
```

The addarena.html form

The `form` data will be submitted with the POST method. Once the **Add Arena** button is pushed, the data inside the entry forms are submitted:

```
<form method="post" class="form">
  Name: {{form.name}}<br>
  Longitude: {{ form.longitude(class_ = 'form-control first-input last-
input', placeholder = form.longitude.data, ) }} <br>
  Latitude: {{ form.latitude(class_ = 'form-control first-input last-
input', placeholder = form.latitude.data, ) }} <br>
    <input type="submit" value="Add Arena">
  </form>
</body>
</html>
```

Clicking on the button will submit the data to the view function. The data will be processed, and a **success** JSON message returned:

```
← → C ⌂  ⓘ 127.0.0.1:5000/nba/api/v0.1/arena/add
{
  "added": "success",
  "features": [
    {
      "geometry": {
        "coordinates": [
          -121.286316,
          37.963689
        ],
        "type": "Point"
      },
      "properties": {
        "name": "Stockton Arena"
      },
      "type": "Feature"
    }
  ],
  "type": "FeatureCollection"
}
```

Sending a POST request using the requests library

A new arena can be added using a web request, avoiding the need to use the HTML template. Here is a demonstration of a request using the `requests` library:

```
>>> form = {'longitude':'-109.5', 'latitude':'40.7', 'name':'Test Arena'}
>>> requests.post('http://127.0.0.1:5000/nba/api/v0.1/arena/add', form)
<Response [200]>
```

The POST request is sent to the `'/add'` endpoint, along with the required `form` parameters, as a Python dictionary.

Deleting an arena

Deleting an `arena` (or another resource) can also be done using a view function and a specific endpoint:

```
@app.route('/nba/api/v0.1/arena/delete/<int:arena_id>', methods=['DELETE'])
def delete_arena(arena_id):
    arena = session.query(Arena).delete(arena_id)
    return jsonify({"deleted":"success"})
```

To delete an `arena`, send a request using the `delete` method:

```
>>> import requests
>>>requests.delete('http://127.0.0.1:5000/nba/api/v0.1/arena/delete/30')
```

Running the REST API locally

To run this API application locally, the `app.py` script is passed to the Python executable. This will start the built-in web server on the local machine:

```
C:\Projects\Chapter13\arenaapp>python app.py
 * Running on http://127.0.0.1:5000/ (Press CTRL+C to quit)
```

Once the server is running, navigate to the API endpoint to get responses from the view functions. If the application is complete, however, the local server won't be powerful enough to handle the API requests. Instead, deployment on a production web server is required.

Deploying Flask to IIS

To deploy the new API application on a Microsoft Server with **Internet Information Services** (**IIS**) installed, we have to download some Python code, and an IIS module called **FastCGI**. Once configured, the application will respond to web requests from any allowed machine.

Flask and web servers

While Flask includes a local web server for testing purposes, it is not designed for production deployments. Flask works best with web servers like Apache or IIS. While there is a lot of literature on how to deploy Flask with Apache, it is less common to find good instructions on how to deploy it using IIS. As most GIS professionals work with Windows servers or have access to them, these instructions will focus on deployment with IIS 7.

WSGI

The **Web Server Gateway Interface** (**WSGI**) is a Python specification that allows for a Python executable to be used to respond to web requests. WSGI is built into Python web frameworks such as Flask and Django.

To enable the use of the Flask web framework to serve web pages, some configuration of IIS is required, including the installation of an IIS **Common Gateway Interface** (**CGI**) module called FastCGI, and the installation of a Python module called **WFastCGI**. With these two additions, the IIS web server will connect to the code behind the API application.

Installing the WFastCGI module and FastCGI

Use the Web Platform Installer, available here: `http://www.microsoft.com/web/downloads/platform.aspx` (if it's not already installed). Use the search bar in the top-right, and enter `WFastCGI`. The search results will appear and will list available WFastCGI versions for both Python 2.x and Python 3.x. Select the version for Python 3.6 and run the installer.

This installation adds two important components to the required tech stack. The FastCGI module is added to IIS, and the WFastCGI Python code is added to a new Python installation. This new installation will be added at `C:\Python36`, unless there is an existing version in that location (not counting Python versions within an ArcGIS10.X Python installation).

Within this new installation, a file called `wfastcgi.py` is added in the `C:\Python36\Scripts` (or equivalent) folder. This file should be copied into the site folder, next to the `app.py` file.

Configuring FastCGI

Open IIS, and click on the **Default Web Site**. Within the features view of the Content Pane, select the **Handler Mappings** icon. Double-click to open it. Select **Add Module Mapping** from the right pane. When the **Add Module Mapping** interface appears, enter the following:

- Add an asterisk (*) to the request path entry.
- Select the **FastCGI** module from the **Module Selection List**.
- If you copied the `wfastcgi.py` file into the code path and the code is at `C:\website`, enter this into the executable entry: `C:\Python36\python.exe|C:\website\wfastcgi.py`.
- Optionally, the `wfastcgi.py` file in the `Scripts` folder can be used. Here is the setup: `C:\Python36\python.exe|C:\Python36\Scripts\wfastcgi.py`.
- Click on **Request Restrictions** and uncheck the **Invoke handler only if request is mapped to:** if it is checked. Click **OK**.
- Click **OK** on the **Add Module Mapping** interface.
- Click **Yes** on the confirmation.

Root server settings and Environment Variables

Go to the `root` server settings and click on the **FastCGI Settings** icon. Double-click on the argument that matches the path added in the previous section. The **Edit FastCGI Application** interface will open.

- Click on the **EnvironmentVariables (Collection)** entry. An ellipsis (...) will appear. Double-click on the ellipsis to edit the environment variables.
- Click the **Add** button to add a new variable.

- Add PYTHONPATH to the **Name** entry.
- Add the path to the site code (for example C:\website\) to the value entry.
- Click the **Add** button to add a second variable.
- Add WSGI_HANDLER to the **Name** entry.
- If the site is controlled by a file called app.py, add app.app to the value entry (replacing .py with .app).
- Once the variables have been added, push **OK**. Push **OK** in the **Edit FastCGI Application**.

The site should now be live. Navigate to a REST endpoint using a browser to confirm that the site loads as expected.

Summary

Creating an API with REST specifications is easy with Python web frameworks. Flask makes it simple to coordinate the URL endpoints with request methods and response types. With built-in JSON capabilities, and with the use of the SQLAlchemy and GeoAlchemy2 ORMs, Flask is a perfect framework for creating a geospatial REST API.

In the next chapter, we will cover the use of the CARTOframes module for cloud visualization of geospatial data.

14
Cloud Geodatabase Analysis and Visualization

This chapter will cover **CARTOframes**, a Python package released by location intelligence software company CARTO in November 2017. It offers a Python interface for working with the CARTO stack, enabling integration of CARTO maps, analysis, and data services into data science workflows.

This chapter will cover the following topics:

- The specifics of the CARTOframes Python library
- Getting familiar with the CARTO stack and how CARTOframes interacts with different parts of it
- How to install CARTOframes, its package requirements, and documentation
- The different package dependencies of CARTOframes
- How to get a CARTO API key
- Setting up a CARTO Builder account
- Virtual environments
- Using Jupyter Notebook
- Installing GeoPandas

A Python package created with data scientists in mind, CARTOframes is a data science tool that combines CARTO's SaaS offerings and web mapping tools with Python data science workflows. Released in late 2017 by CARTO (www.carto.com), it is available for download through GitHub and the **Python Package Index (PyPI)** repository.

The package can be seen as a way to integrate CARTO elements with data science workflows, using Jupyter Notebooks as a working environment. This not only makes it attractive to use for data scientists, but also allows you to save and distribute code and workflows through Jupyter Notebooks. These data science workflows can be extended by using CARTO's services, such as hosted, dynamic, or static maps and datasets from CARTO's Data Observatory—all available through CARTO's cloud platform. This platform is accessed through an API key, which needs to be used when using CARTOframes in a Jupyter Notebook. We'll describe how to get an API key and how to install the CARTOframes package shortly.

The package offers functionality to read and write different types of spatial data. For instance, you can write `pandas` dataframes to CARTO tables, as well as read CARTO tables and queries into `pandas` dataframes. The CARTOframes package brings external data location data services from CARTO into the Jupyter Notebook, such as location data services, cloud-based data storage, CARTOColors (a set of custom color palettes built on top of well-known standards for color use on maps), PostGIS, and animated maps.

One good reason for using CARTOframes is because of its plotting capabilities. It is a good alternative to other map-plotting packages such as GeoPandas, `matplotlib`, Folio, and GeoNotebook. All these packages have their advantages and disadvantages. For example, `matplotlib` is not an easy package to learn and requires a lot of code for basic maps. This is not the case with CARTOframes, and the results look impressive, especially because of the use of colors, combined with dynamic images (time-lapses) and easy commands to read, write, query, plot and delete data.

How to install CARTOframes

The CARTOframes library can be best installed by starting Anaconda Navigator and creating a new environment. From there, you can open a terminal and use `pip` install, which will install the library for you. This is currently the only way to install it (there's no `conda` support yet). Use the following command:

```
>>pip install cartoframes
```

Additional resources

CARTOframes documentation can be found, at: `http://CARTOframes.readthedocs.io/en/latest/`.

The current version of CARTOframes is 0.5.5. The PyPi repository for CARTOframes can be accessed here: `https://pypi.python.org/pypi/CARTOframes`.

There's also a GitHub repository with additional information, as one of the many CARTO GitHub repositories: `https://github.com/CARTODB/CARTOframes`.

Jupyter Notebooks

It is recommended to use CARTOframes in Jupyter Notebooks. In the example scripts later in this chapter, we'll be using the CARTOframes package with other geospatial packages, so you might want to install it in a virtual environment together with GeoPandas, so that you'll have access to its dependencies as well. Consult the installation guides for GeoPandas and other libraries in `Chapter 2`, *Introduction to Geospatial Code Libraries*. You can install the Jupyter Notebook app in a separate Python environment with the following command, in a terminal window:

```
>>pip install jupyter
```

The CARTO API key

After installing CARTOframes, we need to create a CARTO API key in order to be able to use the functionality from the library. The library interacts with the CARTO infrastructure, similarly to the ArcGIS API for Python in `Chapter 9`, *ArcGIS API for Python and ArcGIS Online*. The API key can be used for writing dataframes to an account, reading from private tables, and visualizing data on maps. CARTO provides API keys for education and nonprofit uses, among others. If you're a student, you can get access to an API key by signing up to GitHub's student developer pack: `https://education.github.com/pack`.

 Another option is to become a CARTO ambassador: `https://carto.com/community/ambassadors/`.

Package dependencies

CARTOframes depends on a number of Python libraries that are installed automatically once you run the `pip` install command. The following Python libraries are installed:

- `ipython`: Provides a rich toolkit for using Python interactively
- `appdirs`: A small Python module for determining appropriate platform-specific directories
- `carto`: Provides an SDK around CARTO's APIs
- `chardet`: A universal encoding detector for Python 2 and 3
- `colorama`: Enables colored terminal text and cursor positioning in MS Windows
- `decorator`: Preserves the signature of decorated functions consistently across Python releases
- `future`: Offers a compatibility layer between Python 2 and Python 3
- `idna`: Offers support for **Internationalized Domain Names in Applications (IDNA)**
- `ipython-genutils`: Vestigial utilities from IPython
- `jedi`: An autocompletion tool for Python that can be used for text editors
- `numpy`: Performs array processing for numbers, strings, records, and objects
- `pandas`: Offers powerful data structures for data analysis, time series, and statistics
- `parso`: A Python parser that supports error recovery for different Python versions, and more
- `pickleshare`: A small shelve-like datastore with concurrency support
- `prompt-toolkit`: A library for building powerful interactive command lines in Python
- `pygments`: A syntax highlighting package written in Python
- `pyrestcli`: A generic REST client for Python
- `python-dateutil`: Offers extensions to the standard Python `datetime` module
- `pytz`: Provides modern and historical world timezone definitions
- `requests`: An HTTP `requests` library
- `simplegeneric`: Lets you define simple single-dispatch generic functions
- `six`: A Python 2 and 3 compatibility library
- `tqdm`: Offers a fast, extensible progress meter
- `traitlets`: A configuration system for Python applications

- `urllib3`: An HTTP library with thread-safe connection pooling, file post, and more
- `wcwidth`: Measures the number of terminal column cells of wide-character codes
- `webcolors`: A library for working with color names and color value formats defined by HTML and CSS

The CARTO Data Observatory

You can augment the CARTOframes library by using the CARTO Data Observatory, an online data service from CARTO. It provides three things—out-of-the-box location data, access to a catalog of analyzed data methods, and the opportunity to build location intelligence apps on top of fast APIs. This data service was created with the idea in mind that data available on the web has to be searchable, and therefore labeled well. To be able to find this data, provide a context to your data, and use it for spatial analysis is what is possible with this service.

The CARTO Data Observatory is available for CARTO enterprise users, which requires a paid subscription. In this chapter, we won't cover this option, but we mention it here as to give you an idea of what is possible with the CARTOframes library.

Signing up for a CARTO account

To be able to use CARTOframes, and to interact with data stored in the cloud-based PostGIS database service that CARTO offers, it is necessary to sign up for a CARTO account. While free accounts are available, with limited storage capacity and access to existing data resources, it is necessary to have a paid account to use CARTOframes, as these accounts are provided API keys. The API key will be used by CARTOframes to identify the account, with each data request sent to the user's cloud geodatabase.

A free trial of CARTO

By signing up, the account is initially a paid account with access to all CARTO features. The paid account offers a free 30-day trial that can be used to for evaluation purposes. Go to the site `https://carto.com/signup` and create an account:

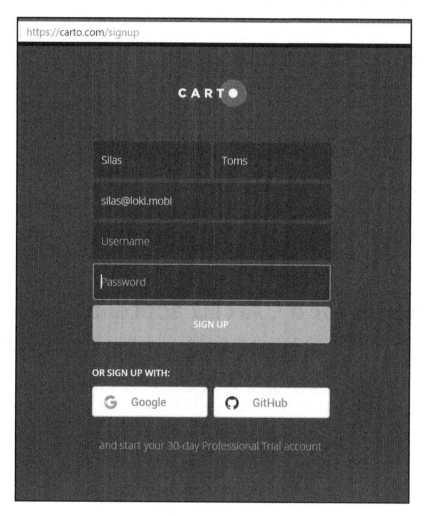

Once the account has been created, the 30-day trial period begins. This will allow you to add data to the cloud database, or to access publicly available data from the CARTO library. It also allows you to easily publish a map. Click on the **NEW MAP** button to get started:

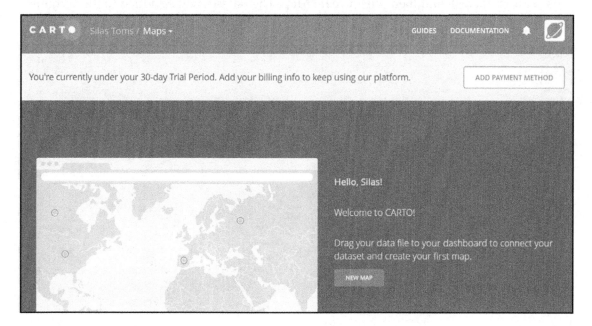

Adding a dataset

Using the **DATA LIBRARY** tab, add the **Portland building footprints** to the map. Select the data set from the list, and then push **Create Map**. The dataset will be added to the account datasets tab, and to the map creation interface called Builder:

The dataset is added as a layer to the map. All aspects of the layer can be manipulated in the map editor, including the color of the layer, the attributes shown, the pop-up window, and more. The basemap can also be adjusted.

Widgets, representing live data from attributes, can be added as well. I've added the **US Census Tracts** layer from the **DATA LIBRARY** to the map, and added a graphing widget that will display values from a selected attribute field. This graph is dynamic, and will adjust the values displayed based on the specific census tracts which are shown in the map window:

Check out the other tabs in Builder, including **DATA, ANALYSIS, STYLE, POP-UP**, and **LEGEND**, to further customize the map. There are a number of adjustments and widgets that will make the data interactive. The map can also be made either public or private, and can be published to the web by pushing the **PUBLISH** button. CARTO's editors and data ingestion interface make it really easy to create and share maps.

The API key

To connect to the CARTO account using CARTOframes, an API key is required. To access it, go to the account dashboard, click on the image in the upper right, and select the **Your API keys** link from the drop-down menu:

The API key is a long string of text used to ensure that the scripts we will write can have access to the account and the datasets associated with it. When it is time to write scripts, copy the key text and assign it to a variable as a Python string within the script:

Adding a dataset

There is a handy method for adding data from your computer to the account. However, when adding shapefiles, all of the data files that make up the shapefile must be in a ZIP file. We'll add the NBA arenas shapefile from `Chapter 11`, *Flask and GeoAlchemy2*, as a ZIP file to the account. Click on the **NEW DATASET** button in the **DATASETS** area of your dashboard:

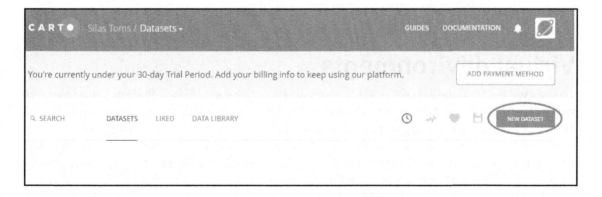

Once the **NEW DATASET** button is pushed, and the **CONNECT DATASET** interface appears, click on **BROWSE** and navigate to the zipped file to upload it:

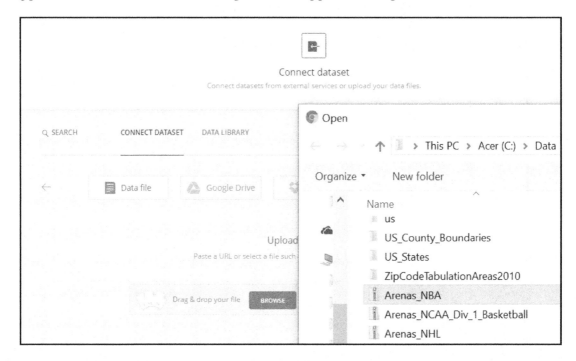

Upon completion of the upload process, the data will be given a URL and can be edited using Builder. It can also be edited using CARTOframes.

Now that the account is set up, and a dataset has been added from a local file as well as from the **DATA LIBRARY**, we need to set up the Python environment on our local machine to be able to connect to the data stored in the account.

Virtual environments

To manage the installation of CARTOframes and the other associated Python 3 modules, we will be using the virtual environments package `virtualenv`. This Python module makes it easy to set up completely separate Python installations on the same computer. Using `virtualenv`, a copy of Python is created, and when activated, all modules that are installed are separate from the main Python installation (in other words, the modules installed inside a virtual environment will not be added to the main `site-packages` folder). This allows for a lot less package management headaches.

Installing virtualenv

Installation of the `virtualenv` package is easy when using `pip` from PyPI (`pypi.org`):

```
pip install virtualenv
```

This command will add `virtualenv` and its supporting modules. Make sure that the main Python installation has been added to the path Windows environment variables so that `virtualenv` can be called from the command line.

Running virtualenv

To create the virtual environment, open a command line and enter the following command structure, `virtualenv {environment name}`. In this case, the name of the environment is `cartoenv`:

```
C:\Packt\PythonScripting\Chapters\Chapter15\Scripts>virtualenv cartoenv
Using base prefix 'c:\\users\\admin\\appdata\\local\\programs\\python\\python36'
New python executable in C:\Packt\PythonScripting\Chapters\Chapter15\Scripts\cartoenv\Scripts\python.exe
Installing setuptools, pip, wheel...done.
```

Inside the folder where `virtualenv` is created, a series of folders are generated with the code files necessary to support Python. There is also a `Lib` folder, which contains the `site-packages` folder that will hold all of the modules installed inside this virtual version of Python:

```
C:\Packt\PythonScripting\Chapters\Chapter15\Scripts\cartoenv>dir
 Volume in drive C is Acer
 Volume Serial Number is CA9C-6B12

 Directory of C:\Packt\PythonScripting\Chapters\Chapter15\Scripts\cartoenv

02/23/2018  12:13 PM    <DIR>          .
02/23/2018  12:13 PM    <DIR>          ..
10/19/2017  12:15 PM    <DIR>          Include
02/23/2018  12:13 PM    <DIR>          Lib
02/23/2018  12:13 PM                60 pip-selfcheck.json
02/23/2018  12:13 PM    <DIR>          Scripts
02/23/2018  12:13 PM    <DIR>          tcl
               1 File(s)             60 bytes
               6 Dir(s)  116,475,166,720 bytes free
```

Activating the virtual environment

To start using the new virtual environment from the command line, pass the following argument inside the folder that holds the virtual environment. This will run the `activate` batch file, and will start the virtual environment:

```
C:\PythonGeospatial3>cartoenv\Scripts\activate
```

Once the virtual environment is activated, the name of the environment will appear before the folder name, indicating that the commands are being run inside the environment and any changes that are performed (such as installing modules) will not affect the main Python installation:

```
(cartoenv) C:\PythonGeospatial3>
```

In a Linux environment, the command source `{environment}/bin/activate` is used instead. When programming in Linux, the commands in the terminal would look like this:

```
silas@ubuntu16:~$ mkdir carto
silas@ubuntu16:~$ cd carto/
silas@ubuntu16:~/carto$ virtualenv cartoenv
New python executable in /home/silas/carto/cartoenv/bin/python
Installing setuptools, pip, wheel...done.
silas@ubuntu16:~/carto$ source cartoenv/bin/activate
(cartoenv) silas@ubuntu16:~/carto$
```

In either OS, to deactivate the virtual environment, pass the `deactivate` command. This will end the virtual session:

```
C:\PythonGeospatial3>cartoenv\Scripts\activate

(cartoenv) C:\PythonGeospatial3>deactivate
C:\PythonGeospatial3>
```

Installing modules in virtualenv

Because each virtual environment is separate from the main Python installation, each environment must have the required modules installed. While this can seem like a pain, `pip` makes it quite easy. After setting up the first virtual environment, a `pip` command called `freeze` allows you to generate a file called `requirements.txt`. This file can be copied into a new virtual environment and using `pip` install, all of the listed modules will be added from PyPI.

To generate a `requirements.txt` file in the current folder, use this command:

```
(cartoenv) C:\Packt\Chapters>pip freeze > requirements.txt
```

After the file has been copied into a new virtual environment folder, activate the environment and pass the following command to read from the file:

```
(newenv) C:\Packt\Chapters>pip install -r requirements.txt
```

Modules to use

For this virtual environment, we will install the two modules CARTOframes and Jupyter. The second module will allow us to run Jupyter Notebooks, which are specialized browser-based coding environments.

Activate the virtual environment, and install the modules within the virtual environment with the following commands:

```
(cartoenv) C:\Packt\Chapters>pip install cartoframes
(cartoenv) C:\Packt\Chapters>pip install jupyter
```

All of the required modules will also be downloaded and installed, along with the two that we are installing directly. Using `pip` and `virtualenv` makes package installation and management simple and quick.

Using Jupyter Notebook

We have covered the basic installation of Jupyter Notebook in Chapter 1, *Package Installation and Management* and in the previous chapter at various instances to run code and get the desired output.

Here, we will be using Jupyter Notebook for CARTOframes to connect to an account and analyze geospatial data and display it.

Connecting to an account

In the first code box, we will import the CARTOframes module, and pass the API key string along with the base URL, which is generated from your CARTO username as `https://{username}.carto.com`. In this case, the URL is `https://lokiintelligent.carto.com`:

In this code block, the API key and the URL are passed to the `CartoContext` class, and a `CartoContext` connect object is returned and assigned to the variable `cc`. With this object, we can now interact with the datasets associated with our account, load datasets into the account, and even generate maps directly in the Jupyter Notebook.

Once the code has been entered into the section, push the **Run** button to execute the code in the current section. Any output will appear in an **Out** section, underneath the code run. This section can include maps, tables, and even graphs—Jupyter Notebooks are often used in scientific computing because of this ability to instantly produce graphs and to save them within the Notebook.

Saving credentials

The CARTO account credentials can be saved and accessed later by using the `Credentials` library:

```
from cartoframes import Credentials
creds = Credentials(username='{username}', key='{password}')
creds.save()
```

Accessing a dataset

To access the NBA arenas dataset that we loaded into the account, we are going to use the `CartoContext read` method, passing the name of the dataset we want to interact with as a string. In a Jupyter Notebook **In** section, run the following code:

```
import cartoframes
APIKEY = "{YOUR API KEY}"
cc = cartoframes.CartoContext(base_url='https://{username}.carto.com/',
api_key=APIKEY)
df = cc.read('arenas_nba')
print(df)
```

Using `CartoContext`, the account is accessed. With the `cc` object, the `read` method creates a `DataFrame` object from the NBA `arenas` dataset. The `DataFrame` object is what is queried or updated.

The `print` statement will produce a table with values from the NBA `arenas` dataset, which has been loaded into a CARTOframe object:

```
In [2]:   import cartoframes
          APIKEY = "1353407a098fef50ec1b6324c437d6d52617b890"
          cc = cartoframes.CartoContext(base_url='https://lokiintelligent.carto.com/', api_
          df = cc.read('arenas_nba')
          print(df)
```

	address1	address2	capacity	city
cartodb_id				
1	601 Biscayne Boulevard	None	19600	Miami
2	1 Sports Parkway	None	17317	Sacramento
3	301 West South Temple	None	19911	Salt Lake City

Individual columns can be access using dot notation (for example, df.address1) or using keys (for example, df['address1']):

```
In [3]:  df.address1

Out[3]:  cartodb_id
         1                601 Biscayne Boulevard
         2                     1 Sports Parkway
         3                301 West South Temple
         4                     191 Beale Street
         5                     1 Center Court
         6                     7000 Coliseum Way
         7                    1601 Girod Street
         8                      1 Center Court
         9                600 West Amelia Street
         10               1001 North 4th Street
         11                  2500 Victory Avenue
         12                    100 Legends Way
         13                  1000 Chopper Circle
         14                   1 Philips Drive NW
         15              1902 West Madison Street
         16               3601 South Broad Street
         17                       50 Route 120
         18                 4 Pennsylvania Plaza
         19                    601 F Street NW
```

Selecting individual rows

To select a specific row within the Pandas dataframe derived from the CARTO account dataset, a conditional statement can be passed to the object in brackets. Here, the NBA arenas dataset's team column is queried by passing the name of an NBA team as a parameter:

```
df[df.team=='Toronto Raptors']
```

Loading a CSV dataset

To load a dataset into the account using CARTOframes, we will use the `pandas` library again, which is installed with the Jupyter modules. Pandas allow us to read data from a CSV (and other file formats), loading it into a Pandas dataframe (a special data object that allows for a multitude of data-manipulation methods, as well as producing output). Then, using `CartoContext`, the dataframe is written (as a table) to the account:

```
import pandas as pd
APIKEY = "{YOUR API KEY}"
cc = cartoframes.CartoContext(base_url='https://{username}.carto.com/',
api_key=APIKEY)
df = pd.read_csv(r'Path\to\sacramento.csv')
cc.write(df, 'sacramento_addresses')
```

This will write the CSV table, imported as a dataframe, into the CARTO account **DATASETS** section:

```
In [28]: import pandas as pd
         df = pd.read_csv(r'C:\Data\us\ca\sacramento.csv')
         cc.write(df, 'sacramento_addresses')

         c:\packt\pythonscripting\chapters\chapter15\scripts\cartoenv\lib\site-packages\IPython\core\interactiveshell.py:2728: DtypeWarn
         ing: Columns (2) have mixed types. Specify dtype option on import or set low_memory=False.
           interactivity=interactivity, compiler=compiler, result=result)

         The following columns were changed in the CARTO copy of this dataframe:
         LON -> lon
         LAT -> lat
         NUMBER -> number
         STREET -> street
         UNIT -> unit
         CITY -> city
         DISTRICT -> district
         REGION -> region
         POSTCODE -> postcode
         ID -> id
         HASH -> hash
         Table successfully written to CARTO: https://lokiintelligent.carto.com/dataset/sacramento_addresses
```

The imported dataset will not be a geospatial table, but is instead a table that can be queried and joined to spatial data.

Loading a shapefile

Loading geospatial data manually into CARTO is easy, as we explored earlier. It's even easier when using CARTOframes, as it makes automated data management possible. New, updated data files or data from REST APIs can be converted into dataframes and written into the CARTO account.

Shapefiles require the installation of the GeoPandas library, as the geometry requires a GeoPandas `DataFrame` object for data management.

Installing GeoPandas

GeoPandas, as discussed in `Chapter 5`, *Vector Data Analysis*, is the geospatial compliment to Pandas. To be able to create dataframes objects from shapefiles, we have to make sure that GeoPandas is installed and added to the virtual environment. Use `pip install` to add the GeoPandas library:

```
(cartoenv) C:\PythonGeospatial3>pip install geopandas
```

If there are installation issues on Windows, pre-built binaries for GeoPandas and Fiona (which powers GeoPandas) are available here, along with many other Python libraries: `https://www.lfd.uci.edu/~gohlke/pythonlibs`. Install Fiona and GeoPandas from the wheels by downloading them, copying them into a folder, and using `pip install` to install from the wheel. For example, here, Fiona is installed from the wheel file:

```
C:\PythonGeospatial3>pip install Fiona-1.7.11.post1-cp36-cp36m-
win_amd64.whl
```

Writing to CARTO

Writing the shapefile to the CARTO account requires only a `CartoContext` object, a file path, and the usual URL and API key combination. With GeoPandas now installed, the MLB Stadiums shapefile can be loaded into a GeoPandas `DataFrame`, and then written to the CARTO account using the `CartoContext` `write` method:

```
import geopandas as gdp
import cartoframes
APIKEY = "{API KEY}"
cc = cartoframes.CartoContext(base_url='https://{username}.carto.com/',
                              api_key=APIKEY)
shp = r"C:\Data\Stadiums_MLB\Stadiums_MLB.shp"
data = gdp.read_file(shp)
```

```
cc.write(data,"stadiums_mlb")
```

Log in to the CARTO account to confirm that the dataset has been added.

Loading CSV with geometry

To ensure that a table (address data from OpenAddresses in this case) with latitude and longitude columns is imported as a geospatial dataset, we have to use the Shapely library's Point class. Each Point geometry is generated from the LON and LAT fields of the address dataset which has been imported:

```
import geopandas as gdp
import cartoframes
import pandas as pd
from shapely.geometry import Point
APIKEY = "{API KEY}"
cc = cartoframes.CartoContext(base_url='https://{username}.carto.com/',
                              api_key=APIKEY)
address_df = pd.read_csv(r'data/city_of_juneau.csv')
geometry = [Point(xy) for xy in zip(address_df.LON, address_df.LAT)]
address_df = address_df.drop(['LON', 'LAT'], axis=1)
crs = {'init': 'epsg:4326'}
geo_df = gdp.GeoDataFrame(address_df, crs=crs, geometry=geometry)
cc.write(geo_df, 'juneau_addresses')
```

 Ensure that the GeoPandas library is imported before CARTOframes to avoid import errors from the Fiona library.

Geospatial analysis

To perform geospatial analysis, using the cloud datasets, we can connect using CARTOframes and perform spatial queries using a combination of GeoPandas and Shapely. In this example, the NBA arenas dataset is compared against a US States shapefile using an intersects spatial query. If the arena object intersects with a state object, the name of the arena and the state are printed:

```
import geopandas as gdp
import cartoframes
import pandas as pd
APIKEY = "1353407a098fef50ec1b6324c437d6d52617b890"
```

```
cc =
cartoframes.CartoContext(base_url='https://lokiintelligent.carto.com/',
                              api_key=APIKEY)
from shapely.geometry import Point
from shapely.wkb import loads
arenas_df = cc.read('arenas_nba')
shp = r"C:\Data\US_States\US_States.shp"
states_df = gdp.read_file(shp)

for index, orig in states_df.iterrows():
    for index2, ref in arenas_df.iterrows():
        if loads(ref['the_geom'], hex=True).intersects(orig['geometry']):
            print(orig['STATE'], ref['team'])
```

Editing and updating datasets

Because CARTOframes incorporates the Pandas dataframes objects, which can be edited in memory, and writes to the datasets stored in the CARTO account, we can create scripts that will automate the upload of geospatial data. Datasets can be updated entirely, or individual rows and values can be updated using Pandas data methods such as replace. This, coupled with Builder, the CARTO web-map deployment tool, makes it easy to create GIS with a web-map frontend and cloud data storage that can be managed using scripting.

In this example code, the name of the state that contains the NBA arena is found using the intersect query. The names are added to a list, and the list is added to the arena dataframe as a new column called states. The geometry data stored in the arenas dataset are required to be converted into Shapely objects, using the loads module:

```
import geopandas as gdp
import cartoframes
import pandas as pd
from shapely.wkb import loads
APIKEY = "API KEY"
cc = cartoframes.CartoContext(base_url='https://{username}.carto.com/',
                api_key=APIKEY)
arenas_df = cc.read('arenas_nba')
shp = r"C:\Data\US_States\US_States.shp"
states_df = gdp.read_file(shp)
data = []
for index, ref in arenas_df.iterrows():
  check = 0
  for index2, orig in states_df.iterrows():
    if loads(ref['the_geom'], hex=True).intersects(orig['geometry']):
      data.append(orig['STATE'])
```

```
        check = 1
    if check == 0:
        data.append(None)
arenas_df['state'] = data
cc.write(arenas_df,'arenas_nba', overwrite=True)
```

overwrite=True

With each update to the datasets, the changes must be written to the CARTO account. To overwrite data in the cloud database with new data, the `overwrite` parameter must be set to `True`:

```
cc.write(data,"stadiums_mlb",'overwrite=True')
```

Creating a map

Because of the interactivity of Jupyter Notebooks, code and code output exist together. This is great when dealing with geospatial data, as it makes it easy to create a map of the data. In this example, the NBA `arenas` and MLB stadiums datasets are added to a map over a `BaseMap` object:

```
from cartoframes import Layer, BaseMap, styling
cc.map(layers=[BaseMap('light'),
                Layer('arenas_nba',),
                Layer('stadiums_mlb')], interactive=True)
```

The output produced is as follows:

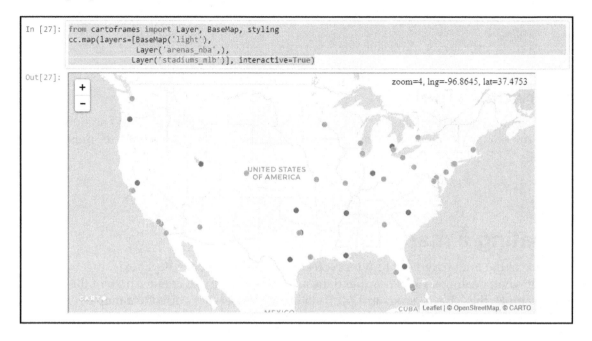

```
In [27]:  from cartoframes import Layer, BaseMap, styling
          cc.map(layers=[BaseMap('light'),
                     Layer('arenas_nba',),
                     Layer('stadiums_mlb')], interactive=True)
```

Summary

This chapter covered the following topics. First, we introduced the CARTOframes Python library and discussed how it relates to other parts of the CARTO stack, such as CARTO Builder and CARTO Data Observatory. Next, we explained how to install the CARTOframes library, what other Python packages it depends on, and where to look for documentation. Because CARTOframes uses data from CARTO Builder, we explained how to set up a CARTO Builder account. In the example scripts that make up the rest of the chapter, we saw how the library integrates `pandas` dataframes, how to work with tables, and how to make maps and combine them with other geospatial libraries, such as Shapely and GeoPandas.

In the next chapter, we will cover another module that utilizes Jupyter Notebooks and cartographic visualizations, MapboxGL—Jupyter.

Automating Cloud Cartography 15

Mapbox has become synonymous with mobile mapping and data visualizations. In addition to their basemap styling toolset, which has been adopted by app developers and cartographers, they are also producing interesting mapping tools written in Python and JavaScript.

Combining those two useful languages into one package, Mapbox recently released the new MapboxGL—Jupyter Python module. This new module allows for instant data visualization creation within a Jupyter Notebook environment. Along with the Mapbox Python SDK, a module that allows API access to account services, Python make it easy to add Mapbox tools and services to enterprise geospatial applications.

In this chapter, we'll learn:

- How to create a Mapbox account to generate access tokens
- How to style a custom basemap
- Read/write access to cloud data and basemaps
- How to create a choropleth map
- How to create a graduated circle visualization

All things cartographic

Founded in 2010 by Eric Gunderson, Mapbox has expanded rapidly and grown beyond its startup roots to become a leader in the cartographic renaissance. Their MapboxGL JavaScript API is a useful library for creating interactive web maps and data visualizations. They have contributed multiple open mapping specifications, including vector tiles, to the geospatial community.

With a core focus on providing custom basemap tiles to map and app developers, Mapbox has positioned themselves as the leading software company for web mapping and mobile applications. The two Python modules used in this chapter allow GIS managers and developers to integrate their services and tools into an enterprise geographic information ecosystem.

How to integrate Mapbox into your GIS

With their JavaScript libraries and the new MapboxGL—Jupyter Python module, Mapbox tools are easier than ever to use. Geospatial developers and programmers can integrate their tools into existing GIS workflows or can create new maps and apps that take advantage of the suite of offerings by Mapbox.

Mapbox, like CARTO, allows for account-based cloud data storage. However, their focus is less on analytical tools and more on cartographic tools. For mapping teams, large and small, using Mapbox tools eases the cost of creating and supporting a custom basemap for interactive web maps, and offers greater savings over other map tile options such as the Google Maps API.

Mapbox Studio makes it easy to create a map with a cartographic look and feel that can match the branding of the company or department. The basemaps can be built using existing styles and overlaid with your organization's layers, or a completely new basemap can be designed. It even allows for styling to be based on an image that is dropped into the studio, assigning colors to features based on a histogram generated from the pixels in the image.

Mapbox tools

Employing leaders in the geospatial field (such as Mapbox open source lead Sean Gillies, a major developer of Shapely, Fiona, and Rasterio), Mapbox has contributed to analysis and mapping Python libraries that are available under open source license. Their new MapboxGL—Jupyter library represents a new way to take advantage of their suite of tools in combination with other Python modules (such as Pandas/GeoPandas) and multiple data types, such as GeoJSON, CSVs, and even shapefiles.

Besides the new Python module, Mapbox's open source tools include the MapboxGL JavaScript library, built on the **Web Graphics Library** (**WebGL**), and the Mapbox Python SDK.

MapboxGL.js

MapboxGL is built on top of `Leaflet.js`, a well-known JavaScript mapping library. Released in 2011, Leaflet supports a wide variety of well-known web mapping applications, including Foursquare, Craigslist, and Pinterest. The developer of Leaflet, Vladimir Agafonkin, has been working for Mapbox since 2013.

Building on the original Leaflet development effort, `MapboxGL.js` incorporates the WebGL library, which takes advantage of the HTML 5 `canvas` tag to support web graphics without a plug-in. `MapboxGL.js` supports vector tiles, as well as 3D environments that zoom and pan smoothly. It supports GeoJSON overlays as well as markers and shapes. Events, including clicks, zooms, and pans, can be used to trigger data processing functions, making it perfect for interactive web mapping applications.

Mapbox Python SDK

The Mapbox Python SDK is used to access most Mapbox services, including directions, geocoding, analytics, and datasets. Low-level access to the cloud-based services supporting data editing and upload, administrative management, and location-based queries, allows for enterprise integration with, and extension of, local GIS.

Installing the Python SDK

Use `pip` to install the Python SDK, allowing API access to the Mapbox services. This module is not required to use the MapboxGL—Jupyter tools, but it is useful for uploads and queries:

```
C:\Python3Geospatial>pip install mapbox
```

 Download the Mapbox Python SDK here:
https://github.com/mapbox/mapbox-sdk-py.

Getting started with Mapbox

To get started using Mapbox tools and Mapbox Studio, you'll need to sign up for an account. This will allow you to generate API keys that are required for adding Mapbox basemap tiles to web maps, as well as to create the custom basemaps that will differentiate your maps. With this account, you can also load data into the cloud to use within your maps.

Signing up for a Mapbox account

To use Mapbox tools and basemaps, you must sign up for an account. This is a straightforward process and involves supplying a username, an email, and a password:

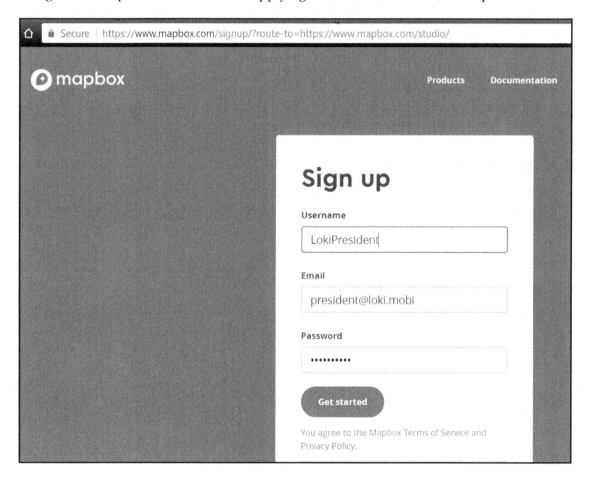

Once you are signed up, you'll be taken to the **Account Dashboard**, where API access token can be generated and **Mapbox Studio** can be accessed. The **Dashboard** also has your account statistics on the number of API calls to the variety of services available, including directions, geocoding, and datasets.

Creating an API token

With the new account comes the **Account Dashboard**, which supplies an API access token by default. This public access token or key begins with **pk** and is a long string of characters. This API access token is used to authenticate all of the maps and apps that will be built using this account. Copy the string of characters and add it to your maps:

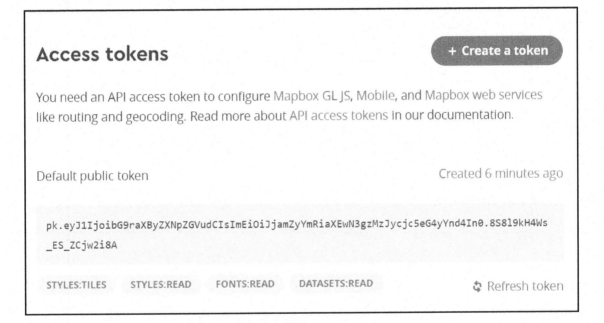

To create a new API access token, push the **Create a token** button and select the access levels that it will allow:

Token name

LokiApps

8 / 128

Select token scopes

All tokens, regardless of the scopes included, are able to view styles, tilesets, and geocode locations for the token's owner. Learn more.

Public scopes

☑ STYLES:TILES   ☑ STYLES:READ   ☑ FONTS:READ

☑ DATASETS:READ

Secret scopes

☐ SCOPES:LIST   ☐ MAP:READ   ☐ MAP:WRITE

☐ USER:READ   ☐ USER:WRITE   ☐ UPLOADS:READ

☐ UPLOADS:LIST   ☐ UPLOADS:WRITE   ☐ STYLES:WRITE

☐ STYLES:LIST   ☐ TOKENS:READ   ☐ TOKENS:WRITE

☐ DATASETS:LIST   ☐ DATASETS:WRITE   ☐ TILESETS:LIST

☐ TILESETS:READ   ☐ TILESETS:WRITE

(Cancel)   (**Create token**)

Within the JavaScript code, the API access token is passed to the MapboxGL object to enable access to tiles and tools. Here is a simple web map using HTML/JavaScript as an example of how the access token is used to create a map. Replace the access token mentioned in the following code with your own public access token:

```
<html><head>
<script
src='https://api.tiles.mapbox.com/mapbox-gl-js/v0.44.1/mapbox-gl.js'></scri
pt>
<link
href='https://api.tiles.mapbox.com/mapbox-gl-js/v0.44.1/mapbox-gl.css'
rel='stylesheet' />
</head><body>
<div id='map' style='width: 400px; height: 300px;'></div>
<script>
mapboxgl.accessToken =
'pk.eyJ1IjoibG9raXByZXNpZGVud0.8S819kH4Ws_ES_ZCjw2i8A';
var map = new mapboxgl.Map({
    container: 'map',
    style: 'mapbox://styles/mapbox/streets-v9'
});
</script></body></html>
```

Save this code as "index.html", and open it using a browser to see the simple map. Make sure that you replace the API access token in the earlier example with your own key, or the map will not appear.

 Explore the documentation to understand the various configurations available for the API access token:
https://www.mapbox.com/help/how-access-tokens-work/.

Adding data to a Mapbox account

Mapbox supports the use of your own data. Not only can you style basemap tiles, but you can even add your own data to the tiles to make them more relevant to your customers or users. This can be managed programmatically using the Mapbox Python SDK and the uploads and datasets APIs.

To upload data, you must create a secret API access token. These are created using the same **Create a token** process detailed earlier, but include secret scopes. Choose the following scopes to allow for dataset and tileset read and write capabilities:

- **DATASETS:WRITE**
- **UPLOADS:READ**
- **UPLOADS:WRITE**
- **TILESETS:READ**
- **TILESETS:WRITE**

 Read more about loading data into your Mapbox account here:
https://www.mapbox.com/help/how-uploads-work/.

Tilesets

Tilesets are rasters which are tiled to create **slippy maps**, allowing them to overlay on a basemap. They can be generated from vector data to create custom basemaps with your own data featured. Using the `Uploader` class from the Mapbox Python SDK, GeoJSON files and shapefiles can be programmatically loaded as tilesets into your cloud account.

 Read more about tilesets here:
https://www.mapbox.com/api-documentation/#tilesets.

Datasets

Datasets are GeoJSON layers, which can be more frequently edited than tilesets. While you can upload datasets using the **Account Dashboard**, to load a dataset larger than 5 MB you must use the datasets API.

 Read more about datasets here:
https://www.mapbox.com/api-documentation/#datasets.

Example – uploading a GeoJSON dataset

The `mapbox` module has a `Datasets` class that is used to create and populated datasets in the account. This demonstration code will read from a zip code GeoJSON file and load one zip code GeoJSON object into a new dataset. Pass the secret access token to the `Datasets` class:

```
from mapbox import Datasets
import json
datasets = Datasets(access_token='{secrettoken}')
create_resp = datasets.create(name="Bay Area Zips",
            description = "ZTCA zones for the Bay Area")
listing_resp = datasets.list()
dataset_id = [ds['id'] for ds in listing_resp.json()][0]
data = json.load(open(r'ztca_bayarea.geojson'))
for count,feature in enumerate(data['features'][:1]):
    resp = datasets.update_feature(dataset_id, count, feature)
```

This will add one zip code to the layer, which can be viewed from the **Account Dashboard**:

Example – uploading data as a tileset

Tilesets can be added to custom basemap styles, making it possible to quickly load your data layers. This demonstration code uses the secret token with read and write capabilities to upload a GeoJSON file as a tileset using the Mapbox Python SDK:

```
token = 'sk.eyJ1IjoibG9oZGqIn0.Y-qlJfzFzr3MGkOPPbtZ5g' #example secret
token
from mapbox import Uploader
import uuid
set_id = uuid.uuid4().hex
service = Uploader(access_token=token)
with open('ztca_bayarea.geojson', 'rb') as src:
    response = service.upload(src, set_id)
print(response)
```

If the response returned is a `201` response, the upload has succeeded.

 Read more about the Uploads API here:
https://www.mapbox.com/api-documentation/?language=Python.

Mapbox Studio

Creating a custom basemap can be a time-consuming process for even experienced cartographers. To help ease this process, Mapbox engineers have used **Open Street Map (OSM)** data to generate pre-built custom basemaps that can be used in commercial and non-commercial applications. Using Mapbox Studio, these styles can also be adjusted to add more custom touches. Also, basemaps can be built from the ground up to create a specific look for your application:

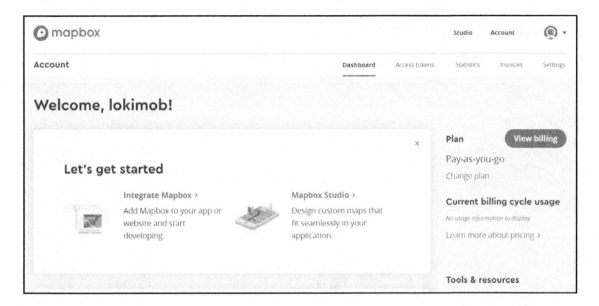

To access Mapbox Studio, log into the **Account Dashboard** and click the **Mapbox Studio** link. In this Studio environment, you can manage basemaps, tilesets, and datasets.

Customizing a basemap

Click the **New Style** button and select the **Satellite Streets** theme:

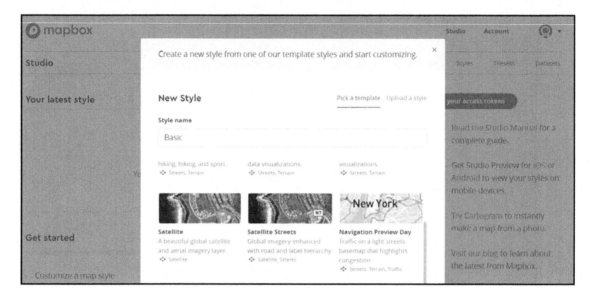

A quick tutorial explains the customization options. A variety of available layers have been added, and both their labeling and styling can be adjusted by clicking on the layers in the table of contents. New layers can be added as well, including account tilesets:

Map zoom levels, bearing, pitch, and initial coordinates can be adjusted. Using the **Map position** menu, these map parameters can be changed and locked as the default position using the **Lock** button at the bottom:

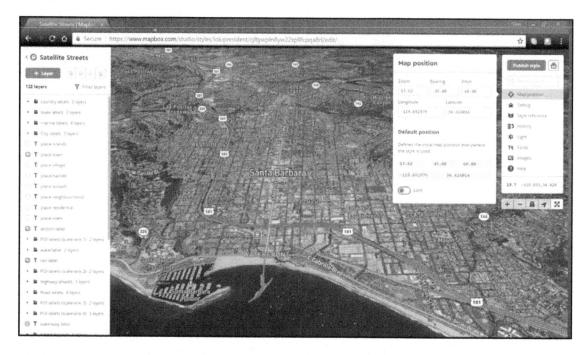

Explore other styling options, such as label colors and layer scale levels. Once you have completed the customizations, publish the style by clicking the **Publish style** button. The style URL is added to MapboxGL visualizations for these Jupyter Notebook exercises or in web maps.

Adding a tileset

To add your data to the basemap style, push the Layer button and select a tileset from the available selection. The zip codes tileset loaded earlier using the Mapbox Python SDK should be available, and can be added to the basemap and styled:

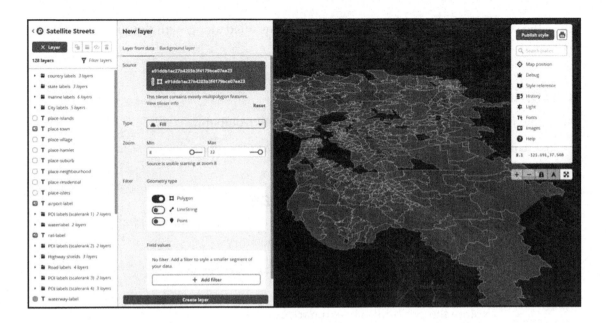

Virtual environment

Start a virtual environment using `virtualenv` (see the previous chapter for installation) and use `pip` to install the modules listed as follows. If you had a folder path of `C:\Python3Geospatial`, `virtualenv` will create a virtual environment folder, here called `mapboxenv`, which can be activated as shown:

```
C:\Python3Geospatial>virtualenv mapboxenv
Using base prefix
'c:\\users\\admin\\appdata\\local\\programs\\python\\python36'
New python executable in C:\Python3Geospatial\mapboxenv\python.exe
Installing setuptools, pip, wheel...done.

C:\Python3Geospatial>mapboxenv\Scripts\activate
```

Installing MapboxGL – Jupyter

The MapboxGL—Jupyter library is available using `pip` from the `PyPI.org` repository:

```
(mapboxenv) C:\Python3Geospatial>pip install mapboxgl
```

All of the supporting modules will be located and installed along with the core libraries created by Mapbox.

Installing Jupyter Notebooks

Install the Jupyter Notebooks library in the virtual environment:

```
(mapboxenv) C:\Python3Geospatial>pip install jupyter
```

Installing Pandas and GeoPandas

Pandas should already be installed, as it is installed with GeoPandas, but if it has not yet been installed, use `pip` to find it in the `PyPI.org` repository:

```
(mapboxenv) C:\Python3Geospatial>pip install geopandas
```

 If you have any issues installing these modules on a Windows computer, explore the pre-built wheel binaries here (use `pip` to install them after download):
https://www.lfd.uci.edu/~gohlke/pythonlibs/.

Using the Jupyter Notebook server

Starting a Jupyter Notebook server is easy. When using a virtual environment, you'll need to activate the environment first, and then start the server. If not, make sure that Python and the location of the Notebook server are in the path environment variable.

Open the command prompt and enter `jupyter notebook` to start the server:

```
(mapboxenv) C:\Python3Geospatial>jupyter notebook
```

The server will start and indicate the specifics of its port number and a token that can be used to relog into the web browser:

```
C:\Users\admin>jupyter notebook
[I 23:00:19.649 NotebookApp] Serving notebooks from local directory: C:\Users\admin
[I 23:03:07.379 NotebookApp] 0 active kernels
[I 23:03:07.381 NotebookApp] The Jupyter Notebook is running at:
[I 23:03:07.382 NotebookApp] http://localhost:8888/?token=1ad280d3b980dc6578f3964000824e
[I 23:03:07.390 NotebookApp] Use Control-C to stop this server and shut down all kernels
[C 23:03:07.398 NotebookApp]

    Copy/paste this URL into your browser when you connect for the first time,
    to login with a token:
        http://localhost:8888/?token=1ad280d3b980dc6578f3964000824ebd19f6eb743ab47bef
[I 23:03:08.493 NotebookApp] Accepting one-time-token-authenticated connection from ::1
[I 23:03:09.431 NotebookApp] Kernel started: 2a1ffde6-64c0-4529-9ff7-63a199fecde6
[W 23:03:10.083 NotebookApp] 404 GET /nbextensions/widgets/notebook/js/extension.js?v=20
host:8888/notebooks/MapboxGL_Chapter.ipynb
```

Starting the server will open a browser window in the system browser. The server address is localhost, and the default port is 8888. The browser will open at http://localhost:8888/tree:

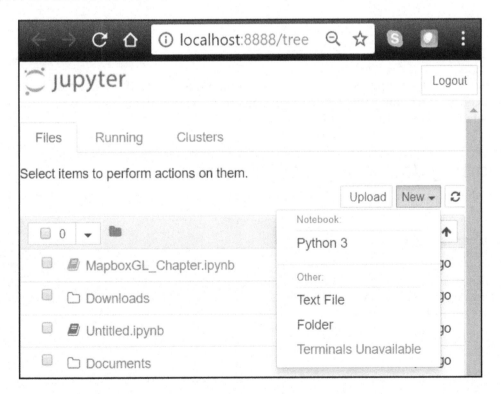

Click the **New** button to create a new Notebook. Select the Python version from the Notebook section, and the new Notebook will open in a second tab. This Notebook should be renamed, as it quickly becomes difficult to organize Notebooks that are untitled:

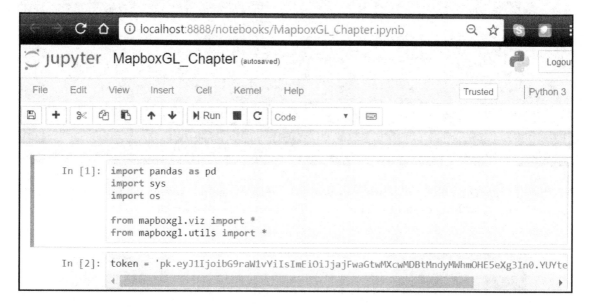

Once the window has opened, the coding environment is live. In this example, we will import census tract data using GeoPandas, convert it to point data, select specific columns, and visualize it using MapboxGL—Jupyter.

Importing data using GeoPandas

Import the required modules and assign the API key to a variable. These commands should be added into Jupyter Notebook cells:

```
import geopandas as gpd
import pandas as pd
import os
from mapboxgl.utils import *
from mapboxgl.viz import *
token = '{user API Key}'
```

The API key can also be assigned to a Windows path environment variable (for example, "MAPBOX_ACCESS_TOKEN") and called using the os module:

```
token = os.getenv("MAPBOX_ACCESS_TOKEN")
```

Creating point data from polygons

The Bay Area census tracts GeoJSON file has population data with polygon geometry. To create the first visualization we need to convert the geometry type to point:

```
tracts = gpd.read_file(r'tracts_bayarea.geojson')
tracts['centroids'] = tracts.centroid
tract_points = tracts
tract_points = tract_points.set_geometry('centroids')
tract_points.plot()
```

The output of the previous code is as follows:

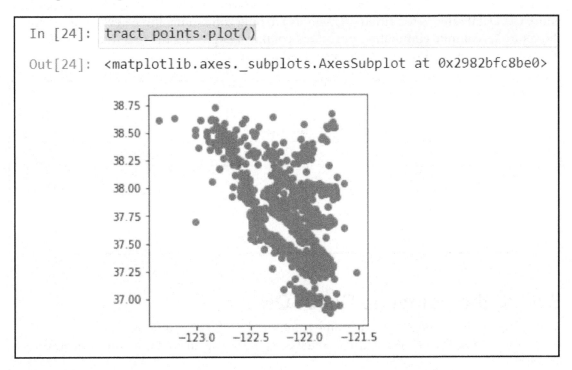

Data cleanup

This data visualization will compare the male and female population in the Bay Area. To generate the circle visualization, we can rename and eliminate unnecessary columns using Geopandas' dataframe manipulation:

```
tract_points['Total Population'] =
tract_points['ACS_15_5YR_S0101_with_ann_Total; Estimate; Total population']
tract_points['Male Population'] =
tract_points['ACS_15_5YR_S0101_with_ann_Male; Estimate; Total population']
tract_points['Female Population'] =
tract_points['ACS_15_5YR_S0101_with_ann_Female; Estimate; Total
population']
tract_points = tract_points[['Total Population',
                'Male Population','Female Population',
                'centroids' ]]
```

This code created three new columns from three existing columns, by passing the name of the new columns and assigning the data values to be equal to the existing column. Then, the entire GeoDataFrame is rewritten (in memory) to only contain the three new columns and the centroids column, eliminating unwanted columns. Exploring the first five rows of the new GeoDataFrame allows us to see the new data structure:

```
In [53]: tract_points[:5]
```

Out[53]:

	Total Population	Male Population	Female Population	centroids
0	4893	2395	2498	POINT (-122.2925253413085 38.00295823758501)
1	6444	3097	3347	POINT (-121.7468504262252 36.95049874202599)
2	3736	1757	1979	POINT (-122.2594490259385 37.8916373721222)
3	4347	2301	2046	POINT (-122.3459716556987 37.97616227082723)
4	1952	984	968	POINT (-122.303938838024 37.8657801574032)

Saving the points as GeoJSON

Saving the newly cleaned GeoDataFrame is required for loading into the Mapbox `CircleViz` class. The GeoJSON driver must be specified, as the default output file format is shapefile:

```
tract_points.to_file('tract_points.geojson',driver="GeoJSON")
```

Adding the points to a map

To simply see the points on the map, we can supply a few parameters and call the `show` property of the `CircleViz` object:

```
viz = CircleViz('tract_points.geojson', access_token=token,
                radius = 2, center = (-122, 37.75), zoom = 8)
viz.show()
```

The previous code will produce the output as follows:

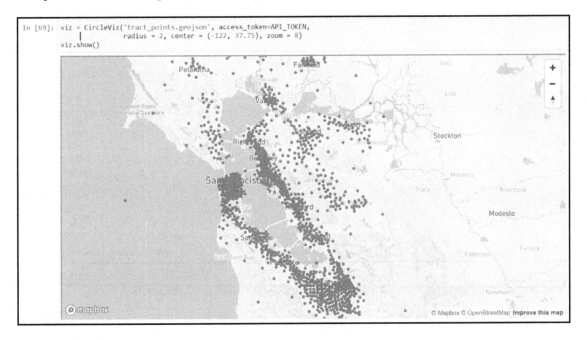

To classify the data, we can set color stops for specific fields, passing class breaks as a list with associated color information:

```
color_stops = [
    [0.0, 'rgb(255,255,204)'],      [500.0, 'rgb(255,237,160)'],
    [1000.0, 'rgb(252,78,42)'],     [2500.0, 'rgb(227,26,28)'],
    [5000.0, 'rgb(189,0,38)'],
    [max(tract_points['Total Population']),'rgb(128,0,38)']
]
viz.color_property = 'Total Population'
viz.color_function_type = 'interpolate'
viz.color_stops = color_stops
viz.radius = 1
```

```
viz.center = (-122, 37.75)
viz.zoom = 8

viz.show()
```

The output will look like this:

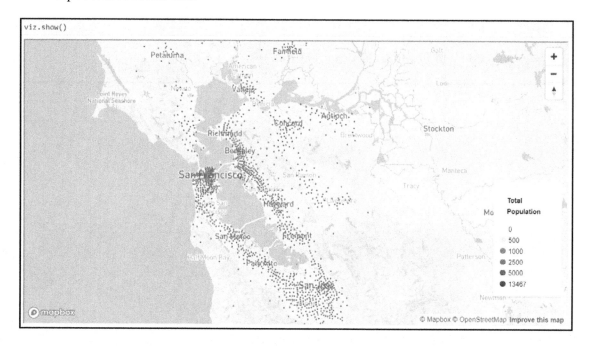

Add some new fields to the `tract_points` GeoDataFrame and resave it:

```
tract_points['Percent Male'] = tract_points['Male
Population']/tract_points['Total Population']
tract_points['Percent Female'] = tract_points['Female
Population']/tract_points['Total Population']
tract_points.to_file("tract_points2.geojson", driver="GeoJSON")
```

Creating a graduated color visualization

This code will manually assign colors to specific sections of the data, breaking the data into categories. This also assigns specific radius sizes to data so that the visualization will convey information with both color and circle size:

```
color_stops = [
    [0.0, 'rgb(107,174,214)'],      [3000.0, 'rgb(116,196,118)'],
    [8000.0, 'rgb(254,153,41)'],
    [max(tract_points['Total Population']), 'rgb(222,45,38)'],
]

minmax = [min(tract_points['Percent Male']),
          max(tract_points['Percent Male'])]
diff = minmax[1] - minmax[0]
radius_stops = [
    [round(minmax[0],2), 4.0],
    [round(minmax[0]+(diff/6.0),2), 7.0],
    [round(minmax[1]-(diff/2.0),2), 10.0],
    [minmax[1], 15.0],]
```

With these radius sizes and color ranges set, they can be applied to two fields within the new GeoJSON: `Total Population` and `Percent Male`. For this visualization, the size of the circle will indicate the male percentage of the population, and the color will indicate the total population:

```
vizGrad = GraduatedCircleViz('tract_points2.geojson', access_token=token)

vizGrad.color_function_type = 'interpolate'
vizGrad.color_stops = color_stops
vizGrad.color_property = 'Total Population'
vizGrad.color_default = 'grey'
vizGrad.opacity = 0.75

vizGrad.radius_property = 'Percent Male'
vizGrad.radius_stops = radius_stops
vizGrad.radius_function_type = 'interpolate'
vizGrad.radius_default = 1

vizGrad.center = (-122, 37.75)
vizGrad.zoom = 9
vizGrad.show()
```

This will produce an interactive map like this:

Automatically setting colors, sizes, and breaks

Instead of manually setting the colors, radius sizes, and breaks, MapboxGL—Jupyter includes utilites (such as `create_color_stops`) that create a match between colors (or sizes) and break values. The color schema is set by passing the `YlOrRd` keyword (which means **Yellow Orange Red**). Also, we can adjust the basemap using another pre-set style or our own custom styles by setting the visualization style to the style URL:

```
measure_color = 'Percent Male'
color_breaks = [round(tract_points[measure_color].quantile(q=x*0.1),3) for
x in range(1, 11,3)]
color_stops = create_color_stops(color_breaks, colors='YlOrRd')
measure_radius = 'Total Population'
radius_breaks = [round(tract_points[measure_radius].quantile(q=x*0.1),1)
for x in range(2, 12,2)]
radius_stops = create_radius_stops(radius_breaks, 5.0, 20)
vizGrad = GraduatedCircleViz('tract_points2.geojson',
                        access_token=token,
                        color_property = measure_color,
                        color_stops = color_stops,
                        radius_property = measure_radius,
```

```
                    radius_stops = radius_stops,
                    stroke_color = 'black',
                    stroke_width = 0.5,
                    center = (-122, 37.75),
                    zoom = 9,
                    opacity=0.75)
vizGrad.style='mapbox://styles/mapbox/dark-v9'
vizGrad.show()
```

The dark basemap allows for the graduated circle visualizations to be more clearly seen:

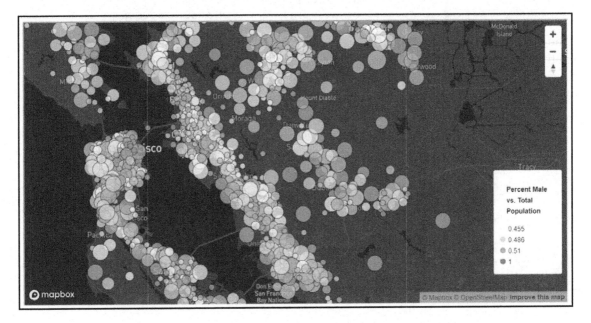

Explore the visualization options available in the documentation here:
`https://github.com/mapbox/mapboxgl-jupyter/blob/master/docs-mark`
`down/viz.md.`

Explore the data utilities available here:
`https://github.com/mapbox/mapboxgl-jupyter/blob/master/docs-`
`markdown/utils.md.`

Explore the color ramps available here:
`https://github.com/mapbox/mapboxgl-jupyter/blob/master/mapboxgl/`
`colors.py.`

Creating a choropleth map

With a choropleth map, we can display a polygon GeoJSON file. Using the `tracts` GeoDataFrame, we'll create another GeoDataFrame with polygon `geometry` and one tabular field, and save it to a file as `GeoJSON`:

```
tract_poly = tracts
tract_poly['Male Population'] = tract_poly['ACS_15_5YR_S0101_with_ann_Male;
Estimate; Total population']
tract_poly = tract_poly[['Male Population','geometry' ]]
tract_poly.to_file('tracts_bayarea2.geojson', driver="GeoJSON")
```

The visualization is created using the `ChoroplethViz` class. The basemap style is the URL of the satellite imagery style created earlier in the *MapBox Studio,* section of the chapter:

```
vizClor = ChoroplethViz('tracts_bayarea2.geojson',
    access_token=API_TOKEN,
    color_property='Male Population',
    color_stops=create_color_stops([0, 2000, 3000,5000,7000, 15000],
    colors='YlOrRd'),
    color_function_type='interpolate',
    line_stroke='-',
    line_color='rgb(128,0,38)',
    line_width=1,
    opacity=0.6,
    center=(-122, 37.75),
    zoom=9)
vizClor.style='mapbox://styles/lokipresident/cjftywpln22sp9fcpqa8rl'
vizClor.show()
```

The output generated is as follows:

Saving the map

To save the choropleth map, use the `create_html` method of the visualization:

```
with open('mpop.html', 'w') as f:
    f.write(vizClor.create_html())
```

To view the saved HTML file locally, open command prompt and start a local HTTP server using Python in the same folder as the saved HTML file. Then, open a browser at `http://localhost:8000/mpop.html` to see the map:

```
C:\Python3Geospatial>python -m http.server
Serving HTTP on 0.0.0.0 port 8000 (http://0.0.0.0:8000/) ...
```

Creating a heat map

Use the `HeatmapViz` class to generate a heat map from the data:

```
measure = 'Female Population'
heatmap_color_stops = create_color_stops([0.01, 0.25, 0.5, 0.75, 1],
colors='PuRd')
```

```
heatmap_radius_stops = [[0, 3], [14, 100]]
color_breaks = [round(tract_poly[measure].quantile(q=x*0.1), 2) for x in
range(2,10)]
color_stops = create_color_stops(color_breaks, colors='Spectral')
heatmap_weight_stops = create_weight_stops(color_breaks)
vizheat = HeatmapViz('tracts_points2.geojson',
                access_token=token,
                weight_property = "Female Population",
                weight_stops = heatmap_weight_stops,
                color_stops = heatmap_color_stops,
                radius_stops = heatmap_radius_stops,
                opacity = 0.8,
                center=(-122, 37.78),
                zoom=7,
                below_layer='waterway-label'
              )
vizheat.show()
```

Uploading data using the Mapbox Python SDK

Storing datasets in the account and joining them to other tabular data is possible using MapboxGL—Jupyter and the Mapbox Python SDK. Loading a GeoJSON file requires specific permissions assigned only to secret API access tokens. To ensure that the API token used has the correct scope, you may have to generate a new API token. Go to your **Account Dashboard** and generate a new token, and ensure that you check the read and write capabilities for uploads and datasets as shown in the *Getting started with Mapbox* section.

Creating the dataset

The first step is to create a dataset, if you haven't created it already. This code generates an empty dataset in the account, which will have a name and description as provided to the `datasets.create` method:

```
from mapbox import Datasets
import json
datasets = Datasets(access_token={secrettoken})
create_resp = datasets.create(name="Bay Area Zips",
              description = "ZTCA zones for the Bay Area")
```

Loading the data into the dataset

To load the data into the new dataset, we will iterate through the features contained in the zip codes GeoJSON, writing them all to the dataset (instead of just one as demonstrated earlier). As this file is larger than 5MB, it must be loaded using the API, which is accessed using the `mapbox` module. The ID of the dataset (retrieved using the `datasets.list` method), the row ID, and the `feature`, are all required parameters for the `update_feature` method:

```
listing_resp = datasets.list()
dataset_id = [ds['id'] for ds in listing_resp.json()][0]
data = json.load(open(r'ztca_bayarea.geojson'))
for count,feature in enumerate(data['features']):
    resp = datasets.update_feature(dataset_id, count, feature)
```

The completed dataset now looks like this in Mapbox Studio:

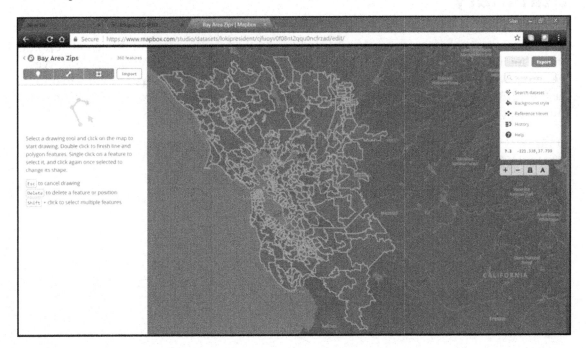

Reading data from a dataset

To read the JSON data stored in the dataset, use the `read_dataset` method:

```
datasets.read_dataset(dataset_id).json()
```

Deleting a row

To delete a specific row from the dataset, pass the dataset ID and the row ID to the `datasets.delete_feature` method:

```
resp = datasets.delete_feature(dataset_id, 0)
```

Summary

In this chapter, we learned how to use the MapboxGL—Jupyter and Mapbox Python SDK to create data visualizations and to upload data into the Mapbox account. We created point data visualizations, choropleth maps, heat maps, and graduated circle visualizations. We learned how to style a custom basemap, how to add it to an HTML map, and how to add custom tilesets to the basemap. We learned how to use GeoPandas to convert Polygon data into point data, and how to visualize the result.

In the next chapter, we will explore the use of Python modules and Hadoop to perform geospatial analysis.

16
Python Geoprocessing with Hadoop

Most of the examples in this book worked with relatively small datasets using a single computer. But as data gets larger, the datasets and even individual files may be spread out over a cluster of machines. Working with big data requires different tools. In this chapter, you will learn how to use Apache Hadoop to work with big data, and the Esri GIS tools for Hadoop to work with the big data spatially.

This chapter will teach you how to:

- Install Linux
- Install and run Docker
- Install and configure a Hadoop environment
- Work with files in HDFS
- Basic queries using Hive
- Install the Esri GIS tools for Hadoop
- Perform spatial queries in Hive

What is Hadoop?

Hadoop is an open-source framework for working with large quantities of data spread across a single computer to thousands of computers. Hadoop is composed of four modules:

- **Hadoop Core**
- **Hadoop Distributed File System (HDFS)**
- **Yet Another Resource Negotiator (YARN)**
- **MapReduce**

The Hadoop Core makes up the components needed to run the other three modules. HDFS is a Java-based file system that has been designed to be distributed and is capable of storing large files across many machines. By large files, we are talking terabytes. YARN manages the resources and scheduling in your Hadoop framework. The MapReduce engine allows you to process data in parallel.

There are several other projects that can be installed to work with the Hadoop framework. In this chapter, you will use Hive and Ambari. Hive allows you to read and write data using SQL. You will use Hive to run the spatial queries on your data at the end of the chapter. Ambari provides a web user interface to Hadoop and Hive. In this chapter, you will use it to upload files and to enter your queries.

Now that you have an overview of Hadoop, the next section will show you how to set up your environment.

Installing the Hadoop framework

In this chapter, you will not configure each of the Hadoop framework components yourself. You will run a Docker image, which requires you to install Docker. Currently, Docker runs on Windows 10 Pro or Enterprise, but it runs much better on Linux or Mac. Hadoop also runs on Windows but requires you to build it from source, and so it will be much easier to run it on Linux. Also, the Docker image you will use is running Linux, so getting familiar with Linux may be beneficial. In this section, you will learn how to install Linux.

Installing Linux

The first step to set up the Hadoop framework is to install Linux. You will need to get a copy of a Linux operating system. There are many flavors of Linux. You can choose whichever version you like, however, this chapter was written using CentOS 7 because most of the tools you will be installing have also been tested on CentOS. CentOS is a Red Hat-based version of Linux. You can download an ISO at: `https://www.centos.org/`. Select **Get CentOS Now**. Then, select DVD image. Choose a mirror to download the ISO.

After downloading the image, you can burn it to a disk using Windows. Once you have burned the disk, place it in the machine that will run Linux and start it. The installation will prompt you along the way. Two steps to pay attention to are the software selection step and the partitioning. For software selection, choose **GNOME Desktop**. This will provide a sufficient base system with a popular GUI. If you have another file system on the computer, you can overwrite it or select the free space on the partitioning screen.

For a more detailed explanation of how to install Linux, Google is your friend. There are many excellent walkthroughs and YouTube videos that will walk you through it. Unfortunately, it looks as though the CentOS website does not have an installation manual for CentOS 7.

Installing Docker

Docker provides the software so that you can run containers. A **container** is an executable that contains everything you need to run the software it contains. For example, if I have a Linux system configured to run Hadoop, Hive, and Ambari, and I create a container from it, I can give you the container, and when you run it, it will contain everything you need for that system to work, no matter the configuration or software installed on your computer. The same applies if I give that container image to any other person. It will always run the same. A container is not a virtual machine. A virtual machine is an abstraction at the hardware level and a container is an abstraction at the application layer. A container has everything you need to run a piece of software. For this chapter, that is all you need to know.

Now that you have Linux installed and have an understanding of what Docker is, you can install a copy of Docker. Using your terminal, enter the following command:

```
curl -fsSL https://get.docker.com/ | sh
```

The preceding command uses the `curl` application to download and install the latest version of Docker. The parameters tell `curl` to, in order, fail silently on server errors, do not show progress, report any errors, and redirect if the server says the location has changed. The output of the `curl` command is piped - | - to the `sh` (Bash shell) to execute.

When Docker has installed, you can run it by executing the following command:

```
sudo systemctl start docker
```

The previous command uses `sudo` to run the command as an administrator (`root`). Think of this as right-clicking in Windows and selecting the **Run as administrator** option. The next command is `systemctl`. This is how you start services in Linux. Lastly, `start docker` does exactly that, it starts `docker`. If you receive an error when executing the earlier mentioned command that mentions sudoers, your user may not have permission to run applications as the `root`. You will need to log in as the `root` (or use the `su` command) and edit the text file at `/etc/sudoers`. Add the following line:

```
your username  ALL=(ALL) ALL
```

The previous line will give you permission to use sudo. Your /etc/sudoers file should look like the following screenshot:

```
## Next comes the main part: which users can run what software on
## which machines (the sudoers file can be shared between multiple
## systems).
## Syntax:
##
##      user    MACHINE=COMMANDS
##
## The COMMANDS section may have other options added to it.
##
## Allow root to run any commands anywhere
root    ALL=(ALL)       ALL
pcrickard       ALL=(ALL)       ALL
## Allows members of the 'sys' group to run networking, software,
## service management apps and more.
# %sys ALL = NETWORKING, SOFTWARE, SERVICES, STORAGE, DELEGATING, PROCESSES, LOCATE, DRIVERS

## Allows people in group wheel to run all commands
%wheel  ALL=(ALL)       ALL

## Same thing without a password
# %wheel         ALL=(ALL)       NOPASSWD: ALL
```

Now that you have docker running, you can download the image we will load which contains the Hadoop framework.

Install Hortonworks

Instead of installing Hadoop and all the other components, you will use a preconfigured Docker image. Hortonworks has a Data Platform Sandbox that already has a container which you can load in Docker. To download it, go to https://hortonworks.com/downloads/#sandbox and select **DOWNLOAD FOR DOCKER**.

You will also need to install the start_sandox_hdp_version.sh script. This will simplify the launching of the container in Docker. You can download the script from GitHub at: https://gist.github.com/orendain/8d05c5ac0eecf226a6fed24a79e5d71a.

Now you will need to load the image in Docker. The following command will show you how:

```
docker load -i <image name>
```

The previous command loads the image into Docker. The image name will be similar to `HDP_2.6.3_docker_10_11_2017.tar`, but it will change depending on your version. To see that the sandbox has been loaded, run the following command:

```
docker images
```

The output, if you have no other containers, should look as it does in the following screenshot:

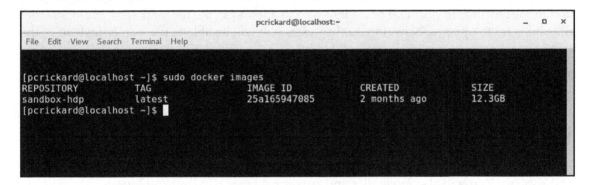

In order to use the web-based GUI Ambari, you will want to have a domain name established for the sandbox. To do that, you will need the IP address of the container. You can get it by running two commands:

```
docker ps
docker inspect <container ID>
```

The first command will have the `container ID`, and the second command will take the `container ID` and return a lot of information, with the IP address being towards the end. Or, you can take advantage of the Linux command line and just get the IP address by using the following command:

```
docker inspect $(docker ps --format "{{.ID}}") --format="{{json
.NetworkSettings.IPAddress}}"
```

The previous command wraps the previously mentioned commands into a single command. The `docker inspect` command takes the output of `docker ps` as the `container ID`. It does so by wrapping it in `$()`, but it also passes a filter so that only the `ID` is returned. Then, the `inspect` command also includes a filter to only return the IP address. The text between the `{{}}` is a Go template. The output of this command should be an IP address, for example, 172.17.0.2.

Now that you have the IP address of the image, you should update your host's file using the following command:

```
echo '172.17.0.2 sandbox.hortonworks.com sandbox-hdp.hortonworks.com
sandbox-hdf.hortonworks.com' | sudo tee -a /etc/hosts
```

The previous command redirects the output of the echo—which is the text you want in your /etc/hosts file and sends it to the sudo tee -a /etc/hosts command. This second command uses sudo to run as root. The tee command sends the output to a file and to the terminal (STDOUT). The -a tells tee to append to the file, and /etc/hosts is the file you want to append. Now, in your browser, you will be able to use names instead of the IP address.

Now you are ready to launch the image and browse to your Hadoop framework.

Hadoop basics

In this section, you will launch your Hadoop image and learn how to connect using ssh and Ambari. You will also move files and perform a basic Hive query. Once you understand how to interact with the framework, the next section will show you how to use a spatial query.

First, from the terminal, launch the Hortonworks Sandbox using the provided Bash script. The following command will show you how:

```
sudo sh start_sandbox-hdp.sh
```

The previous command executes the script you downloaded with the sandbox. Again, it used sudo to run as root. Depending on your machine, it may take some time to completely load and start all the services. When it is done, your terminal should look like it does in the following screenshot:

```
                              pcrickard@localhost:~                        _  □  ×

File  Edit  View  Search  Terminal  Help
Ambari Agent successfully started
Agent PID at: /var/run/ambari-agent/ambari-agent.pid
Agent out at: /var/log/ambari-agent/ambari-agent.out
Agent log at: /var/log/ambari-agent/ambari-agent.log
Starting shellinaboxd:                                    [  OK  ]
Waiting for ambari agent to connect
............       "state" : "INSTALLED",
Waiting for ambari services to start
.............................................................................
.............................................................................
.............................................................................
.............................................................................
.............................................................................
.............................................................................
.............................................................................
.............................................................................
.............................................................................
.............................................................................
.............................................................................
.............................................................................
.............................................................................
.............................................................................
.............................................................................
.............................................................Starting t
utorials...                                               [  Ok  ]

Started Hortonworks HDP container
[pcrickard@localhost ~]$
```

Connecting via Secure Shell

Now that the sandbox is running, you can connect using Secure Shell (SSH). The secure shell allows you to log in remotely to another machine. Open a new terminal and enter the following command:

```
ssh raj_ops@127.0.0.1 –p2222
```

The previous command uses `ssh` to connect as user `raj_ops` to the `localhost` (`127.0.0.1`) on port `2222`. You will get a warning that the authenticity of the host cannot be established. We did not create any keys for `ssh`. Just type `yes` and you will be prompted for the password. The user `raj_ops` has the password `raj_ops`. Your terminal prompt should now look like the following line:

```
[raj_ops@sandbox-hdp ~]$
```

If your terminal is like it is in the previous code, you are now logged into the container.

 For more information on users, their permissions, and configuring the sandbox, go to the following page: `https://hortonworks.com/tutorial/learning-the-ropes-of-the-hortonworks-sandbox/`

You can now use most Linux commands to navigate the container. You can now download and move files around, run Hive, and all your other tools from the command line. This section has already been heavy enough on Linux, so you will not use the command line exclusively in this chapter. Instead, the next section will show you how to execute these tasks in Ambari, a web-based GUI for executing tasks.

Ambari

Ambari is a UI for making the management of Hadoop easier. In the previous section, you learned how to implement `ssh` into the container. From there you could manage Hadoop, run Hive queries, download data, and add it to the HDFS file system. Ambari makes all of this much simpler, especially if you are not familiar with the command line. To open Ambari, browse to the URL as: `http://sandbox.hortonworks.com:8080/`.

 The Ambari URL depends on your installation. If you have followed the instructions in this chapter, then this will be your URL. You must also have started the server from the Docker image.

You will be directed to the Ambari login page. Enter the user/password combination of raj_ops/raj_ops, as shown in the following screenshot:

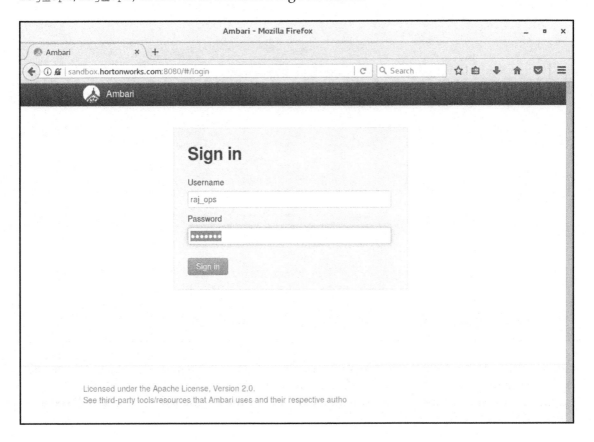

After logging in, you will see the Ambari **Dashboard**. It will look like it does in the following screenshot:

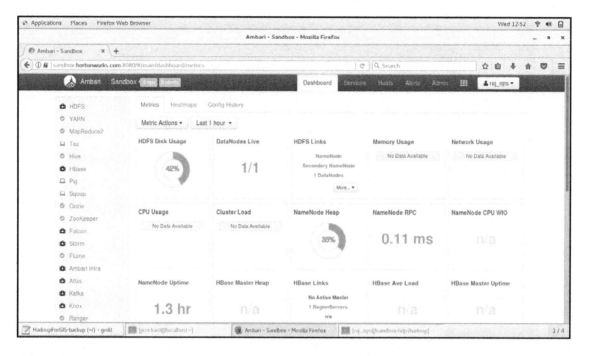

On the left, you have a list of services. The main portion of the window contains the metrics, and the top menu bar has tabs for different functions. In this chapter, you will use the square comprised of nine smaller squares. Hover over the square icon and you will see a drop-down for the files view.

This is the `root` directory of the HDFS file system.

When connected to the container via `ssh`, run the `hdfs dfs -ls /` command and you will see the same directory structure.

From here, you can upload files. To try it out, open a text editor and create a simple CSV. This example will use the following data:

```
40, Paul
23, Fred
72, Mary
16, Helen
16, Steve
```

Save the CSV file and then click the **Upload** button in Ambari. You will be able to drag and drop the CSV to the browser. Ambari added the file to the HDFS file system on the container:

☐ mr-history	--	2017-11-10 07:38	mapred	hadoop	drwxrwxrwx
☐ ranger	--	2017-11-10 07:37	hdfs	hdfs	drwxr-xr-x
☐ sample.csv	0.1 kB	2018-01-31 13:03	raj_ops	hdfs	-rw-r--r--
☐ spark2-history	--	2018-01-31 13:03	spark	hadoop	drwxrwxrwx

Now that you have data loaded in the container, you can query it in Hive using SQL. Using the square icon again, select the drop-down for **Hive View 2.0**. You should see a workspace as follows:

In **Hive**, you have worksheets. On the worksheet, you have the database you are connected to, which in this case is the **default**. Underneath that, you have the main query window. To the right, you have a list of existing tables. Lastly, scrolling down, you will see the **Execute** button, and under that is where the results will be loaded.

In the query pane, enter the SQL query as follows:

```
SELECT * FROM sample_07
```

The previous query is a basic select all in SQL. The results will be shown as follows:

sample_07.code	sample_07.description	sample_07.total_emp	sample_07.salary
00-0000	All Occupations	134354250	40690
11-0000	Management occupations	6003930	96150
11-1011	Chief executives	299160	151370
11-1021	General and operations managers	1655410	103780
11-1031	Legislators	61110	33880
11-2011	Advertising and promotions managers	36300	91100
11-2021	Marketing managers	165240	113400
11-2022	Sales managers	322170	106790
11-2031	Public relations managers	47210	97170
11-3011	Administrative services managers	239360	76370
11-3021	Computer and information systems managers	264990	113880
11-3031	Financial managers	484390	106200

Esri GIS tools for Hadoop

With your environment set up and some basic knowledge of Ambari, HDFS, and Hive, you will now learn how to add a spatial component to your queries. To do so, we will use the Esri GIS tools for Hadoop.

The first step is to download the files located at the GitHub repository, which is located at: `https://github.com/Esri/gis-tools-for-hadoop`. You will be using Ambari to move the files to HDFS not the container, so download these files to your local machine.

 Esri has a tutorial for downloading the files by using `ssh` to connect to the container and then using `git` to clone the repository. You can follow these instructions here: `https://github.com/Esri/gis-tools-for-hadoop/wiki/GIS-Tools-for-Hadoop-for-Beginners`.

You can download the files by using the GitHub **Clone or download** button on the right-hand side of the repository. To unzip the archive, use one of the following commands:

```
unzip gis-tools-for-hadoop-master.zip
unzip gis-tools-for-hadoop-master.zip -d /home/pcrickard
```

The first command will unzip the file in the current directory, which is most likely the `Downloads` folder of your home directory. The second command will unzip the file, but by passing `-d` and a path, it will unzip to that location. In this case, this is the `root` of my home directory.

Now that you have the files unzipped, you can open the **Files View** in Ambari by selecting it from the box icon drop-down menu. Select **Upload** and a modal will open, allowing you to drop a file. On your local machine, browse to the location of the Esri **Java ARchive** (JAR) files. If you moved the zip to your home directory, the path will be similar to `/home/pcrickard/gis-tools-for-hadoop-master/samples/lib`. You will have three JAR files:

- `esri-geometry-api-2.0.0.jar`
- `spatial-sdk-hive-2.0.0.jar`
- `spatial-sdk-json-2.0.0.jar`

Move each of these three files to the `root` folder in Ambari. This is the `/` directory, which is the default location that opens when you launch **Files View**.

Next, you would normally move the data to HDFS as well, however, you did that in the previous example. In this example, you will leave the data files on your local machine and you will learn how you can load them into a Hive table without being on HDFS.

Now you are ready to execute the spatial query in Hive. From the box icon drop-down, select **Hive View 2.0**. In the query pane, enter the following code:

```
add jar hdfs:///esri-geometry-api-2.0.0.jar;
add jar hdfs:///spatial-sdk-json-2.0.0.jar;
add jar hdfs:///spatial-sdk-hive-2.0.0.jar;

create temporary function ST_Point as 'com.esri.hadoop.hive.ST_Point';
create temporary function ST_Contains as
'com.esri.hadoop.hive.ST_Contains';

drop table earthquakes;
drop table counties;

CREATE TABLE earthquakes (earthquake_date STRING, latitude DOUBLE,
longitude DOUBLE, depth DOUBLE, magnitude DOUBLE,magtype string, mbstations
string, gap string, distance string, rms string, source string, eventid
string)
ROW FORMAT DELIMITED FIELDS TERMINATED BY ','
STORED AS TEXTFILE;

CREATE TABLE counties (Area string, Perimeter string, State string, County
string, Name string, BoundaryShape binary)
ROW FORMAT SERDE 'com.esri.hadoop.hive.serde.EsriJsonSerDe'
STORED AS INPUTFORMAT 'com.esri.json.hadoop.EnclosedEsriJsonInputFormat'
OUTPUTFORMAT 'org.apache.hadoop.hive.ql.io.HiveIgnoreKeyTextOutputFormat';

LOAD DATA LOCAL INPATH '/gis-tools-for-hadoop-
master/samples/data/earthquake-data/earthquakes.csv' OVERWRITE INTO TABLE
earthquakes;

LOAD DATA LOCAL INPATH '/gis-tools-for-hadoop-master/samples/data/counties-
data/california-counties.json' OVERWRITE INTO TABLE counties;

SELECT counties.name, count(*) cnt FROM counties
JOIN earthquakes
WHERE ST_Contains(counties.boundaryshape, ST_Point(earthquakes.longitude,
earthquakes.latitude))
GROUP BY counties.name
ORDER BY cnt desc;
```

Running the preceding code will take some time depending on your machine. The end result will look like it does in the following image:

counties.name	cnt
Kern	36
San Bernardino	35
Imperial	28
Inyo	20
Los Angeles	18
Monterey	14
Riverside	14
Santa Clara	12
Fresno	11
San Benito	11
San Diego	7
Santa Cruz	5
San Luis Obispo	3
Ventura	3
Orange	2

The previous code and results were presented without explanation so that you could get the example to work and see the output. Following that, the code will be explained block by block.

The first block of code is shown as follows:

```
add jar hdfs:///esri-geometry-api-2.0.0.jar;
add jar hdfs:///spatial-sdk-json-2.0.0.jar;
add jar hdfs:///spatial-sdk-hive-2.0.0.jar;

create temporary function ST_Point as 'com.esri.hadoop.hive.ST_Point';
create temporary function ST_Contains as
'com.esri.hadoop.hive.ST_Contains';
```

This block adds the JAR files from the HDFS location. In this case, it is the / folder. Once the code loads the JAR files, it can then create the functions ST_Point and ST_Contains by calling the classes in the JAR files. A JAR file may contain many Java files (classes). The order of the add jar statements matter.

The following block drops two tables—earthquakes and counties. If you had never run the example, you could skip these lines:

```
drop table earthquakes;
drop table counties;
```

Next, the code creates the tables for earthquakes and counties. The earthquakes table is created and each field and type are passed to CREATE. The row format is specified as CSV—the ', '. Lastly, it is in a text file:

```
CREATE TABLE earthquakes (earthquake_date STRING, latitude DOUBLE,
longitude DOUBLE, depth DOUBLE, magnitude DOUBLE,magtype string, mbstations
string, gap string, distance string, rms string, source
string, eventid string)
ROW FORMAT DELIMITED FIELDS TERMINATED BY ','
STORED AS TEXTFILE;
```

The `counties` table is created in a similar fashion by passing the field names and types to `CREATE`, but the data is in JSON format and will use the `com.esri.hadoop.hive.serde.EsriJSonSerDe` class in the JAR `spatial-sdk-json-2.0.0` that you imported. `STORED AS INPUTFORMAT` and `OUTPUTFORMAT` are required for Hive to know how to parse and work with the JSON data:

```
CREATE TABLE counties (Area string, Perimeter string, State string, County
string, Name string, BoundaryShape binary)
ROW FORMAT SERDE 'com.esri.hadoop.hive.serde.EsriJsonSerDe'
STORED AS INPUTFORMAT 'com.esri.json.hadoop.EnclosedEsriJsonInputFormat'
OUTPUTFORMAT 'org.apache.hadoop.hive.ql.io.HiveIgnoreKeyTextOutputFormat';
```

The next two blocks load the data into the created tables. The data exists on your local machine and not on HDFS. To use the local data without first loading it in HDFS, you can use the `LOCAL` command with `LOAD DATA INPATH` and specify the local path of the data:

```
LOAD DATA LOCAL INPATH '/gis-tools-for-hadoop-
master/samples/data/earthquake-data/earthquakes.csv' OVERWRITE INTO TABLE
earthquakes;

LOAD DATA LOCAL INPATH '/gis-tools-for-hadoop-master/samples/data/counties-
data/california-counties.json' OVERWRITE INTO TABLE counties;
```

With the JAR files loaded and the tables created and populated with data, you can now run a spatial query using the two defined functions—`ST_Point` and `ST_Contains`. These are used as in the examples from `Chapter 3`, *Introduction to Geodatabases*:

```
SELECT counties.name, count(*) cnt FROM counties
JOIN earthquakes
WHERE ST_Contains(counties.boundaryshape,
ST_Point(earthquakes.longitude, earthquakes.latitude))
GROUP BY counties.name
ORDER BY cnt desc;
```

The previous query selects the `name` of the county and the `count` of earthquakes by passing the county geometry and the location of each earthquake as a point to `ST_Contains`. The results are shown as follows:

counties.name	cnt
Kern	36
San Bernardino	35
Imperial	28
Inyo	20
Los Angeles	18
Monterey	14
Riverside	14
Santa Clara	12
Fresno	11
San Benito	11
San Diego	7
Santa Cruz	5
San Luis Obispo	3
Ventura	3
Orange	2

HDFS and Hive in Python

This book is about Python for geospatial development, so in this section, you will learn how to use Python for HDFS operations and Hive queries. There are several database wrapper libraries with Python and Hadoop, but it does not seem like a single library has become a standout go-to library, and others, like Snakebite, don't appear ready to run on Python 3. In this section, you will learn how to use two libraries—PyHive and PyWebHDFS. You will also learn how you can use the Python subprocess module to execute HDFS and Hive commands.

To get PyHive, you can use `conda` and the following command:

```
conda install -c blaze pyhive
```

You may also need to install the `sasl` library:

```
conda install -c blaze sasl
```

The previous libraries will give you the ability to run Hive queries from Python. You will also want to be able to move files to HDFS. To do so, you can install `pywebhdfs`:

```
conda install -c conda-forge pywebhdfs
```

The preceding command will install the library, and as always, you can also use `pip` install or use any other method.

With the libraries installed, let's first look at `pywebhdfs`.

 The documentation for `pywebhdfs` is located at: `http://pythonhosted.org/pywebhdfs/`

To make a connection in Python, you need to know the location of your Hive server. If you have followed this chapter, particularly the configuration changes in `/etc/hosts`—you can do so using the following code:

```
from pywebhdfs.webhdfs import PyWebHdfsClient as h
hdfs=h(host='sandbox.hortonworks.com',port='50070',user_name='raj_ops')
```

The previous code imports the `PyWebHdfsClient` as h. It then creates the connection to the HDFS file system running in the container. The container is mapped to `sandbox.hortonworks.com`, and HDFS is on port `50070`. Since the examples have been using the `raj_ops` user, the code did so as well.

The functions now available to the `hdfs` variable are similar to your standard terminal commands, but with a different name—`mkdir` is now `make_dir` and `ls` is `list_dir`. To delete a file or directory, you will use `delete_file_dir`. The `make` and `delete` commands will return `True` if they are successful.

Let's look at the `root` directory of our HDFS file system using Python:

```
ls=hdfs.list_dir('/')
```

The previous code issued the `list_dir` command (`ls` equivalent) and assigned it to `ls`. The result is a dictionary with all the files and folders in the directory.

To see a single record, you can use the following code:

```
ls['FileStatuses']['FileStatus'][0]
```

The previous code gets to the individual records by using the dictionary keys `FileStatuses` and `FileStatus`.

> To get the keys in a dictionary, you can use `.keys()`. `ls.keys()` which returns `[FileStatuses]`, and `ls['FileStatuses'].keys()` which returns `['FileStatus']`.

The output of the previous code is shown as follows:

```
{'accessTime': 0, 'blockSize': 0, 'childrenNum': 1, 'fileId': 16404,
'group': 'hadoop', 'length': 0, 'modificationTime': 1510325976603, 'owner':
'yarn', 'pathSuffix': 'app-logs', 'permission': '777', 'replication': 0,
'storagePolicy': 0, 'type': 'DIRECTORY'}
```

Each file or directory contains several pieces of data, but most importantly the type, owner, and permissions.

The first step to running a Hive query example is to move our data files from the local machine to HDFS. Using Python, you can accomplish this using the following code:

```
hdfs.make_dir('/samples',permission=755)
f=open('/home/pcrickard/sample.csv')
d=f.read()
hdfs.create_file('/samples/sample.csv',d)
```

The previous code creates a directory called samples with the permissions 755. In Linux, permissions are based on read (4), write (2), and execute (1) for three types of users—owner, and group, other. So, permissions of 755 mean that the owner has read, write, and execute permissions (4+2+1 =7), and that the group and others have read and execute (4+1=5).

Next, the code opens and reads the CSV file we want to transfer to HDFS and assigns it to the variable d. The code then creates the sample.csv file in the samples directory, passing the contents of d.

To verify that the file was created, you can read the contents of the file using the following code:

```
hdfs.read_file('/samples/sample.csv')
```

The output of the previous code will be a string of the CSV file. It was created successfully.

Or, you can use the following code to get the status and details of the file:

```
hdfs.get_file_dir_status('/samples/sample.csv')
```

The previous code will return the details as follows, but only if the file or directory exists. If it does not, the preceding code will raise a FileNotFound error. You can wrap the preceding code in a try...except block:

```
{'FileStatus': {'accessTime': 1517929744092, 'blockSize': 134217728,
'childrenNum': 0, 'fileId': 22842, 'group': 'hdfs', 'length': 47,
'modificationTime': 1517929744461, 'owner': 'raj_ops', 'pathSuffix': '',
'permission': '755', 'replication': 1, 'storagePolicy': 0, 'type': 'FILE'}}
```

With the data file transferred to HDFS, you can move on to querying the data with Hive.

The documentation for PyHive is located at: https://github.com/dropbox/PyHive

Using pyhive, the following code will create a table:

```
from pyhive import hive
c=hive.connect('sandbox.hortonworks.com').cursor()
c.execute('CREATE TABLE FromPython (age int, name string)  ROW FORMAT
DELIMITED FIELDS TERMINATED BY ","')
```

The previous code imports `pyhive` as `hive`. It creates a connection and gets the `cursor`. Lastly, it executes a Hive statement. Once you have the connection and the `cursor`, you can make your SQL queries by wrapping them in the `.execute()` method. To load the data from the CSV in HDFS into the table and then to select all, you would use the following code:

```
c.execute("LOAD DATA INPATH '/samples/sample.csv' OVERWRITE INTO TABLE
FromPython")
c.execute("SELECT * FROM FromPython")
result=c.fetchall()
```

The preceding code uses the `execute()` method two more times to load the data and then executes select all. Using `fetchall()`, the results are passed to the `result` variable and will look like they do in the following output:

```
[(40, ' Paul'), (23, ' Fred'), (72, ' Mary'), (16, ' Helen'), (16, '
Steve')]
```

Working with `pyhive` is just like working with `psycopg2` — the Python library for connecting to PostgreSQL. Most database wrapper libraries are very similar in that you make a connection, get a `cursor`, and then execute statements. Results can be retrieved by grabbing all, one, or next (iterable).

Summary

In this chapter, you learned how to set up a Hadoop environment. This required you to install Linux and Docker to download an image from Hortonworks, and to learn the ropes of that environment. Much of this chapter was spent on the environment and how to perform a spatial query using the GUI tools provided. This is because the Hadoop environment is complex and without a proper understanding, it would be hard to fully understand how to use it with Python. Lastly, you learned how to use HDFS and Hive in Python. The Python libraries for working with Hadoop, Hive, and HDFS are still developing. This chapter provided you with a foundation so that when these libraries improve, you will have enough knowledge of Hadoop and the accompanying technologies to implement these new Python libraries.

Other Books You May Enjoy

If you enjoyed this book, you may be interested in these other books by Packt:

ArcGIS Pro 2.x Cookbook
Tripp Corbin, GISP

ISBN: 978-1-78829-903-9

- Edit data using standard tools and topology
- Convert and link data together using joins and relates
- Create and share data using Projections and Coordinate Systems
- Access and collect data in the field using ArcGIS Collector
- Perform proximity analysis and map clusters with hotspot analysis
- Use the 3D Analyst Extension and perform advanced 3D analysis
- Share maps and data using ArcGIS Online via web and mobile apps

Mapping with ArcGIS Pro

Amy Rock, Ryan Malhoski

ISBN: 978-1-78829-800-1

- Using ArcGIS Pro to create visually stunning maps and make confident cartographic decisions
- Leverage precise layout grids that will organize and guide the placement of map elements
- Make appropriate decisions about color and symbols
- Critically evaluate and choose the perfect projection for your data
- Create clear webmaps that focus the reader's attention using ArcGIS Online's Smart Mapping capabilities

Leave a review - let other readers know what you think

Please share your thoughts on this book with others by leaving a review on the site that you bought it from. If you purchased the book from Amazon, please leave us an honest review on this book's Amazon page. This is vital so that other potential readers can see and use your unbiased opinion to make purchasing decisions, we can understand what our customers think about our products, and our authors can see your feedback on the title that they have worked with Packt to create. It will only take a few minutes of your time, but is valuable to other potential customers, our authors, and Packt. Thank you!

Index

Made in the USA
Monee, IL
05 November 2019